Anita,)

May the Lord

bless you

through these

devotionals !,

THE ANCHOR HOLDS
A BOOK OF DEVOTIONALS

RON CROWE

WESTBOW
PRESS®
A DIVISION OF THOMAS NELSON
& ZONDERVAN

WestBow Press books may be ordered through booksellers or by contacting:

WestBow Press
A Division of Thomas Nelson & Zondervan
1663 Liberty Drive
Bloomington, IN 47403
www.westbowpress.com
1 (866) 928-1240

ISBN: 978-1-9736-3942-8 (sc)
ISBN: 978-1-9736-3943-5 (hc)
ISBN: 978-1-9736-3941-1 (e)

Library of Congress Control Number: 2019907715

Print information available on the last page.

WestBow Press rev. date: 6/14/2019

THE HOLY BIBLE SCRIPTURE CITATIONS

Each Bible verse used in part or in whole in each devotional is listed and cited in the "Scripture Meditation" section at the bottom of each devotional page.

To my wife, Karen Wilder Crowe. Without her support and assistance, publishing the book would not have been possible. She is the most compassionate person I have ever known. After fifty-two years of marriage, I still marvel at the lengths she will go to help those she knows and does not know. So, you can imagine how much she assists me. Once again, Karen stepped forward with full and sacrificial support of my work for the Lord.

Karen is a three-time cancer survivor. She knows that the travel and other plans that she placed on hold so that I could·write devotionals could mean the same as canceling the trips. Yet, Karen never wavered in her support of my work; she never complained; and she never hesitated to help me in any way that she could. In fact, Karen is still supporting and assisting me, because this ministry has just begun. I am not surprised, because this is way that our Lord taught Karen to be.

ENDORSEMENTS

From Stan Buckley, Founder and Executive Director of But God Ministries: "Interesting! Accurate! Meaningful! Ron Crowe has done a magnificent job sharing the Word of God and the hope of the Gospel. He has beautifully shared the Scriptures and even given us an Action Plan to apply biblical truth to our lives. Plus, all proceeds go to Christian organizations doing good work! Be encouraged. Make a difference. Buy this book!"

From Dr. Kevin L. Cooper, Pastor, Grace Crossing Baptist Church: "'The Anchor Holds' gives the reader an excellent devotional experience designed to satisfy the longing for something stable in our lives. Through personal experience and confident study of God's Word Ron shares with us an exceptional path to knowing more about our anchor in Christ. The Action and Scripture Meditation included in each devotional reading continually point the reader's attention back to the certainty of God and His Word."

FOREWORD
BY CHARLES CHISOLM

You may be silently asking, "Why should I read these devotionals?" The best reason is that these devotionals are literally inspired by God and written for His glory and kingdom. How do I know this? I am a close friend of the author, Ron Crowe, and personally know of the peaks and valleys that he has been through during the past three years in writing the devotionals.

The valleys were trials or roadblocks. There were things like being consumed with pain for weeks, having sudden vision challenges, sitting with a friend in the hospital night after night while his friend's wife died, having a live coal get *inside* his boot (yes, it actually happened) and onto flesh, thereby causing a deep third-degree burn requiring surgery and a skin graft, knowing that his wife beat cancer three times (the last time, noncurable stage four) but is only a doctor's visit away from hearing *it has returned*, and finally the simple uncertainty and apprehension of writing his first book. God took Ron's hand and led him through every one of these problems. He responded to the Lord's guidance, love, and comfort, but Ron will tell you that he did not overcome the pitfalls; God did.

The peaks were blessings such as sharing a sampling of the devotionals with individuals who had a specific need and then seeing God be glorified as the individuals applied the devotionals to their lives. Ron also glorified the Lord by applying the devotionals to his own life. And on three occasions, Ron retreated for a week from the noise and distractions of the world to better hear God, who then used those times to get him refocused and rejuvenated. But the greatest blessing is just beginning, and you can share in this blessing.

The Anchor Holds is the result of God's vision to Ron to write a book(s) containing devotionals on the topics and scripture He would provide through inspiration. God also instructed Ron to ensure that all—not part—of the book's or books' proceeds will be used for funding mission and evangelism work. Ron has created a not-for-profit corporation to receive and disperse all the funds pursuant to the Lord's instructions. A seven-member independent board governs the corporation.

Everyone who buys *The Anchor Holds,* reads the devotionals, meditates on the devotionals, and applies the devotionals to their daily lives will aid in carrying out the will of God in extending His kingdom, which will glorify Him. The bonus is that all who apply the devotionals will experience an increased closeness to God. So, read and be blessed and thereby bless others to the glory of God and His kingdom.

ACKNOWLEDGMENTS

I always marvel at the love and goodness of God's people. As I needed varying kinds of assistance, I asked and received the help. It was that simple. God's people came through in a loving and encouraging way. And due to my inexperience in book writing, I needed a lot of assistance.

First, Karen Crowe, Beverly Shelton, Dr. Joe Young, Charles Chisolm and his late wife, Nikki, and Rickey Gray were kind enough to review the devotionals as I wrote them. So, the devotionals were in very raw form. All were patient, responsive, and encouraging in assisting me. Thank you so much.

A hearty thank you also goes to Sherye Greene, Lee Thigpen, and Cecilia Norwood. Sherye was kind enough to share her lessons learned as a Christian book author. Lee and Cecilia often found me knocking on their office door seeking immediate help of some kind, and both responded in an encouraging and helpful manner.

Last but certainly not least is Martha Stockstill. She reviewed in detail every single devotional. Her help sometimes created additional discussions through email or over the telephone. Her vast knowledge of English and lengthy experience of assisting authors like me is impressive. After working with her a short time, I learned that her knowledge of theology matches that of her English understanding.

Martha's assistance has been vital on several levels, including teaching an *ole dawg* some things about English that I should have already known. I still have an occasional nightmare about split infinitives. Martha, your help was invaluable, and I am eternally grateful. Thanks ever so much.

Again, thank you very much to each of you. You all had an important part in making this book a reality.

INTRODUCTION

It is difficult for me to describe how surprised I was when the Lord gave me a vision to write a devotional book. Questions raced through my mind. *How can I write a book, since I habitually destroy the English language verbally? Where would I find topics for devotionals? Do I know enough about theology? Even if I could manage to write a book of devotionals, how would I get it published?* Then it hit me. Consideration of these questions was being disobedient. So, I told God that I would do as He said.

The Lord then gave me the rest of the vision. He said He would inspire each topic and the scripture to use. He added that He wanted all of the proceeds from this book and later books to be used to aid in extending His kingdom. Our Anchor Ministries (OAM) is a nonprofit corporation, which was created to receive and disperse all the funds according to the Lord's will. God inspired the devotionals, so *The Anchor Holds* is His book.

Note that each devotional has an "Action" and a "Scripture Meditation" section. Each Action section contains suggested steps to take in applying the devotional thought. The Scripture Meditation section is for your reflections and is a list of each complete Bible verse(s) used within the devotional. Unless otherwise noted, the scripture verses are taken from the New King James Version.

Most of us go through times when we need some good devotional thoughts regarding a specific topic. So be sure to refer to the "Index of Devotional Categories," which begins on page 201.

I would be remiss if I did not inform you that the writing and publishing of *The Anchor Holds* has been more than just a journey. It has been truly a humbling and spiritual journey. I am deeply humbled that the Lord trusted me to write His devotional book. His glory shone throughout the journey, as He was faithful in doing what He said He would do. I still feel the blessings of His love, mercy, grace, and guidance.

Oh, Satan and his minions tried hard to prevent *The Anchor Holds* from becoming a reality. But the Lord was in my corner, and He is the Anchor of my soul. Every time I needed help, all I had to do was reach for His extended hand. Satan continued to initiate battles, but he lost every single one.

God is faithful in every way. I continue to feel the hallowed blessings of being comforted by the renewed closeness to Him and being in His protective arms.

It is my prayer that you will be blessed in even greater ways as you read each devotional and glorify God by applying each devotional thought in *The Anchor Holds*.

THE ANCHOR HOLDS

We all have experienced times when we felt like our lives were being tossed around the way ocean waves toss huge ships as if they were mere toys. We may have felt like we were drowning in a sea of trials. The problems sap our strength and health.

Many of our storms cannot be avoided. Christ Jesus told us we would have trials and tribulations. This is the inherent nature of our world. Two important questions concern our response to our trials. Do we try to save ourselves from drowning in our problems? Or do we trust our Lord, Christ Jesus, to help us navigate the storms?

Jesus is the answer for all believers. He is our soul's Anchor, and His hold is absolute and steady. (See Hebrews 6:19 below.) As the Anchor of our soul, Jesus is anchored to Heaven. He has transformed the hope of salvation into an unbreakable promise. Our Anchor will hold us throughout any storm.

You may ask, "How does my Anchor help me with my trials, though?" Jesus will calm your fears and assist, lead, and uphold you throughout your storms and problems because He is always with you. (See Isaiah 41:10 below.) You can be assured that He will help you.

Jesus and God are one. Jesus will use His righteous right hand to take your hand and lead you through the tribulations. He will never leave you, because you are anchored to Him whose promises are anchored in His Word. His Word is anchored in His faithfulness, and His faithfulness is anchored in His love.

As the Lord leads us through a storm, He will strengthen and help us. The storm will remain, but Jesus will calm and comfort us. We will no longer feel tossed about in a sea. Despite our problems, the peace we will experience will glorify God, while nonbelievers marvel at our calmness and comfort.

When you think you are drowning in trials, where will you put your trust? Yourself? Family? Friends? Jesus? Trust the Anchor of your soul, Jesus, because the Anchor holds.

Action: Pray for wisdom to rely on Jesus to lead you through the storms of life. Thank Him for helping and comforting you. Praise Him for being the Anchor of your soul.

Scripture Meditation: Hebrews 6:19: "This hope we have as an anchor of the soul, both sure and steadfast, and which enters the Presence behind the veil." Isaiah 41:10: "Fear not, for I am with you; be not dismayed, for I am your God. I will strengthen you, yes, I will help you, I will uphold you with My righteous right hand."

WHO IS THIS JESUS?

Who Is this Jesus? There are many correct answers, making it difficult to list them all. A few are Son of God, Messiah, Lord, Savior, Prince of Peace, and Immanuel. You probably have a favorite name for Jesus. I have one—God with us. Lord God chose the name Immanuel, which means "God with us." (See Matthew 1:23 below.) Jesus is the full deity of God, as He is God, and He is with us. He always has been and always will be.

Jesus created the earth, the stars, sun, moon, and mankind. He created you and me. He was in the middle of all the riches and glory of Heaven, but He left it all for you and me. He wanted us to have a way to be freed from our sins. So, He became fully man in the humblest of ways.

Jesus was born of a virgin and was placed in a manger. He grew up in poverty. Jesus began a three-year ministry of serving others at age thirty. He walked wherever He went. Jesus taught and preached to the masses. He never owned a home. He never had a formal education. So, why did Jesus leave the richness and splendor of Heaven?

Jesus became fully man for you, me, and everyone else. He wanted all of us to spend eternity in Heaven with God the Father. Jesus knew that for this to be possible, we had to be sin-free, and He had to be the sacrificial payment for everyone's sins.

Jesus became the sacrifice by allowing Himself to be nailed to a cross, where he died. He was buried in a borrowed tomb. God the Father resurrected Jesus after three days, making Him our gateway to Heaven. We can be confident that Jesus is our gateway because He said He was. (See John 14:6 below.) All who believe in Jesus can pass through Him into Heaven. For anyone to believe in Jesus though, he or she must be told the good news of Jesus.

Do you share the good news of Jesus, the Gospel, at every opportunity? If not, are you willing to begin to always tell others about Jesus?

Action: Learn as much as you can about Jesus. Be intentional in telling others about Him. Pray for opportunities to tell others about Jesus and for the Holy Spirit to guide you in sharing the good news of Jesus. Praise God for His Son and your salvation.

Scripture Meditation: Matthew 1:23: "'Behold, the virgin shall be with child, and bear a Son, and they shall call His name Immanuel,' which is translated, 'God with us.'" John 14:6: "Jesus said to him, 'I am the way, the truth, and the life. No one comes to the Father except through Me.'"

THE ONE AND ONLY WAY

Jim and Ritchie had recently become friends. Jim asked Richie, "Are you a Christian?"

Ritchie said, "Yes, I have worked hard to help other people. I have spent a lot of money buying food for the poor. I have even picked up homeless individuals, bought them new clothes, and carried them home so they could bathe and shave. The list of my good works is my ticket to eternal life with God in Heaven."

Jim said, "Think about what Jesus said about the way to Heaven. He said that He is the only way to Heaven. (See John 14:6 below.) His gateway is your ticket to eternal life. Jesus has never said that there are additional ways to enter eternal life. He simply said that He is the way. *The way* means the only way. Those who proclaim other ways to Heaven are wrong."

Ritchie responded, "But there are other Bible verses where we are taught to do good works."

Jim said, "Those good-works verses are directed to those who believe in Jesus. Believers' good works will earn them rewards in Heaven, not entrance into Heaven. Again, Jesus is the only way. He also said that we all would have eternal life if we believe in Him. (See John 3:16 below.) Our belief in Jesus is God's free and loving salvation plan that opens the door to Heaven for us."

"Wow!" Ritchie exclaimed. "Good works are just as important as I thought, but believing in Jesus is more important and is the key to salvation!"

Do you see what God has done? Every Christian does the same thing to gain entrance into Heaven—believes in Jesus. So, all believers will have the same standing. There will be no rich or poor, strong or weak, or healthy or sick. There will be no social classes, temptations to sin, or sorrow. Yet there will be happiness that exceeds our understanding.

Do you fully believe that Jesus is the only way to eternal life?

Action: Believe and accept that Jesus is the one and only way to eternal life with God in Heaven. Accept Jesus as your Lord and Savior if you have not already done so. Praise God for His salvation plan through which you can be free from the bondage of your sin and have eternal life.

Scripture Meditation: John 14:6: "Jesus said to him, 'I am the way, the truth, and the life. No one comes to the Father except through Me.'" John 3:16: "'For God so loved the world that He gave His only begotten Son, that whoever believes in Him should not perish but have everlasting life.'"

IS JESUS LORD OF YOUR WHOLE LIFE?

What role does Jesus occupy in your life? Most of us probably are thinking, *Easy question. Jesus is my Lord and Savior.* Is He really? Or do we place Him on the shelf to make Him available when we need Him? Are you now getting uneasy? I am! Frankly, it is shameful how we limit Jesus to just part of our lives.

A fellow church member and I once visited a family that did not belong to our church. The kids in the family attended our Sunday school. The parents did not. We wanted to share the good news of Jesus with the parents. It did not go well.

The mother excused herself. The only response we could get from the father was that he believed Jesus was the Son of God and that He was good for kids, and that was why he dropped off his kids for Sunday school. The man had relegated Jesus to a position like a toy good for ages three through fourteen. His theory seemed to be that we outgrow our need for Jesus.

Jesus is not a toy, emergency responder, or anything else that we make of Him for our convenience. Jesus is our Lord, and we cannot do anything properly without abiding in Him. (See John 15:5 below.) We need Jesus regardless of our age—be it nine or ninety-nine.

Jesus made possible all that we have accomplished and attained. Sometimes we take full credit for our achievements instead of giving Him the glory. Rather than patting ourselves on the back, we need to fully abide in Jesus. But how?

We need to believe in Jesus, obey Him, and accept Him as Lord over every aspect of our lives. He stands ready, as He is our Savior, the Son of God, the Prince of Peace, our High Priest, our Sustainer, the King of kings, the Lord of lords, our Mediator, and the holder of even more positions. He has us covered. Fully abide in Him or flounder. Without Him, you cannot do anything.

Is Jesus the Lord of your whole life or just part of your life?

Action: Allow Jesus to be the Lord of your life—not part but *whole*. Pray to God, asking for forgiveness for not fully abiding in Jesus and not allowing Him to fully abide in you. Then enjoy the peace Jesus provides.

Scripture Meditation: John 15:5: "'I am the vine, you are the branches. He who abides in Me, and I in him, bears much fruit; for without Me you can do nothing.'"

FAITH OR WASTE?

Two coworkers, Will and Sam, were having lunch together. Will, a Baptist deacon, asked Sam, "Do you know Jesus?"

Sam said, "Yes, I do. I was saved at age thirteen, but I stopped attending church as a young adult."

Will then asked, "If you do not mind my asking, how do you nourish your relationship with Jesus?"

Sam seemed to be uncomfortable with the last question, but he answered, "Sundays are my Sam-time days. I kind of drifted away from Christ Jesus. During bad times, I pray to God for help. Then I get my Bible out and read some. I admit this only lasts for a few days. One day, though, I will join a church." What a contrast from the spiritual life of Will, who tries to maintain a daily quiet time with God and tries to do His will continually.

Keep in mind the differences between Will and Sam and think about the biblical truth that believers need patient endurance to carry out the will of God. (See Hebrews 10:36 [NLT] below.) Faith produces a lasting patience, and Will seems to have more faith than Sam does.

When we are righteous, we live by faith, but when we turn our backs to the Lord, we offend Him. (See Hebrews 10:38 [NLT] below.) Undoubtedly, Will is pleasing God by faithfully living in Him. Sam, though, seems to be living his life in a way that displeases God. Sam fears he may lose the temporal joy of worldly ways. He is wasting his time on earth. He has backslidden.

Sam said that he would someday turn back to God. Sam does not need to tarry, for Jesus is coming again without delay. (See Hebrews 10:37 [NLT] below.) Sam should use Will as a role model and restore his relationship with God so that he also can have an abundant life on earth.

Each of us has a limited time on earth. Will you live your earthly time by faith in our Lord or through waste?

Action: Be faithful and seek the will of God by communing with Him each day. Be obedient to His will. Pray for the strength and perseverance in your daily walk with the Lord. Praise God for being your strength and sustainer.

Scripture Meditation: Hebrews 10:36–38 (NLT): "Patient endurance is what you need now, so that you will continue to do God's will. Then you will receive all that he has promised. 'For in just a little while, the Coming One will come and not delay. And my righteous ones will live by faith. But I will take no pleasure in anyone who turns away.'"

CONFORMER OR TRANSFORMER?

Conflicts between the ways of the world and God have always existed. The existence of these conflicts tempts Christians to conform to the world. The success in overcoming the temptations is determined by the level of each believer's obedience to God. The temptations are now greater because some individuals with a national voice are trying to force Christians to conform to the world. A United States senator is one example.

The senator publicly announced that he would vote against confirming a man who was appointed to a public office because of the man's Christian beliefs. The man had stated that anyone who did not believe that Jesus was the only way to Heaven would die a spiritual death. The senator said that the man was intolerant because of his Christian belief. The man remained faithful to God and refused to conform to the senator's worldly viewpoint.

The man was strongly tempted to be worldly while considering his two choices. He knew that the final vote on his confirmation would be close even without the temptation. He could appease the senator by conforming to the customs and beliefs of the world, or he could obey God by continuing to think more like God so he would further understand the perfect will of God. (See Romans 12:2 [NLT] below.) The decision was very difficult for the man, yet he overcame the temptation and wisely chose to obey God and His truths. The previous transformation of the man was critical to his ability to obey the Lord.

"Allowing the Lord to change a believer's way of thinking seems to be the key to bolstering one's strength in warding off temptations. So how does God change our way of thinking?" you ask. He changes our thinking through our studying and meditating on His Word and our communicating with Him through prayer. As our time with the Lord becomes more regular, our thinking transforms to be more like God's. Our transformed thinking reveals the good and pleasing will of God.

You, I, and all other believers are more likely to face greater temptations than ever before. When you are tempted, will you be a conformer or a transformer?

Action: Transform your thinking daily by being with the Lord in prayer and in His Word. Pray for strength and perseverance in keeping your daily appointments with Him. Thank Him for leading you through your transformation.

Scripture Meditation: Romans 12:2 (NLT): "Don't copy the behavior and customs of this world, but let God transform you into a new person by changing the way you think. Then you will learn to know God's will for you, which is good and pleasing and perfect."

IS YOUR WISDOM WISE?

Whoa! Does today's topic imply that some wisdom is not wise? It sure does. We all probably know that wisdom is knowledge of what is correct and truthful. But knowledge alone does not make one wise. For wisdom to be wise, it must be applied correctly. The knowledge has to be applied with true and insightful discernment.

There are two types of wisdom—God's wisdom and earthly wisdom. God's wisdom is from above and is for His followers. Earthly wisdom is of the world and is advocated by Satan.

The wisdom of God does not allow for any bias, but it does create mercy, peace, kindness, and understanding toward everyone. (See James 3:17 below.) James's description of God's wisdom reads like a depiction of Jesus's character. We are Jesus's disciples. We should get wisdom from God so we can be more like Jesus in our walk with God.

Worldly wisdom does not come from God. It comes from Satan and is evil and demonic and promotes chaos, sinful practices, pride, and self-centeredness. (See James 3:15–16 below.) It is easy to see Satan's influence in worldly wisdom. Confusion, anger, pornography, fear, and a "me first" attitude seem to be prevalent at times.

Surely the contrast between the wisdom of God and the wisdom of the world is apparent to you. God's wisdom is very wise when applied. It enables us to be more like Jesus. This pleases God and glorifies Him. The worldly wisdom produces self-seeking and foolishness, which pleases the evil one.

Every believer has access to the wisdom from above. All we need to do is ask God for wisdom, but we must ask in faith without any doubts that He will supply the wisdom. Also, we need to apply the wisdom in our serving Jesus. We can use either God's wise wisdom or Satan's evil wisdom. Choose God's wisdom.

Action: Pray for the Holy Spirit to examine your heart for any wisdom not from God, to replace the worldly wisdom with that of His, and to guide you in applying the wisdom from above. As your life becomes an overflowing reservoir of peace, love, self-control, and other fruits of the Spirit, praise and thank God.

Scripture Meditation: James 3:15–17: "This wisdom does not descend from above, but is earthly, sensual, demonic. For where envy and self-seeking exist, confusion and every evil thing are there. But the wisdom that is from above is first pure, then peaceable, gentle, willing to yield, full of mercy and good fruits, without partiality and without hypocrisy."

DISCOURAGED? DON'T BE!

Crime is rampant. More and more people are selecting irresponsibility as the preferred way of life. Society is amusing itself into destruction. We seem to be becoming a "gimme, gimme" culture. Earning a living appears to be no longer fashionable to many. There is a new adage: what's yours is mine. Government is shifting from protecting to providing. Discouragement just might be the feeling of the day most of the time.

The daily news is discouraging. But Christians do not have to be discouraged. Nor should we be. God is alive and well. He is still with us. God has not changed. His greatest work occurred when all appeared to be lost.

Do not despair. Not only is God still with you, He loves you. God loved you in the past. He loves you now. And He will always love you. (See Jeremiah 31:3 below.) Jeremiah relates great and comforting words from God. Let these words of God draw you out of the doldrums of discouragement. Then march on. It gets even better.

One of the biblical psalmists told God that he was always with Him, that He guided the psalmist by His hand and counseled him, and that He would receive him to glory. (See Psalm 73:23–24 below.) You, like the psalmist, are a child of God. He also will take your hand to lead and guide you. Wow! The hand that formed the earth, dug out the Grand Canyon, and was nailed to the cross is the same hand that will take hold of yours and guide you all the way to eternal life. Your discouragement will melt away and be replaced by God's peace and comfort flowing through His loving hand.

Are you willing to take hold of God's extended hand? Go ahead. He will not force you to take His hand. Be like the psalmist. Reach for and take His hand now. The Lord is waiting. The results will comfort you beyond your expectations.

Action: Accept God's hand and tell God that He is the strength of you and your heart forever. Pray for strength and boldness in following the Lord's lead through all the mayhem the world throws at you. Let your newfound comfort and peace radiate to unbelievers as you bask in calmness amid disorder.

Scripture Meditation: Jeremiah 31:3: "The Lord has appeared of old to me, saying: 'Yes, I have loved you with an everlasting love; therefore with lovingkindness I have drawn you.'" Psalm 73:23–24: "Nevertheless I am continually with You; You hold me by my right hand. You will guide me with Your counsel, and afterward receive me to glory."

MY BEST REQUEST TO THE LORD IS ...

Ponder the title. Do not just casually think about it. Get still and reflect on it. What would be your greatest request to God? You may have many good requests, making it difficult to choose just one. No problem. Use King David as a mentor.

David said the Lord was his salvation and light. He depended on the Lord. From God, David sought strength, wisdom, protection from his enemies, and other things. The Lord said, "David is a man who wants a heart like Mine and seeks to obey Me." (See Acts 13:22 below.) Wow! Do you think David had trouble identifying his greatest request to God? Yes, I believe he did. He only named one though.

David wanted and sought to live in the house of the Lord for the rest of his life. (See Psalm 27:4 below.) Think about it. David did not say he just wanted to talk with God. David really wanted more. He wanted to move in with the Lord and live with Him forever.

I almost hear you thinking, *Yeah, but David is a better person than I am.* You're wrong. David was also a sinner, a murderer. So, you too can reside with the Lord.

Jesus said that He and God the Father are willing to move in and live with all believers, if we truly believe in and obey Him and His Father. (See John 14:23 below.) Jesus knows that we will fail Him and God the Father through sin. Still, they both love us and will abide in us. Wow. How great is this?

Are you ready to name the greatest request you would make to God?

Action: Keep the commands and instructions of Jesus by loving Him with all your heart. Pray for the Holy Spirit to guide you in showing your love for Jesus each day. Revel in the Lord residing with you.

Scripture Meditation: Acts 13:22: "And when He [God] had removed him [that is, Saul], He raised up for them David as king, to whom also He gave testimony and said, 'I have found David the son of Jesse, a man after My own heart, who will do all My will.'" Psalm 27:4: "One thing I have desired of the Lord, that will I seek: That I may dwell in the house of the Lord all the days of my life, to behold the beauty of the Lord, and to inquire in His temple." John 14:23: "Jesus answered and said to him, 'If anyone loves Me, he will keep My word; and My Father will love him, and We will come to him and make Our home with him.'"

I LOVE THE PRAISES OF ...

It happens often. It should not happen. Yet it does. We feel guilty. We say, "Enough. It will not happen again." But it probably will and does happen again. So, what is this "it"?

"It" is a sad event. A Christian has a good opportunity to state publicly that Christ Jesus is the Messiah and our Lord. The believer remains silent. Another chance to plant a seed of the good news of Jesus is lost. Why did he or she remain silent?

Did the Christian lack the courage to speak? Could be. Was he or she afraid of saying the wrong thing? Maybe. What about being overcome with anxiety? I doubt it. So, why did the believer not speak up for his or her Lord?

The usual reason is that one's pride rears its ugly head, causing him or her to fear losing praises of mankind. This is a sin against God. Placing the praise of humans above that of God is placing mankind above God. (See John 12:42–43 below.) Is this true for many other Christians?

Believers sometimes do love the praise of man more than the praise of God. God sacrificed His Son for us. Then we repay Him by loving the praise of man more than His praise. The praises of humans create instant but temporary gratification that falls away like the autumn leaves. The praise of God is different and better than that of humans. The Lord's praises will not fall away from us like the praises of mankind.

God's praise is everlasting. Our faith holds us until the glorious return of Lord Jesus. Then every believer's praise will come from God the Father. (See 1 Corinthians 4:5 below.) Also, Jesus will help us build our faith so we can stand fast for the praise of God. Jesus has told us that we can bear much fruit by abiding in Him. Bearing fruit purifies our hearts so we are truly deserving of God's praise.

Will you seek the praise of God?

Action: Pray for strength and guidance in faithfully seeking the Lord's will in all you do. Know that the praise of God will most assuredly await you.

Scripture Meditation: John 12:42–43: "Nevertheless even among the rulers many believed in Him, but because of the Pharisees they did not confess Him, lest they should be put out of the synagogue; for they loved the praise of men more than the praise of God." First Corinthians 4:5: "Therefore judge nothing before the time, until the Lord comes, who will both bring to light the hidden things of darkness and reveal the counsels of the hearts. Then each one's praise will come from God."

FAITHFUL, FAITHLESS, OR IN BETWEEN?

We all should evaluate our faith from time to time to determine if our acts of faith have become a meaningless routine instead of joyful deeds of obedience to our Lord. We can start by using 2 Timothy 2:11–13, which many consider to be a statement of faith recited by the early church believers. The statement is a good gauge of our faith in Jesus.

Our faith in Jesus is very important. It is our faith in Him that gives us victory over death. Our spiritual identification and participation with Jesus in His death, burial, and resurrection bring us eternal life with Him and victory over sin, death, and Satan. (See 2 Timothy 2:11 below.) Knowing that dying with Jesus brings us eternal life with Him should comfort our whole inner being.

Our endurance is evidence of the status of our faith in Jesus. Failure to persevere indicates a weaker faith in Him. The stronger our faith, the more we endure all the trials and tribulations that are thrown at us. Reigning with Christ eternally is our reward, but rejecting Christ is denying Him, demonstrates no faith in Him, and brings eternal separation from God. (See 2 Timothy 2:12 below.) Our faith may even waver at times, but the Lord's faith stays steady.

Look at 2 Timothy 2:13 below. Some may be faithless, but Jesus is always faithful. A faithless person is one who never had a true "saving faith," regardless of what he or she may say. Yet Jesus is faithful in following God's will to judge nonbelievers and to save believers. If we are faithless and remain so, we will be judged rather than saved.

What does your evaluation say about your faith? How strongly do you believe that dying with Christ brings you eternal life? Enduring suffering for Christ will permit you to reign with Jesus, whose faithfulness is whole and perfect. Regardless of how you score your faith, it is less than perfect.

Will you seek to achieve a stronger faith?

Action: Be intentional in following Jesus. Use the Word of God the Father to strengthen your faith as Jesus did. Also, pray daily for the Holy Spirit to help you keep your soul and spirit fixed on Jesus. The victory will be yours. You can count on it.

Scripture Meditation: Second Timothy 2:11–13: "This is a faithful saying: For if we died with Him, we shall also live with Him. If we endure, we shall also reign with Him. If we deny Him, He also will deny us. If we are faithless, He remains faithful; He cannot deny Himself."

BE A TEAM PLAYER

We all have experienced being a member of a team that worked toward an end or goal. Much of what we do involves being with one or more persons working to achieve something. It may have been in sports, our careers, civic activities, or our Christian service. We all can say, "I have been there, done that." We are veterans at being team members, but are we good team players?

Good team players work at carrying out their tasks within the team structure, whether formal or informal. Other team members might attempt to accomplish their work outside the team framework. Our Lord intended for us to serve Him within a teamwork structure. For example, consider the spreading of the Gospel—the good news of Jesus.

Christ Jesus knew we would need help in witnessing for Him, so He sent a helper, the Holy Spirit, to aid everyone who believes in Him. (See John 15:26–27 below.) Spreading the Gospel requires teamwork. As we tell others about Jesus, the Holy Spirit will persuade the hearers. This is how unbelievers are saved. We have no power without the Holy Spirit. To be successful in evangelizing, we must team up and work with the Holy Spirit.

Believers often become so determined to spread the Gospel that they forget about their teammate—the Holy Spirit. This is when we learn just how powerless we are without the Spirit. We eagerly tell individuals about our Lord Jesus, but we end up walking away disappointed because no one seemed to absorb the truth of Jesus. We were not a team player. We let God down. The evil one, Satan, rejoices in our failure.

Be aware that Satan, the prince of darkness, will do his best to convince you that you do not know exactly what to say in your attempts to testify about Jesus. Do not listen to Satan. He is a liar. Ignore him and his lies. Your teammate, the Holy Spirit, will guide you in determining what to say.

Are you always working with the Holy Spirit in your evangelistic efforts?

Action: Be intentional in always praying for the Holy Spirit to lead the way in your efforts to tell people about Jesus. You explain. Let the Spirit convince. Rejoice with the angels in Heaven every time you assist in leading someone to accept our Lord. Thank God for allowing you to serve Him.

Scripture Meditation: John 15:26–27: "'But when the Helper comes, whom I shall send to you from the Father, the Spirit of truth who proceeds from the Father, He will testify of Me. And you also will bear witness, because you have been with Me from the beginning.'"

LISTENING TO JESUS OR SATAN?

We all have probably experienced being in the middle of a tug-of-war between Christ Jesus and Satan. This is spiritual warfare.

Satan uses trickery and lies in his quest to convince us to live under his guidance. He tries to trick us into believing that some sins are too insignificant for God's attention; some sins are not really sins; and these and other purported sins will give us an abundant life.

Jesus wants us to have an abundant life, but this cannot be achieved through sin. He wants us to walk with the guidance of His helper, the Holy Spirit. Obedience to Jesus will provide us with an abundant life through the fruits of the spirit—love, joy, peace, longsuffering, kindness, goodness, faithfulness, gentleness, and self-control.

Jesus is all-powerful. Satan is not. The most powerful weapon Satan had was the power of death that mankind feared due to the enslavement to sin. As sinners, we were headed toward a spiritual death. But Jesus's death on the cross and resurrection removed Satan's power of death and provided an option for us to break the chains of sin. (See Hebrews 2:14 below.)

We, as believers in Jesus, share in His victory. By believing in Him, we no longer have to be afraid of death or continue to be enslaved by sin. (See Hebrews 2:15 below.) Satan's greatest power has been crushed. Satan is a now a weaker adversary, but we still listen to him sometimes. Why?

Satan cannot force us to do anything, but he can tempt us through lies and trickery. We all have weaknesses; Satan zeros in on each weakness and attacks. His goal is to deceive us into self-destruction. But Jesus has supplied us with more than ample tools (Himself, the Holy Spirit, the armor of God, and other believers) to use in keeping Satan at bay.

Satan is not going away. We can fight Him the Lord's way, or we can be more susceptible to Satan's deceit. As Jesus's disciples, we should fight the Lord's way. Are you willing?

Action: Fight Satan daily by allowing the Holy Spirit to guide you, obeying Jesus, absorbing God's Word, putting on the armor of God, and requesting other believers to intercede for you in prayer. Pray for strength and perseverance in fighting Satan.

Scripture Meditation: Hebrews 2:14–15: "Inasmuch then as the children have partaken of flesh and blood, He [Jesus] Himself likewise shared in the same, that through death He might destroy him who had the power of death, that is, the devil, and release those who through fear of death were all their lifetime subject to bondage."

MARCHING TO ZION

When anyone accepts Jesus as his or her Lord and Savior, the person begins a march to Zion. Many Christians enjoy singing the old hymn "We're Marching to Zion," but some believers find the march to be long, difficult, and filled with many barriers. Other believers view the march as short, easy, and joyful, with fewer trials. Yet many do not know what Zion is, why we are marching to it, or what the march represents.

Look at Hebrews 12:2 below. Zion is actually Mount Zion and is a synonym for the heavenly city of our God and is called Jerusalem. As Christians, Mount Zion is our designated destination—an eternity of bliss with God. Zion also has a countless number of angels. When we reach Zion, we will join the angels in worshipping God for all eternity. We all should eagerly look forward to the glorious day that we arrive in Zion.

The march to Zion is each Christian's individual life pathway for following Jesus, who enabled the march through His death on the cross and His resurrection. Our journeys will involve challenges along the way.

Challenges are trials or roadblocks and may or may not be beyond our control. They may be testing or molding by God, our failing to avoid Satan's tricks, or our disobeying God. The more we obey Jesus, the fewer barriers we will run into. Yet we will still face plenty of tribulations.

As we obediently march along our path, following Jesus, we will share in His peace as He comforts us, and the Holy Spirit will supply us with spiritual energy. Jesus loves us and wants to help us in our march. He will be with us every step of the way, keeping us focused on the goal of reaching Mount Zion. Our march sometimes will be very difficult but joyful because of our obedience to the Lord. God will be glorified as we happily march along toward Zion.

Do you feel the joy and the peace of the Lord while marching to Zion, or does your march seem to be a continuous struggle? Your trial-scarred march, though difficult, can still be joyful and peaceful.

Action: Pray daily for the Lord to guide you through your problems and to wrap you in His peace and comfort. Bask in His love and joy. Also, ask Jesus to have the Holy Spirit give you a tug when you begin to stray from your march. Praise God for your pathway to Mount Zion.

Scripture Meditation: Hebrews 12:2: "But you have come to Mount Zion and to the city of the living God, the heavenly Jerusalem, to an innumerable company of angels."

FROM JESUS: STOP WORRYING!

Worrying is common, though needless. Jesus taught that we should not worry about our lives, including our health, food, drink, and other daily needs. His command even included not worrying about tomorrow. (See Matthew 6:25, 34 below.) Jesus said to stop worrying, but worrying seems to be part of our inner makeup.

We often think worrying is justified. A loved one is critically ill. Your job is in jeopardy. Your creditors are hounding you. Are these valid worries? Jesus said that He had a better alternative—a heart-comforting peace. (See John 14:27 below.) Jesus wants us to trade our worries for His peace, if we will allow Him. Note my example.

In January 2013, my wife was diagnosed with an atypical return of cancer. The doctor said that the cancer was stage four and could not be cured. We could try to force the cancer into remission through aggressive use of chemotherapy. Worry consumed me for two days. I was haunted by silently wondering if her death was imminent.

I asked God to guide me in caring for my wife. He let me know I could not adequately take care of her while obsessed with worry. I *felt* Him saying, "You give Jesus your worries, and He will give you His peace." I simply said okay. My worries evaporated as Jesus's peace filled me and left me with an unexpected comfort.

I then knew that whatever happened would be the best for her. The cancer was in remission after only half of the treatments. She began a lifetime maintenance plan of taking chemo pills daily. Her doctor stopped the plan after four years. She is doing really well now. God is in control, and we both bask in Jesus's peace.

Do you worry about your circumstance(s)?

Action: Ask God for the strength to obey Jesus's command not to worry and for you to be filled with Jesus's peace. Your calmness will be a witness for the love, mercy, and grace of the Lord.

Scripture Meditation: Matthew 6:25, 34: "'Therefore I say to you, do not worry about your life, what you will eat or what you will drink; nor about your body, what you will put on. Is not life more than food and the body more than clothing? Therefore do not worry about tomorrow, for tomorrow will worry about its own things. Sufficient for the day is its own trouble.'" John 14:27: "Peace I leave with you, My peace I give to you; not as the world gives do I give to you. Let not your heart be troubled, neither let it be afraid."

LIGHT OR DARKNESS?

Have you ever thought about if you are projecting light or darkness during your daily life? Note that in the Bible, light represents all that is good, while darkness means all that is bad—sin. When we are light, we please God. When we are darkness, we please Satan.

Some think that they always radiate light because they are Christians. After all, Christians do follow God and fellowship with Him through Jesus. God does radiate light constantly, as there is no darkness in Him. So, some Christians think they project light only because they follow God, who is light. They could not be more mistaken. Their unacknowledged sin blots out God's light. Apparently, they are not listening to the Holy Spirit.

The Bible says that all men and women are sinners. For any of us to say we always project light is claiming that we never sin and never emanate darkness. The apostle John taught that when someone says he or she does not sin, the person is untruthful. (See 1 John 1:8 below.) When we claim to be sinless, we are lying to God, others, and ourselves.

With this attitude, our sin is compounded. The sin reflects darkness. Then our saying that we have no sin is an additional sin and creates more darkness. This puts us in a filthy hole.

We can get out of the hole by being truthful about our sin and seeking forgiveness. We know that the Lord is faithfully committed to forgiving our sins, if we confess them. (See 1 John 1:9 below.) God is faithful to His word. He will forgive us.

We should also be faithful by confessing our sins and seeking forgiveness. Our forgiven sins are cast aside rather than compounded. We can then project more light, just as our Lord wants us to do.

Are you willing to acknowledge your sin and seek forgiveness?

Action: Pray for the Holy Spirit to convict you of any sin not confessed. Confess the sins to God and ask for His forgiveness. Others will see your light and seek what you have—joyful and peaceful daily living, whether your circumstances are good or bad.

Scripture Meditation: First John 1:8–9: "If we say that we have no sin, we deceive ourselves, and the truth is not in us. If we confess our sins, He is faithful and just to forgive us our sins and to cleanse us from all unrighteousness."

HE WILL COME

Currently, the United States is in a morality nosedive, and the changes in our moral fiber are affecting the Christian community. Some believers question why Jesus has not yet come for His followers. Some other believers are no longer spreading the Gospel with nonbelievers when possible. Some Christians are even beginning to question whether Jesus is coming for us as He said. Their doubts about Jesus's return vary from being major to minor.

Never doubt Jesus. He is faithful to His word. Paul explained that Jesus will come down from Heaven into the clouds with a shout; the dead believers will rise from their graves; then those believers who are alive will ascend with the other believers to meet Jesus; and all believers will then be with the Lord for all eternity. (See 1 Thessalonians 4:16–17 below.) Jesus will come at the perfect time for His people. Do not doubt His coming.

Any doubt of His coming reveals weaknesses in our faith in Jesus. Our faith needs to be strong, like that of Louis in the following story.

Ray and Louis were World War l soldiers and close friends who vowed to help each other regardless of the circumstances. During a trench battle, their unit left their trench to attack the enemy's trench. Enemy firepower caused a retreat. But Louis did not get back. He was critically wounded.

Ray heard Louis calling for him. Ray wanted to go get him, but his commander said no. Finally, Ray's commander let him go. He found Louis and dragged him to their trench while under enemy fire. Louis died during the process. Ray's commander told him that he risked his life for nothing. Ray said that he had to go. He added that Louis told him, "I knew you would come, Ray."

Compare your faith in Jesus with Louis's faith in Ray. Are you just hoping that Jesus will come, or do you know that He will come?

Action: In prayer, ask God to forgive you for any weaknesses in your faith in Jesus's coming, and for the Holy Spirit to nudge you when your faith might waver. Refer to 1 Thessalonians 4:16–17 below any time that doubt of His coming creeps into your mind.

Scripture Meditation: First Thessalonians 4:16–17: "For the Lord Himself will descend from heaven with a shout, with the voice of an archangel, and with the trumpet of God. And the dead in Christ will rise first. Then we who are alive and remain shall be caught up together with them in the clouds to meet the Lord in the air. And thus we shall always be with the Lord."

DESENSITIZED?

For many years, America's citizens were reminded that the spread of communism could occur in our country through systematic desensitization, without the citizenry even realizing it. The process was likened to placing a frog in a pan of water on a stove. Low heat was started and over time increased slowly until the water killed the frog through scalding. The frog never leaped out of the pan because it became desensitized to the heat.

Today, we live in a time when more and more people are becoming desensitized to the depravity of sin. We are constantly bombarded with news of immoralities, causing our minds to slowly view more sins as nonsins. More and more people celebrate these immoral ways. As Christians, we must not fall into the trap of desensitization. Fortunately, a nephew of Abraham, Lot, is an example for us.

Lot was a sinner. Still, he hated the depravity of the sin occurring in Sodom, where he lived, but he never allowed his righteousness to be numbed by the evil and lewd conduct occurring constantly. (See 2 Peter 2:8 below.) God decided to destroy Sodom along with Gomorrah with fire, as an example of the fruit of an ungodly lifestyle. But first, God had Lot delivered out of Sodom before its destruction. (See 2 Peter 2:4, 6–7 below).

God will still deliver the righteous, for He is faithful in saving the godly from temptations and sin and letting the ungodly languish until punishment after the coming Day of Judgment. (See 2 Peter 2:9 below.) It is far better for us to be spared by God than to be judged on Judgment Day.

The ball is in our court. It is essential that we all answer this question: are we going to be like Lot or the frog in the pan?

Action: Be like Lot. Do not let the wickedness of sin around you desensitize your heart. Pray to Jesus for continual discernment in recognizing all sins as what they truly are—abominations to God. Praise Jesus for loving you and His coming for you at the heavenly Father's prescribed time. Then Jesus's light will shine through you into a dark world.

Scripture Meditation: Second Peter 2:4, 6–9: "For ... God ... turning the cities of Sodom and Gomorrah into ashes, condemned them to destruction, making them an example to those who afterward would live ungodly; and delivered righteous Lot, who was oppressed by the filthy conduct of the wicked (for that righteous man, dwelling among them, tormented his righteous soul from day to day by seeing and hearing their lawless deeds)—then the Lord knows how to deliver the godly out of temptations and to reserve the unjust under punishment for the day of judgment."

ARE YOU HOLY?

Has anyone ever asked you if you are holy? I'm guessing probably not, so I am asking. Are you holy? Before you answer, reflect on the meaning of *holy* as it relates to mankind—a sincere, devoted, and loving service to God and His church. Strive to be honest with yourself and answer the question.

If, like so many Christians, your answer is no, because you are a sinner and only God is holy, you are wrong. This answer comes from Satan, not God. Both the apostle Paul and the Lord told us to be holy. (See 1 Peter 1:15–16 below.) God knows we are imperfect, so our holiness is also. Still, His Word commands us to be holy. His command is not a suggestion.

God's Word means what it says. We need to be about the business of being holy. We are able to become holy or increase our holiness by continually striving to become like God. The more we are like Him, the holier we are and the more we glorify Him and sin less.

"What can we do that would make us more like God?" you ask. We can be more like Him by obeying our Lord and Savior, Jesus the Christ. The Holy Spirit, who we received in our hearts when we accepted Jesus, will guide and direct us. Not only is God glorified by these actions, but also He is pleased with us.

As we endeavor to achieve holiness in our lives, we should be mindful that attempts through the desire or lust of the flesh bring failures. The devil would have us believe the opposite. Do not be fooled by his wiles. Satan would tell us that our imperfection prevents us from being holy. Listen to him and you will only fail while having anxiety and worry.

Do you see the contrast? Seek holiness through worldly or fleshy desires and become a failure while living in worry, anxiety, and dejection. But seek holiness through Jesus and be a success while living in joy, comfort, and peace. It should be an easy choice for everyone.

Will you seek holiness from the world or from God?

Action: Take resolute steps in following Jesus daily and obeying His commands, so that you create or increase your holiness. Pray for strength and perseverance in following Jesus as the Holy Spirit guides you. Praise God as your holiness grows. Know your actions are bringing glory to God.

Scripture Meditation: First Peter 1:15–16: "But as He who called you is holy, you also be holy in all your conduct, because it is written, 'Be holy, for I am holy.'"

PAY IT FORWARD

We all suffer from troubles. Having to endure trials during our stay on earth is a common thread running through us. The type of problems and the amount of suffering vary from trouble to trouble and person to person. Most of the trials create anguish. So, we seek comfort. But where do we find our comfort?

As Christians, we know that true comfort comes only from our God and Him alone. (See 2 Corinthians 1:3 below.) As great as the Lord's comfort is, it is not an end in itself.

The comfort that we receive from God is not intended for us to just enjoy it. God also wants us to take the comfort we receive and use it to help others. (See 2 Corinthians 1:4 below.) The help could be in the form of testimony, care giving, encouragement, or any other needed assistance. The Holy Spirit will let you know how to assist God in comforting others.

You may remember when "pay it forward" was popular in our society. The phrase was born as the title to a movie featuring paying it forward. The idea was that when someone did something really nice for us, we should do the same for someone else. We were to pay it forward. This is an example of what God wants us to do—receive His comfort and forward it to others.

Paying it forward is being obedient to Jesus. We are His agent. (See 2 Corinthians 1:5 below.) The more we suffer, the more comfort we will receive from Jesus.

Think about this. The more we suffer, the more comfort we receive. The more comfort we receive, the more we will be able to pass on. The more comfort we pass on, the more we please God. The more we please God, the more He is glorified.

Are you paying it forward? If not, will you begin to do so?

Action: Pray for Jesus to give to you His peace and comfort as you navigate your troubles. Praise Him for His comfort. Pray for guidance in directing you to those who need comforting. Pay it forward and revel in the knowledge of Jesus's pleasure in you for bringing glory to God.

Scripture Meditation: Second Corinthians 1:3–5: "Blessed be the God and Father of our Lord Jesus Christ, the Father of mercies and God of all comfort, who comforts us in all our tribulation, that we may be able to comfort those who are in any trouble, with the comfort with which we ourselves are comforted by God. For as the sufferings of Christ abound in us, so our consolation also abounds through Christ."

COMMUNICATE, COMMUNICATE

Suppose we were asked whether we have a personal relationship with Jesus. Most of us would probably say, "Sure I do. I am a Christian." Then we would be asked, "Do you nurture the relationship by spending time communicating with Jesus daily or most every day?" Would our truthful answer embarrass us?

Satan has tricked many Christians into believing they have a good relationship with Jesus without spending time with Him, except for an occasional prayer when something is needed. Satan reminds us of many other things that need to be done so that we feel too busy. We can sit down with Jesus later, but later rarely comes. Jesus taught that if we spend time in His Word, we will be true disciples and know His truths. (See John 8:31–32 below.) But Jesus did not say, "If you have time."

Most believers probably understand the benefits of reading and absorbing the Lord's written word—the Bible. Yet many just do not take the time each day to communicate with Jesus or read the Bible. This is contrary to God's instruction and is illogical.

Have you ever tried to be friends with someone without spending much time with him or her? Satan says you can, but he is lying. It just does not work. The same is true with Jesus. We cannot build a better relationship with Him without spending time and communicating with Him.

Note that spending time with Jesus is more than just praying to Him. True communication is not one-sided. We should allow time for Jesus to communicate with us through His written word and the Holy Spirit. The less time we spend with Him, the less obedient we will be and the less we will hear from Him.

We have to decide each day to spend quality time with Jesus and to read the Bible. Satan cannot prevent us from doing it. Jesus will not force us to do it. He is faithful to our free will. We should use our free will and make time for Jesus.

Action: Be intentional in setting a daily time to spend with Jesus and His Word. Talk to Him in prayer. Praise Him. Give Jesus time to answer you through His Word and through the Holy Spirit. Communicate, communicate. Enjoy learning more of God's truth as your relationship with Jesus grows.

Scripture Meditation: John 8:31–32: "Then Jesus said to those Jews who believed Him, 'If you abide in My word, you are My disciples indeed. And you shall know the truth, and the truth shall make you free.'"

WHOLE WORSHIP

When we sit down for lunch on Monday, we should ask ourselves questions like the following: (1) What points were made in yesterday's sermon at church? (2) What did my Sunday school teacher teach us? (3) Did I honor God this morning? (4) Have I consulted with Jesus concerning my plans for today?

Our answers are indicative of the level at which we are worshiping God. Sadly, for many of us, our answers will contain one or more answers like "I don't remember," "I don't know," or "I am not sure." Having just one of these answers reveals a worship that is less than whole. Having more than one of these answers is even worse.

We all need to raise the level of our worship. We do this by glorifying God, because all things are for His glory. We glorify Him by pleasing Him. And we please God by offering ourselves totally to Jesus and becoming an instrument of righteousness. (See Romans 12:1 [NLT] below.) To improve, we must be living sacrifices to our Master. Many believers call this maturing in Christ. We all should work to become His instruments.

While seeking to be instruments of God, it is imperative that we not overlook preparation. For example, a lady had recently become a Christian. Desperation set in because she could not determine how to find God's will and to serve Him. She wanted to be an instrument for God. Yet she was overlooking His commands in His Word. She became confused and was floundering spiritually as she tried to practice whole worship on her terms rather than God's.

It is not complicated, though Satan says it is. He is lying. God created the earth and mankind to run the earth. Man turned against God by sinning. God is now working to bring individual humans back to Him one by one. As individuals turn to God, they assist Him in His work through whole worship—true and proper worship. But remember that we assist God by His rules, not ours. After all, He is God, and we are not.

Are you willing to make your worship of God true and proper?

Action: Equip yourself to serve God. Listen to, read, absorb, and be a doer of God's Word. Pray for the Holy Spirit to assist you in understanding and in directing you in serving God. Partner with Jesus in your walk with God. Rejoice in God's glory as you please Him.

Scripture Meditation: Romans 12:1 (NIV): "Therefore, I urge you, brothers and sisters, in view of God's mercy, to offer your bodies as a living sacrifice, holy and pleasing to God—this is your true and proper worship."

GOD SEES PERFECTION IN YOU

Almost everyone shares a common characteristic—the inner desire to be liked. Some people spend a lot of time and effort in attempting to make themselves likable. Some others say they do not care if they are disliked. What they probably really mean is that a mutual dislike exists, so they do not care.

Think about it. How strong is your need to be liked? Do you wear the need on your sleeve? Is it hidden deep inside you? Or is it somewhere in between? Regardless, likely the desire is there. Yet the thirst to be liked has been quenched. We just often fail to realize it. God loves us and sees us as perfect.

Okay, so you are now saying, "Wait, I am a sinner. I definitely am not perfect." You are if you are a believer. Once you came to believe in Jesus, you became a child of God, who began sanctifying you; the Holy Spirit entered you, and God no longer remembers your sins. (See Hebrews 10:14–15, 17 below.) Wow! God sees you as having been perfected.

God says He sees all believers as perfect. So we need to act like we are perfect. "But how?" you ask. Look to Jesus. He once commanded that we love everybody—friends and enemies. (See John 13:34 below.) We need to replace our desire to be liked with a love for *all* others. Jesus's solution is not a suggestion. It is a command. The only way to obey is to love everyone. Our obedience allows us to see in others what God sees in us: perfection.

I know you are thinking that some people make it very difficult to love them. So what! We make it difficult for God to love us, but He sees us as perfect. Rid yourself of the desire to be liked. See yourself and others as perfect, just as God does.

Are you committed to loving others as Jesus commanded?

Action: Pray for the Holy Spirit to guide you in seeing what God sees in others—goodness and perfection—and trading your thirst to be liked for love of others. Revel in your newfound love of others.

Scripture Meditation: Hebrews 10:14–15, 17: "For by one offering He has perfected forever those who are being sanctified. But the Holy Spirit also witnesses to us; for after He had said before, then He adds, 'Their sins and their lawless deeds I will remember no more.'" John 13:34: "A new commandment I give to you, that you love one another; as I have loved you, that you also love one another."

LISTENING TO THE HOLY SPIRIT

Kelley and Lucy were discussing their spiritual quiet times. Lucy said, "Most of the time, I cannot understand the scripture passages I read. Sometimes I guess at the meaning and later learn that I was wrong. I feel as though I am not conducting my quiet times correctly. God and Jesus do not seem to be there with me."

Kelley asked, "Are you listening to the Holy Spirit during your quiet times?"

Lucy said, "I read the Bible and then pray to God. Then usually nothing happens, so I end the session."

Maybe Lucy is not concentrating on listening for the Holy Spirit. It is very difficult to listen to the Spirit if one does not *first listen for Him*. We know the Spirit is with Lucy. Jesus said that the Spirit is with all Christians. While with Lucy, the Holy Spirit will lead her in learning God's truth—His Word. (See John 16:13 below.) But first she must listen *for* Him and then *to* Him.

All Christians must listen to the Holy Spirit to understand God's truth. Jesus said that the Spirit does not speak on his own, but He speaks from God's authority. (See John 16:13 below.) God gave His knowledge to Jesus, who passed it on to the Spirit, who gives the knowledge to believers. (See John 16:15 below.) What the Spirit teaches is from God. We must listen to Him.

Part of the Holy Spirit's ministry is to teach us the Word of God. God's Word is His truth. Jesus's truth is God's truth. The Holy Spirit's truth is God's truth. Relying on ourselves to understand God's truth is the same as thinking we know as much as God, Jesus, and the Spirit. Such thinking is dangerous, sinful, and influenced by Satan.

The Word of God is considerably more valuable than gold, silver, gems of all kinds, and other precious jewels combined. Fortunately, we can understand God's Word if we are willing to concentrate on the Holy Spirit's guidance.

Are you listening for and to the Holy Spirit?

Action: Be intentional in listening to the Holy Spirit to guide you in understanding God's truth—His Word. Pray for the Spirit to guide you in recognizing His efforts to teach and lead you. Thank the Lord for sending the Holy Spirit.

Scripture Meditation: John 16:13, 15: "'However, when He, the Spirit of truth, has come, He will guide you into all truth; for He will not speak on His own authority, but whatever He hears He will speak; and He will tell you things to come. All things that the Father has are Mine. Therefore I said that He will take of Mine and declare it to you.'"

DUMP YOUR GRUDGES

Grudge is a word that implies bad meanings. Just a few synonyms for grudge are bitterness, ill will, resentment, spite, and, well, you get the idea. Grudge, like its synonyms, represents or is associated with sin. Strong statement? The truth usually is. So, what makes grudge a sin?

Many of us have held a grudge against someone who did something that hurt us, or others whom we love dearly, or both. We get mad, hold onto the anger, and do not forgive the offender by holding a grudge against him or her. Some still hold the grudge(s). Some even boast about it by stating something like "I don't get mad. I get even."

Grudges are symptomatic of a merciless heart. This is an affront against God—a sin. This sin will be judged harshly, because God does not give mercy to those who do not show mercy to others. (See James 2:13 below.)

Holding on to grudges is unforgiving and brings forth judgment from God. Being unforgiving damages our relationship with God. He will not forgive those who do not forgive others. (See Matthew 6:15 below.) Note that here we are not talking about our previously received salvation. Our current walk with God is damaged. We miss some blessings, and worst of all, we are not as close to our Lord. There is good news, though. Jesus told us how to overcome these sins.

Jesus said that we should reconcile our differences with the offender and God to avoid judgment. To do this, we rid ourselves of all our grudges. God will then forgive us when we forgive others. (See Matthew 6:14 below.) It is simple. If we rid ourselves of our grudges and forgive the offenders, God will forgive us.

We have two choices. Be forgiving, and our relationship with God and the offenders will then be reconciled and joyful. Be unforgiving, and our relationship with God and offenders will continue to be broken. Which will you choose?

Action: Pray for conviction of any grudges you may be holding. Ask for His guidance in cleansing your heart. Get rid of the grudges by forgiving the offender(s). Then pray for forgiveness for your holding of grudges. Know that your light will shine brighter as you joyfully continue your daily walk with the Lord.

Scripture Meditation: James 2:13: "For judgment is without mercy to the one who has shown no mercy. Mercy triumphs over judgment." Matthew 6:14–15: "'For if you forgive men their trespasses, your heavenly Father will also forgive you. But if you do not forgive men their trespasses, neither will your Father forgive your trespasses.'"

JESUS WEPT. HAVE YOU?

We are living in a time when nonbelievers in Jesus are having unprecedented success in ousting God from the public domain. Public reveling in all sorts of evil has replaced condemnation of immorality. As Christians, we seem to be viewing the wrongdoing with disdain toward the participants. Is this what Jesus wants us to do?

When Jesus saw Lazarus was dead, He erupted with tears of grief because His love for Lazarus was so strong. (See John 11:35–36 below.) Jesus knew He was going to resurrect Lazarus in a matter of minutes. Still, Jesus was compassionate. Lazarus had died, and it is normal to grieve when a believer dies physically. But how should we react when nonbelievers are destined to a spiritual death in hell? We look to Jesus for direction.

Jesus's compassion is demonstrated through His love for everyone—His followers, those who have turned their backs to Him, and those who have not heard the good news of His free gift of eternal life. Jesus even loves those who hate Him. He grieves over all people. Not some but all. As Christians, we are Jesus's disciples. We need to follow His lead.

Jesus wept over the physical death of a follower. So, just think how much more He grieves over those who are headed to a spiritual death in hell. The rejoicing of thousands of heavenly angels gives evidence of this when just one nonbeliever accepts Jesus as his or her Lord and Savior. Jesus's love and compassion for the lost drive Him to grieve for them.

Jesus said that we are to love our neighbors as ourselves. (See Matthew 22:39 below.) Your neighbor is everyone you meet. Ask yourself, "Do I love my neighbor enough to mourn and sob over their lost soul, or do I just shrug it off by thinking, *It is their problem*?" If you have a Jesus-like compassion and love, you will present the good news of Jesus to them.

Are your compassion and love strong enough to cause you to weep and lament over lost people and to tell them the good news of Jesus?

Action: Pray for the Holy Spirit to guide you in developing a compassionate and loving heart. Spread the Gospel to your neighbors. Agonize, weep, and pray fervently for lost people even though they may have rejected Jesus. Also ask that their hearts be stirred. Know you are giving the heavenly angels good reasons to continue rejoicing.

Scripture Meditation: John 11:35–36: "Jesus wept. Then the Jews said, 'See how He loved him!'" Matthew 22:39: "And the second is like it: 'You shall love your neighbor as yourself.'"

BEING UNQUALIFIED QUALIFIES YOU

Mr. Earl Rowe's situation is an example of failing to obey God. His church needed a volunteer to manage a new ministry. The church leaders involved began to pray separately for God to lead them to His choice for the ministry. They each felt that the Lord led them to Mr. Rowe. The leaders were confident that Earl would not decline.

Mr. Rowe was asked to lead the new ministry. Earl sincerely felt he was unqualified for the job. The process began to unravel because Mr. Rowe did a lot of thinking and very little praying. His consideration consisted of compiling reasons for being unqualified. His praying was telling God that he was unqualified. So he declined.

Mr. Rowe was mistaken about being unqualified. Had he consulted God's Word, Earl could have seen that his being unqualified was a great qualification for serving God.

God took an old man, Moses, with poor speech and had him take on an Egyptian Pharaoh. A scrawny shepherd boy named David with only a sling and five pebbles was chosen by God to take down a giant in full battle armor. There are other great examples, but perhaps the greatest is God choosing Paul to become the world's best missionary.

Paul was the most unqualified and improbable of them all. He worked hard to exterminate Christians. Yet God chose him to extend God's kingdom throughout the world by planting churches, spreading the Gospel, and making disciples for Jesus.

The power of God that raised Jesus from the dead still chooses the unqualified and instills the necessary ability and tools to accomplish His will. (See Hebrews 13:20–21 below.) God repairs, molds, and instills whatever is needed to ready us for His assignments. God's best work has been accomplished through supposedly unqualified people. We should be elated that He turns our weaknesses into strengths for serving Him.

Will you obey God when He calls on you?

Action: Pray always for discernment to know when God calls you to serve Him in specific ways, be they large or small. Praise Him. Thank Him for choosing you. But most of all, know that He prepares you and obey Him.

Scripture Meditation: Hebrews 13:20–21: "Now may the God of peace who brought up our Lord Jesus from the dead, that great Shepherd of the sheep, through the blood of the everlasting covenant, make you complete in every good work to do His will, working in you what is well pleasing in His sight, through Jesus Christ, to whom be glory forever and ever. Amen."

STANDING FIRM FOR JESUS

You may remember the video of twenty-one Christians executed in the Middle East one day in early 2015. Any who would denounce Jesus would be spared. All refused. So all were beheaded. What a testimony. They gave their all by standing firm for Jesus.

In the United States, persecution usually occurs in nonviolent ways. The most common form of persecution is a person or group that embarrasses, shames, or ridicules Christians. Some persecutors have turned to the judicial courts to seek an oppressive type of persecution by requesting that our Christian ideals be forced out of public view and hearing. How should we respond when we are persecuted in some way? God's Word provides the answer.

Paul taught that there are two possible responses to being persecuted. If we deny that Jesus is who Christians say He is, He will deny us, but if we endure, we will reign with Jesus in Heaven. (See 2 Timothy 2:12 and Luke 12:8–9 below.) Luke's writing agreed with Paul's. We should be comforted knowing that Jesus is confessing us in Heaven as long as we confess Him. Failure to confess Jesus is a form of denying Him. Stand fast for Him.

When persecution strikes any believers, we should respond by boldly and prudently confessing Jesus. This reaction should be the same whether the expected impact is good or dire.

Satan will attempt to sway us from standing up for Christ. The evil one will use trickery or other methods to tempt us to do his will. Satan is able to tempt us, but he does not have the power to force us to do anything. We can control the situation.

Suppose you will be persecuted in some way today. Will your reaction deny Christ Jesus in order to avoid persecution? Or will you hold fast to your belief in Jesus and acknowledge Him as Lord? Would your answer be the same if bodily harm or your life was on the line?

Action: Pray for the Lord to lead you through persecutions and for the strength and courage to stand with Jesus in rebuking those who seek to defile His name. Then bask in the peace and comfort of knowing that Jesus is confessing you in Heaven.

Scripture Meditation: Second Timothy 2:12 states: "If we endure, we shall also reign with Him. If we deny Him, He also will deny us." Luke 12:8–9: "'Also I say to you, whoever confesses Me before men, him the Son of Man will also confess before the angels of God. But he who denies Me before men will be denied before the angels of God.'"

STOP SNUBBING JESUS

Your friends have done it. You have done it. I have done it. Probably all have done it. "It" is dealing wrongfully with a problem dumped in our lap. The problem could be anything—health issue, financial struggle, job complication, and such.

We mull over the problem. Good solutions seem scarce. We talk to our friends about it. We are anxious. We make a decision, only later to find it wasn't the best one. We end up floundering. Then we run to Jesus for help. It is like when all else fails, call Jesus. We snubbed him and acted on our own. Snubbing Jesus is a sin. Yet, because of His love, He will still help us.

Why do we not go to Jesus first? God wants us to pray when we are suffering. (See James 5:15 below.) Instead of first obeying God, we let Satan trick us. The devil tells us that Jesus is too busy to help us, our problem is too small, or other lies. With just one problem, we snubbed Jesus, disobeyed God, and listened to the worst liar of all time. We created a big mess.

Rather than creating messes, we should obey God by giving our burdens to Jesus in prayer because He loves us. (See 1 Peter 5:7 below.) Not only will Jesus lead us to the best solution, He will remove the anxiety the problem created. After all, He is the Prince of Peace. He will always comfort you with His peace. (See 2 Thessalonians 3:16 below.)

Our action should be a no-brainer when a problem strikes. There are two paths available to us. 1) Snub Jesus by acting without Him. This sin creates other sin—disobeying God and listening to Satan. Also, our solution is usually not the best, leaving us floundering and anxious. 2) Pray to Jesus immediately by obeying God and rejecting Satan's lies. We will be left with the best solution while relaxing in the comfort of Jesus's peace.

Who will you trust with your trials—yourself or Jesus?

Action: When problems strike, obey God by praying to Jesus for help. Ask Jesus to lead you through the trial to His solution. Reject Satan by verbally telling him to flee from you. While enjoying the peace of Jesus, praise God for the resolution.

Scripture Meditation: James 5:13: "Is anyone among you suffering? Let him pray. Is anyone cheerful? Let him sing psalms." First Peter 5:7: "Casting all your care upon Him, for He cares for you." Second Thessalonians 3:16: "Now may the Lord of peace Himself give you peace always in every way. The Lord be with you all."

UGH, ANOTHER CHANGE

Change is a dirty word to many of us. Why is this? Some changes are good, especially those we seek. Some others are bad. Many times, the bad changes seem to overshadow the good ones. The bad changes usually force an unwanted mind-set in us. We may feel unsettled, anxious, frustrated, and fearful. Sometimes we have to educate ourselves about the changes. Still, a bad change creates one big nuisance that often influences us to react in a non-Christian manner. A friend related a good example of this.

The friend and his wife were shopping in our local grocery store one day and found most of the food items had been relocated within the store. Some shoppers became angry, some reacted sarcastically, and some joked about the difficulty in finding desired food items. Then the couple heard an ear-piercing scream from another aisle. A lady was screaming because she could not find the items she wanted. She just lost it. Her reaction is symbolic of what change can do to us, if we let it.

A better solution is to seek help from Jesus, who has experience handling change. He left His throne in a perfect Heaven to come to an imperfect earth in order to die on a cross for our benefit. Jesus knows change. He has always been available to assist us, and He continues to be accessible.

Jesus is all-powerful. He has always been with mankind, and He always will be with us. (See Revelation 1:8 below.) We need Jesus's assistance, and He is always available to lead us through the changes we face. Call upon Him. He is waiting on us to faithfully seek his assistance in adapting to changes. And it gets even better.

We have assurance Jesus will not change His desire and ability to lead us through the trials of change. He has not changed, and He never will change. (See Hebrews 13:8 below.) We can depend on Jesus. He will be there for us. We all need to accept this truth and abide by it.

Will you deal with each change alone or will you trust Jesus's help with the changes?

Action: Pray to Jesus. Praise Him for being willing to lead you through changes, and then ask him to show you the way to overcome each change. Then walk through the change with confidence and joy.

Scripture Meditation: Revelation 1:8: "'I am the Alpha and the Omega, the Beginning and the End,' says the Lord, 'who is and who was and who is to come, the Almighty.'" Hebrews 13:8: "Jesus Christ is the same yesterday, today, and forever."

IS YOUR STONE STRONG?

Have you considered the responsibility you received by accepting Jesus Christ as your Lord and Savior? Christians seem to understand easily the Savior part, but the Lord part, not so much. God didn't sacrifice His Son just so we would feel blessed. God saved us so that we could glorify Him by serving Him and humankind through the assistance and guidance of Jesus Christ.

God is building a spiritual temple, and He has made Jesus the cornerstone—a living cornerstone. (See 1 Peter 2:4–5 [NLT] below.) Our salvation makes us living stones for God's temple. God's will demands that our living stones be strong, so He placed in us the responsibility of making our stones strong through our obedience to Him. As God's holy priests, we obey Him by making sacrifices, spiritual sacrifices, through Jesus's assistance (that Lord part). This is a big responsibility. Never fear, though. Obeying God fulfills our priesthood responsibilities and makes our living stones strong.

Holy priests were special servants in the Old Testament. They were cleansed of their sin and had special privileges. They made sacrifices to God.

We are much like the OT priests, but we are more special. We have Jesus. He mediates for us as we make spiritual sacrifices—our priestly duties. These duties include leading others to Christ, praying, serving God, sharing what we have, sacrificing for the betterment of others, praising Him, and other callings. These are all done for the glory of God.

Our obedience as priests determines the strength of our stones and how much glory God receives. Unfortunately, some Christians show up at church, put on their priest robe, go to Sunday school and a worship service for learning, take off their priest robe, and return home. Our godly duties are a Sunday-through-Saturday job. Leave your robe on. Our stones grow stronger as we fulfill the will of God by completing our duties. So, is your stone strong?

Action: Be intentional in making your living stone strong. Pray to Jesus Christ, asking for guidance and discernment in carrying out your priestly duties. Also, ask for the Holy Spirit to show you where you have failed in your duties.

Scripture Meditation: First Peter 2:4–5 (NLT): "You are coming to Christ, who is the living cornerstone of God's temple. He was rejected by people, but he was chosen by God for great honor. And you are living stones that God is building into his spiritual temple. What's more, you are his holy priests. Through the mediation of Jesus Christ, you offer spiritual sacrifices that please God."

BE SPIRIT FILLED

Do your daily actions reflect the presence of the Holy Spirit in you? God commands us to be completely filled with the Spirit. (See Ephesians 5:18 below.) The Holy Spirit dwells within all believers. The Spirit is our conscience and assists Jesus in guiding our lives. Being filled with the Spirit means we allow Him to continually influence our daily lives.

Though the Spirit dwells in believers, we are not filled with the Spirit until we give control of our lives to the Spirit.

Not giving the Spirit control suppresses the Spirit and disobeys God's command to be filled with the Spirit. What a bummer. Our disobedience is a sin against God. Obviously, this displeases Him. Some Christians fail to recognize that the Spirit is in them. This too is a sin. The result of not being with the Spirit is sin. The amount of sin depends how far away we are from being Spirit filled.

There are much happier consequences resulting from obeying God's command to be filled with the Holy Spirit. We develop characteristics such as interacting with others through love, edification, and singing. We have a melodious heart toward God and give thanks to Him for all things through the name of Lord Jesus. We develop personal humility by submitting to one another as well as to Jesus and God the Father.

The above traits transform us into being more like Jesus and closer to Him. Our daily living will then reflect the fruits of the Holy Spirit—love, joy, peace, longsuffering, kindness, goodness, faithfulness, gentleness, self-control. (See Galatians 5:22–23 below.) Once we are filled with the Spirit, we can joyfully serve the Lord each day in ways that glorify Him.

Being filled with the Spirit and not being filled have opposing results. Being Spirit filled is being obedient to God and pleases Him, which creates happiness in us. Not being Spirit filled is disobedient to God. It displeases Him and robs us of the happiness God wants us to have. Will you ensure that you are Spirit filled?

ACTIONS: Be Spirit filled. Pray to God for the Holy Spirit to speak to you daily. Listen to the Holy Spirit. Act under the Spirit's guidance. Let your Spirit-controlled life be a witness for Jesus as you display the fruits of the Spirit. Enjoy your Spirit-filled life each day.

Scripture Meditation: Ephesians 5:18: "And do not be drunk with wine, in which is dissipation; but be filled with the Spirit." Galatians 5:22–23: "But the fruit of the Spirit is love, joy, peace, longsuffering, kindness, goodness, faithfulness, gentleness, self-control. Against such there is no law."

DO YOUR PRAYERS PLEASE GOD?

The prayer life for many Christians is sporadic or barely exists. Some believers live in the "I am so busy" trap. Some others pray only when they have personal problems. Some reserve prayer only for the most important matters in their lives. These and even more reasons are poor excuses. A prayer life that is less than persistent does not fulfill the will of God.

"So, what kind of prayer life does God desire for us to have?" you ask. He commanded us to always pray. (See 1 Thessalonians 5:17 below.) Of course, we cannot pray without a break. We must eat, sleep, work, and such. But we can be like a law enforcement officer.

A law officer is always ready to protect us and enforce the law twenty-four hours a day and seven days a week. Even while off duty, the officer is armed and ready if the need arises. We can be like the officer—armed and ready to pray throughout every day and night.

We must always be ready. We need to pray regularly and persistently about everything in our lives, whether large or small. We should also pray under the guidance of the Holy Spirit, be alert to prayer needs of others, and persevere in praying for our brother and sister saints. (See Ephesians 6:18 below.) Do this and we will not worry about anything. (See Philippians 4:6 below.)

We could then calmly pray while a tornado appears to be headed our way. When we lose our smartphone, we can pray for God to lead us to it. We could easily pray for other people. The reasons for prayer needs are endless. But anytime we pray, we should not ramble on or pray in vain. (See Matthew 6:7 below.)

Does your prayer life please God and demonstrate obedience to His will?

Action: Pray for strength, wisdom, and perseverance in arming yourself always to be ready to pray so Jesus can lead you in all circumstances according to God's will. Praise God for the results and fully enjoy the comfort of knowing your prayers are pleasing God.

Scripture Meditation: First Thessalonians 5:17: "Pray without ceasing." Ephesians 6:18: "[Pray] always with all prayer and supplication in the Spirit, being watchful to this end with all perseverance and supplication for all the saints." Philippians 4:6: "Be anxious for nothing, but in everything by prayer and supplication, with thanksgiving, let your requests be made known to God." Matthew 6:7: "'And when you pray, do not use vain repetitions as the heathen do. For they think that they will be heard for their many words.'"

PRETENDING AND FENCE STRADDLING?

At the end of the morning church service, a lady walked down the aisle and told the pastor she wanted to accept Jesus the Christ into her heart as her Lord and Savior. The pastor led her to Jesus through prayer.

The congregation was very surprised. Everyone thought she had long been a Christian. She had been playing church for more than thirty years. She regularly attended Sunday school, Sunday worship, and Wednesday worship services. She said she had been a pretend Christian. She was working alongside Christians without being part of the family of God. She had not been a true witness.

We all should ask of ourselves, "Am I a pretend Christian?" This question is extremely important. God said that we have a choice between life (good) and death (evil). (See Deuteronomy 30:15 below.) God did not mention any middle ground—being a pretend Christian. One either is a true Christian or is not a Christian. There is no in between.

Everyone is destined to spend eternity either in life (Heaven) or in death (hell). God was and still is serious. He desires for us to have eternal life in Heaven with Him. It is our individual choice and ours alone. We must choose between Heaven and hell. No one can decide for us.

Do not think that anyone can escape the decision by straddling the fence. Pretending or straddling the fence will not get anyone into Heaven.

A no decision is a decision for hell. It is not complicated. Telling God "no" or avoiding a decision will send you to hell. To go to Heaven, you must choose Jesus and then pray: Tell God that Jesus is Lord and that you truly believe Jesus died on the cross and was resurrected from the dead. God will save you. (See Romans 10:9 below.) Jesus is the only gateway to Heaven.

Action: Do not pretend. Do not straddle the fence. Get on your knees. Ask God to forgive you for your sins, and tell Him you believe in Jesus. Also, tell God of your heartfelt belief that Jesus died and was raised from the dead. You will receive the Holy Spirit to help you as you march to Heaven, and your salvation will be secure forever.

Scripture Meditation: Deuteronomy 30:15: "'See, I have set before you today life and good, death and evil.'" Romans 10:9: "If you confess with your mouth the Lord Jesus and believe in your heart that God has raised Him from the dead, you will be saved."

DO YOU REALLY LOVE JESUS?

Today's title is not intended to be offensive, but sometimes we all need a reality check. So, the title is meant to motivate self-evaluations. We need to know how well we are performing our main job, which is to love the Lord and everyone else. We start with loving Jesus, because the more we love Him, the more we will love others.

We are fortunate. Jesus set the standard for us. He said that we are to love our God with all of our inner being—our mind, heart, and soul. (See Matthew 22:37 below.) Tough standard? Of course it is. Jesus is perfect. We are not. Yet we always should attempt to reach His standard. Our efforts will strengthen our walk and fellowship with Him.

Jesus also told us that if we love Him, we will keep His Word and that God will love us. (See John 14:23 below.) The strength of our walk with Jesus is affected by how much we love Him. Wow. Think about it. The more we love Jesus, the closer we will walk with Him and feel the love of God the Father. Naturally, the opposite is true. The less we love Jesus, the further we will be from God. How well we love Jesus greatly depends on how well we focus on Him.

Many Christians seem to think they can adequately love Jesus on Sunday while loving the world Monday through Saturday. This is a part-time love, creating a part-time fellowship with Jesus. It is dangerous. No one can walk in darkness or evil and have fellowship with Jesus. Anyone who says he or she can is not telling the truth. Such a claim is a lie. (See 1 John 1:6 below.)

What about you? Does your love for Jesus please Him and bring joy and comfort to you? Or is your love for Him displayed in a part-time or halfhearted way?

Action: Pray for the Holy Spirit to guide you in training yourself to focus properly on Jesus each day. The increasing focus on Jesus will result in a greater love for Him. Remember the increase of love for Jesus creates a much greater ability to love others.

Scripture Meditation: Matthew 22:37: "Jesus said to him, 'You shall love the Lord your God with all your heart, with all your soul, and with all your mind.'" John 14:23: "Jesus answered and said to him, 'If anyone loves Me, he will keep My word; and My Father will love him, and We will come to him and make Our home with him.'" First John 1:6: "If we say that we have fellowship with Him, and walk in darkness, we lie and do not practice the truth."

WHO SEEKS WHOM?

We are constantly wrestling with challenges. Some seem manageable. Many seem very difficult. We will continue to have problems, because we live in a fallen world. This is normal for both believers and nonbelievers. Problems seem to be everywhere. When we do not see trials, we hear folks talk about them, and this is in addition to our own burdens. This begs the question, "What is this world coming to?" We Christians know the answer. This world will come to an end.

What are we to do before the end comes? We should seek Jesus. He said He wanted us to have full life. He will help us overcome the burdens of the world and have an abundant life. It is Jesus's desire.

Do not be like the lady in a story relayed by a preacher. The lady was sitting on a bus stop bench crying. A stranger asked her, "Is something wrong?" She said, "My husband left me for another woman. He also took what little money we had. I am at my wit's end. I believe Jesus would help me, if He would just look for me and come near to me." Whoa! The lady did not understand Jesus's love. He loves everyone, including those who misunderstand Him.

Jesus will come near to anyone who seeks Him, including the lady. He told us to seek Him, and we should respond by seeking Him. (See Psalm 27:8 below.) Our challenges and all the problems we see and hear about are unable to prevent Jesus from coming to us when we seek Him. Jesus will not force Himself upon us, but He will respond to us in a mighty way.

Jesus will comfort you, give you His peace, and remove your fear as He reminds you that He is with you. He will give you strength as He helps you and lifts you up with His righteous hand. (See Isaiah 41:10 below.) This allows you to joyfully march through your burdens.

What else could we possibly want?

Action: Seek Jesus's face every day by focusing on Him. Use short, one-sentence prayers. They could be "Jesus, I seek your face," or "Jesus, show me the solution to this financial problem," or "Jesus, protect me while I am returning home." This keeps you focused on Him.

Scripture Meditation: Psalm 27:8: "When You said, 'Seek My face,' My heart said to You, 'Your face, Lord, I will seek.'" Isaiah 41:10: "Fear not, for I am with you; be not dismayed, for I am your God. I will strengthen you, yes, I will help you, I will uphold you with My righteous right hand."

DO NOT DOUBT JESUS

Christians rarely admit that we have doubted our Lord Jesus. Yet many have, especially in our prayer lives. Christians often, while mentioning a problem or need, say things like, "I prayed to Jesus, but I do not know if He will provide." Being uncertain has doubt as a companion. Having complete faith in our prayers, though, blocks out doubt. Faith and doubt have opposing meanings and cannot coexist in the same circumstance.

Jesus said that when we really believe, we will receive what we asked for in prayer; the provision is assured. (See Mark 11:24 below.) Any wishing or other uncertain feelings are doubts about whether Jesus will provide and weakens our walk with Him.

The apostle Peter let doubt damage his faith in Jesus. Jesus's disciples were in a boat on the sea. Jesus went close to them while walking on the water. Learning that Jesus was there, Peter called out to Jesus, asking to be commanded to go to Him, if He was there. Jesus told him to come. Peter left the boat and began to walk on the water toward Jesus. Then the wind blew stronger, scaring Peter, and he began to sink. Peter then asked that the Lord save him, and Jesus did. (See Matthew 14:28–31 below.) Peter was walking on water until his focus shifted from Jesus to the wind. The shift in focus brought fear, which created doubt in Peter's mind.

Get the point? When not focusing on Jesus, doubt steps in. Satan tricks us into doubting. Natural occurrences like storms, problems, and such can also shift our focus away from Jesus. It is up to each believer to avoid doubting Jesus by being intentional in maintaining his or her focus on Christ Jesus.

Do you sometimes doubt Jesus?

Action: Pray for strength to maintain your focus on Jesus and not doubt Him during unfortunate events and for wisdom to discern when Satan is trying to trick you. Tell Satan to flee from you.

Scripture Meditation: Mark 11:24: "Therefore I say to you, whatever things you ask when you pray, believe that you receive them, and you will have them." Matthew 14:28–31: "And Peter answered Him and said, 'Lord, if it is You, command me to come to You on the water.' So He said, 'Come.' And when Peter had come down out of the boat, he walked on the water to go to Jesus. But when he saw that the wind was boisterous, he was afraid; and beginning to sink he cried out, saying, 'Lord, save me!' And immediately Jesus stretched out His hand and caught him, and said to him, 'O you of little faith, why did you doubt?'"

SEND HIM PACKING

During the 1960s, many people would respond humorously to getting caught in a supposedly improper act. Many defended themselves by saying that the devil made them do it. This usually generated laughter from those who heard the remark. The statement helped turn bad situations into humor. However, the statement, albeit comical, unwittingly seemed to create a misconception of the biblical truth of Satan.

The devil cannot make or force us to do anything, as noted in the Bible and elsewhere in this book. We need to be ever mindful of this truth so that we can concentrate on what he is able to do as our adversary.

Satan tries to scare and devour us by walking around like a mean lion. (See 1 Peter 5:8 below.) He devours us through temptation and trickery. He tempts us by using our weaknesses to get us to fall victim to our natural worldly desires. He tricks us into committing sins by convincing us we can sin without consequences. The devil's goal is to damage our relationship with our Lord. But we can overcome his wily ways by resisting him.

Know that we can resist Satan because God commanded us to resist him. (See 1 Peter 5:9 below.) God also tells us that we can resist the devil by wearing the whole armor of God in order to overcome the wily ways of Satan. (See Ephesians 6:11 below.) Having the armor of God is wearing the belt of truth and the breastplate of righteousness; covering our feet with the gospel of peace; and using our faith as a shield, the Word of God as a sword, and our salvation as a helmet of protection.

Wearing the whole armor of God coupled with seeking encouragement and prayer support from other believers will effactually build our strength to resist Satan and his helpers. When we do this, we send him packing.

Are you prepared to resist the devil?

Action: Obey God. Resist Satan by putting on the whole armor of God to strengthen you in warding off Satan's wiles. Pray for assistance from Jesus and believers to further strengthen your ability to ward off the devil. Enjoy the peace and comfort of knowing you have sent Satan packing.

Scripture Meditation: First Peter 5:8–9: "Be sober, be vigilant; because your adversary the devil walks about like a roaring lion, seeking whom he may devour. Resist him, steadfast in the faith, knowing that the same sufferings are experienced by your brotherhood in the world." Ephesians 6:11: "Put on the whole armor of God, that you may be able to stand against the wiles of the devil."

WHERE IS YOUR DAILY FOCUS?

A marketing class taught that a brewery was the first known company to use targeted advertising. Their target was a man who worked hard to provide for his family. At the end of most workdays, he looked for a peaceful escape from the anxieties of his job. He arrived home only to be met by his wife, who told him of that day's household problems. He listened at first, but then he thought, *I can't take this*, and went to the refrigerator and grabbed a can of beer.

The man needed a respite from his cares and problems. But the worldly solution he chose would only bring a short, false reprieve. What he needed was a lasting release. One is available. We can give all of our concerns and worries to the Lord. (See 1 Peter 5:7 [NLT] below.) Giving our cares to our Lord is far better than a temporary solution.

So, how do we go about letting Jesus have our concerns and problems? We make Him our primary focus every day. This enables us to feel Jesus's presence and have confidence that He is thinking of us and keeping an eye on our problems because He cares.

Often, focusing on Jesus is difficult. Satan is prowling around, trying to convince us the solutions of the world are better. We should ignore him and maintain our focus on Jesus. For He, not Satan, promotes peace on earth and in Heaven. The more we focus on Jesus, the more our trust in Him grows.

Where is your primary daily focus? Is it on Jesus or anxieties of your career, your family, finances, or other cares? Do you trust Jesus to receive your problems? As a Christian, do you ever pray for the Lord to take your cares from you, and then later wonder why you still have the burdens? Maybe, just maybe, you sometimes ask Jesus to receive your anxieties, but you continue to hold on to them. Retaining our problems indicates a lack of focus on Jesus. Also, as you try to focus on Jesus, maybe one or more new concerns come creeping into the forefront.

Stop shouldering your anxieties. Give your worries and cares to the Lord.

Action: Pray for the Holy Spirit to convict you when your primary focus strays. Then welcome Jesus back into your mind. Speak to Him throughout the day as a way to keep Him in the center of your mind. Tell Jesus you are giving Him your cares. Then let go of them.

Scripture Meditation: First Peter 5:7 (NLT): "Give all your worries and cares to God, for he cares about you."

FULLY HUMBLE YOURSELF

The word *humble* is found eighty-two times in the Bible, while its noun form, humility, is found fourteen times—a total of ninety-six uses. Is this indicative of anything? It sure is. God places great importance on our humbling ourselves. His inspired Word teaches us to be humble before Him. (See James 4:10 below.) It is the will of God that we be humble in His presence.

Most, if not all, of us could truthfully say, "I do humble myself before God." We recognize His sovereignty. But do we fully humble ourselves? We need to look in the mirror and ask, "Do I humble myself before God and then check my humbleness at the door when going out into the world each day?" If so, we are not obeying God.

When dealing with other people, God wants us to use the same humility we display before Him. God also commands us to humbly submit to one another. (See 1 Peter 5:5 below.) It is easy to be humble before people who are charismatic, jovial, insightful leaders and such. Not so with others who are mean, negative, depressive, or sourpusses. So, what should we do?

God's command applies to all of us—everyone. We all submit by serving others. There are no exceptions. God commands that we submit and humble ourselves before everyone.

We humble ourselves in obedience to God by doing away with our selfishness, pride, and conceit and by highly respecting God and all others. (See Philippians 2:3 below.) Failure to do this allows pride to rule and offends God, because He detests pride. (Again, see 1 Peter 5:5 below.) But we please God when we humble ourselves before Him and others. He then continues to shed His grace upon the humble. So, it is our choice. We can fully humble ourselves and receive blessings from God, or yield to pride, causing God to resist us. What is your decision?

Action: Please God by humbling yourself before Him and others. Pray for the Holy Spirit to guide you. As you view all others as being better than yourself, serve them. Notice your pride slides away from your heart, leaving space for the fruit of the Spirit.

Scripture Meditation: James 4:10: "Humble yourselves in the sight of the Lord, and He will lift you up." First Peter 5:5: "Likewise you younger people, submit yourselves to your elders. Yes, all of you be submissive to one another, and be clothed with humility, for 'God resists the proud, but gives grace to the humble.'" Philippians 2:3: "Let nothing be done through selfish ambition or conceit, but in lowliness of mind let each esteem others better than himself."

MADE BY THE BEST

We all have done it. When purchasing something, we sometimes look for the item(s) of the manufacturer considered the best. We desire the finest. Sometimes the product is the best. Other times, it is faulty. When not the best, we complain.

There is no valid reason to complain about how we were made. God created us in His image. (See Genesis 1:27 below.) Our sovereign God is responsible for how we were made. God is perfect, so we should consider ourselves to be marvelously made. Each of us is one of the Lord's masterpieces. What more could we desire? We were made by the best.

I'm guessing many are now saying, "Yeah, but my nose is too big." Or "But I need more beauty." Or "But I am handicapped." Or "But …" Stop it! Which is more important, people's view of you or that of our Creator?

Each day, we consider which clothes we will wear. The decision is usually based on three things, whether consciously or subconsciously: 1) the activities we have planned for the day; 2) the worldview standards for the activities; and 3) the weather. Then we add accessories to our outer wear. Nothing wrong here.

Be careful, though, while selecting what you will wear. Do not be so mindful of selecting your clothes and accessories that you ignore the character and integrity within you. Ensure that you create and maintain an indestructible spirit of gentleness and wisdom, because God will be pleased. (See 1 Peter 3:3–4 below.) So, do you want to appear precious in the sight of God or people?

It is your decision. Remember though, people look at you outward appearance, while God looks at your heart and inner soul. (See 1 Samuel 16:7b below.) Also, you were made in the image of God.

Action: Pray for the Holy Spirit to guide you in keeping Jesus's commands. Notice how your focus starts shifting away from the concern about people's views of you to God's view. Thank and praise God for how He made you.

Scripture Meditation: Genesis 1:27: "So God created man in His own image; in the image of God He created him; male and female He created them." First Samuel 16:7b: "For the Lord does not see as man sees; for man looks at the outward appearance, but the Lord looks at the heart." First Peter 3:3–4: "Do not let your adornment be merely outward—arranging the hair, wearing gold, or putting on fine apparel. Rather let it be the hidden person of the heart, with the incorruptible beauty of a gentle and quiet spirit, which is very precious in the sight of God."

FORGIVING AND BLESSING, OR IGNORING?

Failure to forgive someone fully has to be one of the most common faults among Christians. Who among us has failed to forgive someone? We are persecuted by being deeply hurt, mentally or physically. The greater the hurt, the more difficult it is to forgive. Still, our Lord Jesus told us to forgive those who sin against us.

Jesus did not suggest we forgive others. He commanded it in very clear terms. Jesus told us that God the Father would not forgive us unless we forgive those who hurt us. (See Matthew 6:14–15 below.) Jesus was blunt in His command, which does not leave any wiggle room for argument. Forgive and be forgiven. Do not forgive, and you will not be forgiven.

Failure to forgive triggers a terrible consequence. But we can overcome. Jesus did. He knew His disciple Judas was a coconspirator to His upcoming murder. Yet Jesus called him His friend. (See Matthew 26:50 below.) Jesus, being without sin, could not have called Judas friend without forgiving him.

A mass killer murdered a lady's daughter because her daughter was a Christian. The lady demonstrated Jesus's standard of forgiveness. We all know that the greatest pain of all for parents is to lose a child to death. Yet this mother, through tears of pain, publicly forgave the killer who snatched away her daughter's life. There is only one word to describe her actions. Obedience.

Forgiving others cannot be partial or halfhearted. The forgiveness must be full and true with a follow-up. Follow-up? How? Jesus also expects us to bless and not curse everyone who sinned against us. (See Romans 12:14 below.) Ouch! Forgiving is very difficult, as is blessing those who hurt us. Put the two together, and our obedience is really tested. Yet, perseverance in obeying our Lord will transform our hearts into ones that are more like Him.

Are you willing to forgive and bless everyone who hurts you?

Action: Pray for strength in obeying God to forgive and bless those who hurt you, regardless of the level of pain. Ask God to use this experience to mold your heart into one that is pleasing to Him. Praise God as your transformation becomes a witness for Him.

Scripture Meditation: Matthew 6:14–15: "'For if you forgive men their trespasses, your heavenly Father will also forgive you. But if you do not forgive men their trespasses, neither will your Father forgive your trespasses.'" Matthew 26:50: "But Jesus said to him, 'Friend, why have you come?'" Romans 12:14: "Bless those who persecute you; bless and do not curse."

GOD'S WORD SAYS ...

Think about this. We need a Bible verse to help us, but we cannot find one that applies. We know that at least one verse exists. We either read it at home or heard it at church. We cannot find it, though. Sound familiar? This has happened to all Christians at some point. For some, it's been more regular than for others. But why does it happen? We read the Bible regularly. We listen in Sunday school as the teacher explains some scripture.

Could it be that we are not absorbing God's Word? We hear and read the Word. But we cannot absorb the Word because we do not meditate on it. We are hearing the Word without applying it. God told us through James to apply the Word rather than just listening, which is tricking ourselves. (See James 1:22 below.)

You are probably thinking, *I must be a doer of the Word, as I am not deceiving myself. I have stopped my past wicked ways.* Think again. Reevaluate using James 1:21 below. James said that putting aside your sinning and humbly receiving the absorbed Word would save you from eternal damnation.

We are not instructed to humbly receive God's Word into our minds and hearts. The instruction was to *humbly receive the absorbed or implanted Word.* To absorb or implant the Word of the Lord, we must read it, listen to it, meditate on it, apply it, and sometimes memorize it.

A natural result of implanting God's Word is truly becoming a doer of His Word. Need a Bible verse for a specific instance? Your mind will lead right to it. Jesus promised you would be blessed, for Luke told us that everyone who hears the Word and applies it will be blessed. (See Luke 11:28 below.)

Do you absorb God's Word in your heart? Or do you just wave at the Word as it passes through your eyes and ears? Are you willing to implant His Word?

Action: Implant God's precious Word in your mind and heart by reading, listening to, meditating on, and obeying it. Pray for the Holy Spirit to guide you in keeping His Word. Enjoy the blessing of being able to recall God's Word as needed daily.

Scripture Meditation: James 1:21–22: "Therefore lay aside all filthiness and overflow of wickedness, and receive with meekness the implanted word, which is able to save your souls. But be doers of the word, and not hearers only, deceiving yourselves." Luke 11:28: "But He said, 'More than that, blessed are those who hear the word of God and keep it!'"

BE STRONG. PERSEVERE!

Turn on the television to get the daily news, and you end up feeling disheartened, disgusted, disappointed, or depressed. The news is filled with reports of murders, robberies, rapes, and other crimes. When the TV anchors get to the so-called good news, it seems to be nothing more than people enjoying immoral lifestyles. As Christians, how can we fit into a society with rampant crime and immorality?

The answer is we hitch up our britches and start serving our Lord in a more serious, determined, obedient, and faithful manner. We create a revival across the land by allowing our Lord to begin within us. As we serve God, we should ask Him in prayer to have mercy on us and protect us with His presence and that we trust in Him. (See Psalm 57:1 below.)

Our obedience to the Lord becomes easier with His protection. Remember that we are able to be strong and courageous without any fear because the Lord is always with us. (See Joshua 1:9 below.) We can stand fast and persevere in serving Jesus.

The most important thing we can do while serving Jesus is to be a bright beacon for Him and constantly explaining the way to Him. The last thing Jesus said to His disciples before ascending to Heaven was to go throughout all of the land making and baptizing disciples. (See Matthew 28:19 below.) Jesus's command also applies to us.

Jesus commanded us to spread the Gospel. God said He would be merciful and protect us while we are doing His work. So, we have no reason not to obey Jesus.

Are you ready to be strong and persevere in spreading the Gospel, making disciples, and teaching them to be obedient? Obedience to our Lord would assist in again building a godly nation.

Action: Be strong and persevere. Under the protection of God, spread the news of Jesus. Ask God to continually place before you opportunities to spread the Gospel. Pray for the Holy Spirit to prepare the heart of each person you approach.

Scripture Meditation: Psalm 57:1: "Be merciful to me, O God, be merciful to me! For my soul trusts in You; and in the shadow of Your wings I will make my refuge, until these calamities have passed by." Joshua 1:9: "'Have I not commanded you? Be strong and of good courage; do not be afraid, nor be dismayed, for the Lord your God is with you wherever you go.'" Matthew 28:19: "'Go therefore and make disciples of all the nations, baptizing them in the name of the Father and of the Son and of the Holy Spirit.'"

WILL YOU RECEIVE A NEW NAME?

Have your ever wondered why a nickname is given to so many people? Usually the nickname is given out of an embedded love for the one named. This is especially true when a parent gives a child a nickname. Most of the time, the nickname stays with the person during his or her physical lifetime.

Do you have a nickname? Do you associate the nickname with a love for you within the person who gave you the name? Sure you do. Otherwise, the nickname would have slowly gone away. Well, guess who has a new name waiting for you? Jesus does, if you are a believer.

Jesus promised that everyone who obeys Him by overcoming will receive a new name written on a stone, and no one will see the stone except you and Jesus. (See Revelation 2:17 below.) How great is this! As believers, we will receive a new name that no one else knows except Jesus. You will not know my new name, nor will I know yours.

The name is Jesus's private and personal note to each of us because He loves us, died for us, and was resurrected for us. Jesus and each of us are best friends. We will always be His because He will continue to be our Lord throughout all eternity. And it gets better.

We will receive our new name written on a white stone. During biblical times, a white stone represented acquittal, approval, or a pass to an important event. Think about it. Our secret name is written on a stone as confirmation that we have been forgiven for our sins, and our ticket to Heaven has been guaranteed. Our spot in Heaven is reserved, and our new name is confirmation of our reservation. Woohoo!

Are you Heaven bound? Is Jesus holding a new name for you? If not, you can make your reservation for Heaven by believing in Jesus and accepting Him as your Lord and Savior.

Action: If you are not a Christian but want to go to Heaven, turn from your sins. Ask God to forgive you and for Jesus to come into your heart as your Lord and Savior. Then bask in the love of Jesus and look forward to your secret name. If you are already a believer, praise God for your salvation.

Scripture Meditation: Revelation 2:17: "'He who has an ear, let him hear what the Spirit says to the churches. To him who overcomes I will give some of the hidden manna to eat. And I will give him a white stone, and on the stone a new name written which no one knows except him who receives it.'"

RIGHTEOUS ANGER

Have you heard of righteous anger? Ever had it? God had it. Christ Jesus had it. You can have it. So, what is it? Note that anger can be either good or bad. It is not of itself a sin. Good anger is righteous anger, while bad anger is sinful.

Righteous anger is an unselfish anger toward immorality, crime, ungodly actions, and all other sins against God. It is not a sin. God had no sin, but the Israelites pushed Him into a righteous anger because of their unrelenting sin. Jesus, who was totally sinless, displayed a righteous anger when He saw sinful business being conducted in the temple. He overturned the tables and chairs of the unfair sellers and moneychangers. (See Matthew 21:12 below.) Jesus's motive was pure and unselfish.

Before you say, "Phew, my angry disgust toward the idolatry worship and immorality going on all around me is a righteous anger," think again. When did you develop this righteous anger? Did it develop today, yesterday, last month, or last year? Any time farther back than today means your anger is no longer righteous. Any righteous anger we developed today should not be carried over to the next day. (See Ephesians 4:26 below.) Even righteous anger is to be chunked quickly. Hold onto the anger and it becomes a sin against God. Still, it is difficult to discard anger.

We do not have the knowledge or the discipline of the Lord. Holding onto anger, including righteous anger, allows our emotions to creep in. This is bad. Our emotions are often tainted with sin. The anger begins to fester and turn toward the one who sinned against us. But we do have an escape route to a solution. We know or should know the old tenet, "hate the sin and love the sinner." We all must inject love to rid ourselves of our anger.

We can have righteous anger, but we must ensure that we do not hold on to it.

Action: Pray for the Holy Spirit to remind you to remove all anger quickly, including righteous anger. Also, ask for strength to develop the discipline to love those who anger you. Praise God as stress from anger fades away and is replaced by the comfort of peace and joy.

Scripture Meditation: Matthew 21:12: "Then Jesus went into the temple of God and drove out all those who bought and sold in the temple, and overturned the tables of the money changers and the seats of those who sold doves." Ephesians 4:26: "'Be angry, and do not sin': do not let the sun go down on your wrath."

RECEIVED A MIRACLE LATELY?

An individual is in the middle of financial crisis. He needs a miracle to recover. He knows he can ask God to remove the trial. But he doesn't. Why? The man probably lacks the faith that God will provide a miracle. This is so sad. He is relying on his own power rather than God's power.

God is able and willing to provide any needed miracle, big or small. One of the more memorable miracles in the Bible's New Testament is Jesus's use of five loaves of bread and two fish to feed five thousand people. That, my friends, is quite a miracle. The folks were hungry. Jesus fed them all from a small amount of food and had leftovers.

Do you need a miracle? You may say, "I do, but my situation is extremely dire covering several different parts of my life." Did you know that God can do much, much more than we can envision or request? (See Ephesians 3:20 [NIV] below.) Think about it. Neither you nor I are able to ask for or imagine as much as He can provide.

God is willing to provide a miracle if we ask Him. Don't be shy. Present your needs to the Lord in prayer, not with anxiety but with thanksgiving. (See Philippians 4:6 below.) We must ask in faith, though. Do this, and God will be faithful in answering your request. If we ask with a faithless hope, we probably will be left still hoping.

Some of you are probably thinking, *The Bible is full of God's miracles, but His miracle making was left behind as the world evolved with ever-changing technology.* Your doubts are totally unfounded. God does not change. (See Malachi 3:6 below.) So, God's ability to make miracles is unchanged.

Remember that our eternal God is still capable and willing to provide a miracle when needed. And it does not matter how bad or grim our circumstance may be.

Action: Know that God is able and willing to perform miracles. Stand firm in your faith in Him. In prayer, faithfully petition God to save you from whatever your impossible situation is. Relax as your miracle from God smothers your fear of the impossible plight.

Scripture Meditation: Ephesians 3:20 (NIV): "Now to him who is able to do immeasurably more than all we ask or imagine, according to his power that is at work within us." Philippians 4:6: "Be anxious for nothing, but in everything by prayer and supplication, with thanksgiving, let your requests be made known to God." Malachi 3:6: "'For I am the Lord, I do not change; therefore you are not consumed, O sons of Jacob.'"

WORSHIP: PART-TIME VERSUS FULL-TIME

Our human nature tends to have us compartmentalize our lives. We put our various life parts in separate boxes. This can be a serious problem for Christians.

Christians accept Jesus as Lord, which means He is Lord over each Christian's entire life. For this to be true, we must worship Jesus full-time. To worship Him full-time, we cannot put our worship in a box separate from the other parts of our lives. Otherwise we will be worshipping part-time.

As we limit our worship, we limit sharing in the riches of God's glory. We miss experiencing His peace and comfort each day. Our level of joy and gentleness is lower. And this is just part of the benefits affected. There is something even worse.

Placing a limit on our worship is being disobedient to God. Jesus is our lord. We are His disciples. All that we do we should do in Jesus's name and with thanksgiving to God. (See Colossians 3:16–17 below.) Did you see the word *all*? Everything that we do should be in Jesus's name. This is full-time worshipping. We are commanded to worship Him in our personal lives, professional lives, and all other parts of our lives. We begin worship of God by having Jesus's Word dwell in us.

Instead of compartmentalizing or limiting our worship, we should make Jesus our top priority in every part of our lives. We can do this. We can take Jesus to work with us. We should consult with Him for guidance and wisdom. After work, we need to take Jesus home with us. There, we should continue to call upon Jesus to guide us.

Do you get the picture? Part-time worship is following Jesus part-time. The closer we move to full-time worship, the more we obey God, the more glory we bring to Him, and the greater happiness we enjoy.

Each day, we have a choice: worship Jesus full-time or part-time. Remember, though, full-time worship is obedience to God. Part-time worship is disobedience to Him.

Action: Seek God's forgiveness if you have worship in a separate box. Pray for guidance in working toward full-time worship. Also, ask for the Holy Spirit to convict you if you backslide. Thank and praise God for being your Lord.

Scripture Meditation: Colossians 3:16–17: "Let the word of Christ dwell in you richly in all wisdom, teaching and admonishing one another in psalms and hymns and spiritual songs, singing with grace in your hearts to the Lord. And whatever you do in word or deed, do all in the name of the Lord Jesus, giving thanks to God the Father through Him."

WHAT IS FUELING YOUR CONTENTMENT?

In today's world, we are urged to dream big, set lofty goals, and never be satisfied. If you reach a goal, set a new and higher one. Attaining our goals makes us successful. Or at least in people's eyes. God's eyes may view our goals differently.

Goal setting is great, if it is consistent with God's will. For example, never being satisfied is not God's will for us. Using himself as an example, Paul explained this.

Paul at times needed money. Other times, he had plenty. There were instances when Paul was persecuted. Other times, he abided in the comfort of friends. Yet Paul learned that regardless of what state or condition he was in, he was contented. He further explained that it did not matter if he was hungry, full of food, suffering, well, or penniless; he was contented. (See Philippians 4:11–12 below.) Paul was satisfied in all his situations, whether good or bad. We need to be like him.

We also can attain Paul's attitude, if we depend on Jesus Christ who makes us strong. This aids us in developing a continual attitude of contentment because we are able to do anything while relying on Jesus. (See Philippians 4:13 below.)

Paul's lead teaches us how to want what we have rather than wanting what we don't have. Being satisfied while striving to reach the goal of fulfilling God's will is a very worthy and reachable goal that brings eternal success.

Do you want to be successful before humans or God? Consider your time on earth to be but a speck of sand out of all the sand in the world. Eternity is all the sand. Do you desire success that ends after that single speck passes before you? Or do you want success that continues while the uncountable specks of all the world's sand pass before you one by one? Will you choose humanity's way or God's?

Action: Pray for Jesus to reveal God's will to you. Set achieving His will as your goal. Ask for the Holy Spirit to guide you in working to fulfill God's will. Also, ask Jesus to fill you with His peace as you go about pleasing God. Praise Him for your contentment.

Scripture Meditation: Philippians 4:11–13: "Not that I speak in regard to need, for I have learned in whatever state I am, to be content: I know how to be abased, and I know how to abound. Everywhere and in all things I have learned both to be full and to be hungry, both to abound and to suffer need. I can do all things through Christ who strengthens me."

PEACE OR DESPAIR?

Christians enjoy talking about the peace of God. Have you experienced His peace? Not the world's peace, for there is a huge difference between the peace of the world and God's peace. We do not understand His peace, but it calms our hearts and minds. (See Philippians 4:7 below.) The world's peace is a simple outward calmness easily understood by all.

Jesus stands ready to give to His followers the peace that exceeds our knowledge. He said, "I give to you My peace, which is different and far better than the world's peace. So, be calm and do not fear." (See John 14:27 below.) This peace has a comforting tranquility that goes far beyond any understanding or ability to describe adequately.

Jesus does more than give us His peace. He will guide us through our trials, storms, and tribulations. The Lord said that there is no reason to fear. He will grasp and lead us with His righteous right hand and make us stronger. (See Isaiah 41:10 below.) Again, have you experienced His peace?

Suppose you just learned that you have stage four cancer. Your mind is spinning with all kinds of thoughts, and you are at a fork in the road. One path is the way of peace. The other path is the way of despair. Your human side could send you reeling down the road of despair. This road is heavily populated with self-pity, why me, worry, fear, discouragement, and other miseries. You seek comfort from the world. But this comfort is filled with pity.

The road of peace is filled with true comfort, serenity, tranquility, and such, all of which are far greater than your imagination. Such peace instills self-confidence, which allows you to better face your trials. And you are not alone because the Lord leads you through your dire situations.

When you come to the fork, will you choose peace or despair?

Action: Choose peace by praying to God for His peace and for Jesus to lead you by the hand as you travel through the trial. Know that as you live in God's peace, your light will shine brighter as a witness for Jesus and God the Father.

Scripture Meditation: Philippians 4:7: "And the peace of God, which surpasses all understanding, will guard your hearts and minds through Christ Jesus." John 14:27: "Peace I leave with you, My peace I give to you; not as the world gives do I give to you. Let not your heart be troubled, neither let it be afraid." Isaiah 41:10: "Fear not, for I am with you; be not dismayed, for I am your God. I will strengthen you, yes, I will help you, I will uphold you with My righteous right hand."

TAKE JESUS OFF THE SHELF

As Christians, we are disciples of Jesus. We are to follow, abide in, and serve Him. Most Christians know this, but many other believers put Jesus on a shelf until they feel He is needed for an emergency. Could it be that these Christians have yet to obtain the mind-set of Jesus? As disciples, we should think like Jesus.

A man had accepted Christ as his Lord and Savior as a teenager. For eleven years, he failed to mature as a Christian. He called on Jesus only when he had a problem or trial. Suddenly, he learned that he needed to nurture his mind to be like that of Jesus. Then his whole world changed. He began to seek those he could serve and with whom he could share the good news of Jesus. His closeness to Jesus became a testimony to others.

As that man learned, our thoughts influence our lives. It is that simple. Whatever is in our mind, good or bad, dictates what we do. To please God by properly serving Jesus, we need pure thoughts. Jesus's thoughts were the purest of anyone who ever lived. His mind-set was the perfect model.

We need to have the mind-set of serving others as Jesus did. (See Philippians 2:5 below.) We know this is God's will because He faithfully called us to serve through fellowship with Jesus. (See 1 Corinthians 1:9 below.)

It really is not difficult to seek Jesus's mind-set. He told us we could be like Him by abiding in Him and allowing Him to abide in us. Jesus said that when He and we abide in each other, we will bear a lot of fruit. (See John 15:5 below.) We need to allow Jesus to direct us as we serve Him, for we cannot do anything without Him.

Are you abiding in Jesus or just using Him as an emergency responder?

Action: Remove Jesus from the shelf and allow Him to abide in you. Reciprocate and abide in Him. As you learn to think and act like Jesus, pray for continued success in being like Him. Praise God for His faithfulness and for allowing you to seek Jesus's mind-set.

Scripture Meditation: Philippians 2:5: "Let this mind be in you which was also in Christ Jesus." First Corinthians 1:9: "God is faithful, by whom you were called into the fellowship of His Son, Jesus Christ our Lord." John 15:5: "'I am the vine, you are the branches. He who abides in Me, and I in him, bears much fruit; for without Me you can do nothing.'"

I RECEIVED COMFORT. NOW WHAT?

All Christians have suffered through a life trial. The problem may have been a serious illness, family problem, overdue bills, and such. We all probably reacted the same.

We felt like we were in a jam. We got anxious. We prayed. God comforted us while leading us through the trials. We praised Him for what He had done for us. We reveled in the blessedness for a while. Then our attention shifted back to our daily drudgery. Sound familiar? I'm guessing it does. Is our action correct?

While facing a problem, we all should ask God for help and comfort. The trial is magnified if we attack it alone. The stress can be devastating. But God is able and more than willing to lead us though our tribulations. He desires to comfort and lead us through our problems. God is merciful. So, He will comfort and help us. (See 2 Corinthians 1:3–4 below.) But it does not stop here.

It is the will of God for us to use the comfort we received to comfort others. Some of you may now be saying, "Nobody has ever told that to me." Well, God did through Paul. (See 2 Corinthians 1:4 below). When we receive comfort from God, we should be merciful like Him and comfort those who are suffering when we cross their path. This is an important task that God has placed before us.

We are never to hoard the comfort God has given to us. One of the reasons He gives us comfort is for us to use it in comforting others with problems. It is not just God's desire. He has made it our responsibility.

Be cautious. Simply telling others, "I have been there, done that," is not comforting to most people. It is being flippant. God doesn't want us to be shallow. He never was. We should share our comfort experience in a loving way and tell how it replaced our stress and anxiety with an inner peace. In other words, be testimonial in sharing your comfort.

Action: Use your God-given comfort to help those battling problems. Pray for the Holy Spirit to guide you in assisting others. Praise God for your comfort and the privilege of using it to help others. Enjoy observing others bask in the same comfort you experienced.

Scripture Meditation: Second Corinthians 1:3–4: "Blessed be the God and Father of our Lord Jesus Christ, the Father of mercies and God of all comfort, who comforts us in all our tribulation, that we may be able to comfort those who are in any trouble, with the comfort with which we ourselves are comforted by God."

SHED YOUR COCOON

A man and a woman were talking. He said to her, "What is wrong? You appear to be starving for love. You radiate loneliness and distrust. You greet those you see in church without stopping to talk. Your best friend says you are less socially minded. Most of your friends no longer have time to drop in. You seem to be wrapped in a cocoon. Why?"

"My spouse, coworkers, and some friends have all turned their backs on me," she said.

"Have you asked Jesus to help you? He will, you know," he responded.

"I don't know. It is my fault. I messed up really bad. Most of the people I loved no longer love me. So, I started trying to drink my way back into their love," she said.

He then said to her, "I will pray for you. And please, go to our Lord in prayer, seeking His comfort and help. He will lead you through your problems."

"You don't understand. I am ashamed of myself, disappointed in those I loved, and distrustful of most everyone. I went from walking with Jesus to crawling alone in the mud," she said.

He responded, "Jesus understands how you feel. He has not walked in your shoes. He walked in worse. He was in deeper mud than we can imagine. Some loved ones turned against Him. Many of the people He came to save screamed for Him to be crucified. He was mocked as His shredded body hung on a cross so He could save you and me. So, do not let shame guide you. Jesus didn't."

Jesus's love for everyone is never-ending and never fails. (See Psalm 18:50 [NIV] below.) We all should shed our cocoons. We do not need them. Jesus will give to us a much better solution. He will give us His peace, so do not fear or worry. (See John 14:27 below.) Ask for His peace.

Jesus is ready to help everyone who needs it. His never-ending love bolstered by His arms of peace and comfort is all we need. Jesus will pull us out of the muck. Trust Him.

Action: When someone hurts or disappoints you, in prayer cry out to Jesus. Let Jesus's never-failing love give you peace and comfort as He leads you through the trial. Praise Him as you persevere while resting in His peace.

Scripture Meditation: Psalm 18:50 (NIV): "He gives his king great victories; he shows unfailing love to his anointed, to David and to his descendants forever." John 14:27: "Peace I leave with you, My peace I give to you; not as the world gives do I give to you. Let not your heart be troubled, neither let it be afraid."

ARE YOU EXPERIENCING GOD?

Many believers say they want more from their relationship with God. Guess what? God does too. So, what is the problem? Maybe, just maybe, we do not know God—I mean really know Him.

We say we study the Bible and rarely miss Sunday school and worship services. This is great. We obviously have learned a lot about God. But do we really, really know Him? We have to experience God to truly know Him.

Now, we are saying that we thought we knew God. We selected some church-sponsored ministries in which to take part. We have been faithful to the ministries. Yet we have not experienced God in those activities. What is the problem?

Maybe we learned about God but put our knowledge to work to accomplish our will, not His. We elected to serve in ministries we chose. We did not ask God if that is where He wants us to serve. We probably were afraid God would ask us to step out of our comfort zone. We were wrong. It is a false worry. God will equip and comfort us if we are obedient to His will.

We need to follow God's will, not ours. He will help us. Our Lord, the God of peace, will equip us to do any good work or task that is consistent with His will through Christ Jesus. (See Hebrews 13:20–21 below.) This is pleasing to God and glorifies Him. God has been grooming and equipping us for certain tasks. He will reveal His will for our service if we seek it through prayer and obedience to His Word. This is how we are able to experience God.

Experiencing God broadens your comfort zone to include whatever His will is for you. Are you willing to experience God by adjusting your life to comply with His will? Only you can decide for yourself.

Action: Use your knowledge of God to seek and fulfill His will. Pray for Jesus to assist you and for the Holy Spirit to convict you if you stray from God's will. Enjoy the peace, comfort, and joy of experiencing God. Note that your light will shine with increasing brightness.

Scripture Meditation: Hebrews 13:20–21: "Now may the God of peace who brought up our Lord Jesus from the dead, that great Shepherd of the sheep, through the blood of the everlasting covenant, make you complete in every good work to do His will, working in you what is well pleasing in His sight, through Jesus Christ, to whom be glory forever and ever. Amen."

WRETCHEDNESS VERSUS GOD'S GRACE

It is difficult to describe God's grace. His grace is more than His love, mercy, or any other of His great traits. It is all His traits rolled into one. God's grace is who He is. The grace of man cannot compare to God's grace. John Newton's ever-popular song, "Amazing Grace," just might be the best description of God's grace. Within the first verse, the lyrics indicate that God will save anyone, no matter how wretched.

Can you relate to being wretched? I can. I was bad, yet I was saved more than sixty years ago, and I still feel overwhelmed with emotion when I think of how God's grace washed away my wretchedness with His Son's blood.

Biblical heroes Moses, David, and Paul were murderers. Yet God saved them through His grace. They all proved that our wretchedness is not greater than God's grace. For example, Paul was determined to kill the Christian religion by murdering believers. He ended up doing the opposite because God transformed him. Paul became a missionary, extended the kingdom of God by planting churches, and wrote at least thirteen books in the Bible's New Testament. God's grace was and still is truly amazing.

Do you see what God has done? He created the world and mankind. Man ruined the perfect world by sinning. But God did not give up on humanity. His grace covered humanity with a love that is never ending and is greater than our understanding. God, through His grace, gave His only Son, Jesus, unto death so that anyone could be saved from his or her sins and have eternal life, if he or she truly believes in Jesus. (See John 3:16 below.)

God sacrificed His only Son rather than giving us what we deserve—condemnation. Rather than condemning the world, God, through His grace, chose to save the world through Jesus. (See John 3:17 below.) Wow! Does His grace overwhelm you? It should. It overcomes wretchedness.

Action: Personalize John 3:16 by substituting your name for *the world* and *whoever* and add the word "who" before *believes*. For example, "For God so loved Ron that He gave His only begotten Son, that Ron who believes in Him ..." Use this modified verse to avoid taking God's grace for granted. Pray for guidance in accepting more of God's grace.

Scripture Meditation: John 3:16–17: "For God so loved the world that He gave His only begotten Son, that whoever believes in Him should not perish but have everlasting life. For God did not send His Son into the world to condemn the world, but that the world through Him might be saved."

ARE YOU WHERE GOD WANTS YOU?

Our nature is to seek safety, because we find comfort in security. Some circumstances denote safety. Going to sleep while listening to the pitter-patter of rain hitting the roof. Sitting by the fire on a cold night. Being controversy-free in your job. All are comfortable and safe. Is being secure where God wants you to be though?

"I am God's child, so I must be where God wants me," you say. Did you ask Him? Why haven't you? Are you afraid to step away from the security of your comfort zone? Don't be. God is not only your salvation. He is your light, so is there anyone of whom to be afraid? (See Psalm 27:1 below.) Fear no one.

Be adventurous. Seek God's will. Obey Him by stepping out in faith. Teach a Sunday school class. Change your career. Become a missionary. Change churches. Just obey God. "But He may ask me to do something that I am not capable of or cannot do," you say.

God told Abraham to offer his only son, Isaac, as a sacrifice. The world would consider this murder, yet Abraham obeyed the Lord. He packed up Isaac, wood, and fire. He then left for Mt. Moriah. Isaac noticed that there was no lamb for the offering. (See Genesis 22:7 below.) Abraham said that they would rely on God for the lamb. (See Genesis 22:8 below.) As Abraham was about to slay Isaac for the sacrifice, an angel of the Lord stopped him. Abraham then saw a ram caught in bushes, so he took the ram and used it as an offering. (See Genesis 22:13 below.)

Throw away your self-made safety net; seek God's will and obey Him. There is nothing to fear. God will provide your needs. Step out in faith. Then you will be where God wants you.

Action: Ask God if you are where He wants you to be. If not, ask Him to reveal His will to you. Act through faith to fulfill His will.

Scripture Meditation: Psalm 27:1: "The Lord is my light and my salvation; whom shall I fear? The Lord is the strength of my life; of whom shall I be afraid?" Genesis 22:7–8, 13: "But Isaac spoke to Abraham his father and said, 'My father!' And he said, 'Here I am, my son.' Then he said, 'Look, the fire and the wood, but where is the lamb for a burnt offering?' And Abraham said, 'My son, God will provide for Himself the lamb for a burnt offering.' So the two of them went together. Then Abraham lifted his eyes and looked, and there behind him was a ram caught in a thicket by its horns. So Abraham went and took the ram, and offered it up for a burnt offering instead of his son."

CLOSE TO GOD OR JUST HOPING?

Consider this: What is your status with God? Very close? Wishing to be close? Trying to get closer? Most, if not all of us, probably are not as near to God as we should be. Why is this? There are a lot of possible reasons, and each one reflects our failures, not God's.

God does not fail us. Yet I have heard many Christians say that God is not as close to them as He once was. They say this as if God had moved from them. God did not move. They did. We usually call it backsliding. We must remember that Satan is still prowling around, tempting believers. Sometimes we fall for his tricks.

We fail ourselves, but most of all, we fail God. There is a solution though. Some call it going back to the basics to shore up our Christian foundation. I call it obeying God. James told us to approach God in worship, and He will approach us. (See James 4:8 below.) We act, and God reacts.

Get closer to God by submitting to Him and humbling yourself before Him. Satan will have this quiet and calm voice, telling you that it is useless. He will say God has stepped away from you. Don't fall for the lie. Tell him to get lost. Now proceed toward God.

Reestablishing our lowliness before the Lord eases the way for us to regret and grieve over the sins that caused our backsliding. (See James 4:9 below.) This really scares the evil one even more.

Seek forgiveness from God from a repentant heart. This recognizes His sovereign authority and is submitting to Him. Affirming our allegiance to Him defeats Satan, and he will run from us. (See James 4:7 below.) Don't you just love defeating the devil?

Now that Satan is licking his wounds, don't tarry. Continue to run to God. He is waiting.

Action: In prayer, ask the Holy Spirit to convict you of backsliding. Ask God to forgive you. Submit to Him. Humble yourself before Him. Take comfort in God's presence. Praise God for His closeness.

Scripture Meditation: James 4:7–9: "Therefore submit to God. Resist the devil and he will flee from you. Draw near to God and He will draw near to you. Cleanse your hands, you sinners; and purify your hearts, you double-minded. Lament and mourn and weep! Let your laughter be turned to mourning and your joy to gloom."

HOW RESISTANT ARE YOU?

We all are tempted to sin. Temptations come in a sundry of ways. Some are subtle. Some come openly. And we will continue to face temptations on this side of Heaven. The most important thing is our effort to resist temptations. Are you successful in resisting? Do you succumb to some temptations? The most honest answer is probably yes to both questions.

Our weaknesses determine our resistance-success-to-failure ratio. We will be tested. Satan will use his lies and tricks to ensure we will be provoked to sin. Yet, there is good news. Paul taught that we are able strengthen our resistance to temptations, if we are willing. (See 1 Corinthians 10:13 below.) Mull over this verse and then continue reading.

The ability to resist temptations can be found in numbers. There are many others trying to ward off similar temptations. We can learn from them. We can create joint efforts to fight Satan. We all are capable of resisting because God will not permit us to be tempted beyond what we can handle. Yet He also provides an escape route for us. This should provide a lot of confidence and comfort while attempting to resist temptations. No matter how weak we are, we can overcome. Jesus overcame, and we can too if we ask God for help.

I know what you're probably thinking that Jesus was perfect, and you are not. But He is precisely what we need. We have a High Priest who understands our weaknesses. He has withstood the same temptations as we endure, and He overcame every single enticement placed before Him. (See Hebrews 4:15 below.) Jesus is our High Priest, and He overcame. He has been there and done that.

Hunger was thrown at Jesus. He did not bite. Greed waved its flag at Him. He never yearned for more. Power offered itself to Him. He pushed it away. Jesus refused to sin when tempted. Be like Him.

Action: Tell Satan to get lost. Jesus is your leader. Pray for discernment to distinguish between Satan's tricks and Jesus's guiding hand. Let Jesus lead. Thank and praise God for giving us a loving and sinless High Priest.

Scripture Meditation: First Corinthians 10:13: "No temptation has overtaken you except such as is common to man; but God is faithful, who will not allow you to be tempted beyond what you are able, but with the temptation will also make the way of escape, that you may be able to bear it." Hebrews 4:15: "For we do not have a High Priest who cannot sympathize with our weaknesses, but was in all points tempted as we are, yet without sin."

WHY? (PART I)

Suppose you lived during the time of Christ Jesus's ministry on earth. You heard about Him. Then two of His followers, Peter and John, told you that Jesus was the Son of God and was doing great things. They also said that Jesus was a king, and His kingdom was everlasting but not of this earth. Ten days later, you heard Jesus had been arrested and would be crucified. Why?

You go to see for yourself. And there is Jesus being forced to carry the cross that would kill Him. He is being whipped. His blood is on the street. Strips of flesh are hanging from Him. Jesus can hardly carry the cross. The soldiers continue to flog Him. Jesus doesn't complain. More beatings. More blood. Why?

Somehow, Jesus survives the short trek to Calvary. Then the soldiers nail His hands and feet to a cross and stand it upright. Jesus's bleeding continues. He still doesn't complain. He is spit on, laughed at, and mocked. Why?

Jesus somehow endures the horrific pain without screaming. While struggling to breathe, He even talks to one of two other men being crucified. Jesus does not appear to be angry or ashamed for what is happening. Why?

Jesus looks down at those watching Him. He speaks to a couple of them. You wonder if He sees the soldiers gambling for His clothes. Then Jesus's difficulty in breathing worsens considerably. He is dying. Why?

The grotesque scene gets to you. You scream out, "Jesus, you are the Son of God. You do not have to die. Please, please come down from there!" He turns, and His eyes lock in on your eyes. You say, "Why?"

Jesus says, "It is finished."

You ask, "Finished? What is finished?" Then you remember.

Peter and John had told you that Jesus said that God, through His love, gave His only Son so that everyone believing in Him will have eternal life. (See John 3:16 below.) You say, "Jesus died for me so I could have eternal life because I believe in Him." That is why.

It is simple. Jesus died for everyone, but all will not believe in Him. Do you?

Action: If you believe in Him, accept Him as Lord if you have not already. If you do not believe in Jesus, pray for the Holy Spirit to send a Christian to you to explain Jesus to you.

Scripture Meditation: John 3:16: "For God so loved the world that He gave His only begotten Son, that whoever believes in Him should not perish but have everlasting life."

WHY? (PART II)

You had observed Christ Jesus's death on the cross. As you watched, you were extremely distraught. You asked yourself, "If Jesus is truly the Son of God, how could this happen?" Then as Jesus took His last breath, you remembered that Peter and John had told you Jesus had foretold all the disciples of His death. His dying was sacrificial so we could have eternal life. You became jubilant.

Three days later, you are distraught again. You are no longer sure that you will have eternal life. You keep saying to yourself, "I watched Jesus die. I saw His dead body taken from the cross and carried to a burial cave. For some reason, soldiers came and sealed the tomb." Finally, you ask out loud, "How can a dead man give anyone eternal life?" This question haunts you.

You go looking for Peter and John, thinking that they might be able to help you. Peter sees you coming. He is smiling. You silently ask, "Why is he smiling? Our Lord has been murdered."

Peter welcomes you with open arms and shouts, "Jesus is alive! He arose from the dead! I have seen Him and touched His nail-scarred hands and feet!"

You are speechless. You just look at Peter with a blank expression. He reports Jesus had told them that He would be arrested by evil men, crucified, and then rise up three days later. (See Luke 24:7 below.) Slowly, joy begins to fill you.

Now your depression turns to renewed jubilation. Excitedly, you tell Peter, "Now I get it! Jesus sacrificed His life on the cross to pay the price for my sins! Jesus defeated death by arising from the dead so that I could have eternal life!" Peter agrees. That is what Jesus meant when He said that God did not send Him here to condemn people but to save them. (See John 3:17 below.)

Jesus came to save the world. To be saved, you need to believe in Him in your heart.

Are you ready to be freed from your sins and to know that you will be with the Lord throughout eternity?

Action: Pray that you will not forget that Jesus defeated death by arising from a sealed tomb and eventually ascending back to Heaven. Praise God for your salvation.

Scripture Meditation: Luke 24:7: "'The Son of Man must be delivered into the hands of sinful men, and be crucified, and the third day rise again.'" John 3:17: "'For God did not send His Son into the world to condemn the world, but that the world through Him might be saved.'"

TELLING OTHERS ABOUT JESUS

Over two thousand years ago, Jesus arose from His throne and left Heaven to be born a baby from a virgin womb. Just like you and me, He grew physically, walked along the earth, laughed, became angry, cried, and faced temptations. But unlike you and me, He never succumbed to temptations. His death came by offering Himself as a living sacrifice.

He allowed Himself to be nailed to a cross. There He suffered the most horrific, painful, slow, and torturous death devised by humans. God resurrected Jesus on the third day. The sacrificial death atoned for our sins, and the resurrection confirmed the sacrifice by defeating death. Jesus paid the price of all the past, present, and future sins—my sins, your sins, and all others' sins. This is the good news of Jesus—the Gospel.

Jesus told us to spread the Gospel by going to the nations; making disciples; baptizing the disciples in the name of the Father, Son, and Holy Spirit; and teaching them the things He had taught and commanded. (See Matthew 28:19–20 below.) Jesus's instructions were His last spoken words before returning to Heaven. He also said that He always would be with us spiritually. Jesus clearly made sharing the Gospel a top priority for you and me.

We are commanded to go and spread the Gospel. It is not hard. Yet somehow Satan has convinced many of us that if we do share the news of Jesus, we will be scorned and ridiculed, become friendless, or suffer a sundry of other bad reactions. Yet we must obey Jesus, not Satan.

Have you failed to be obedient to Jesus's command? Do you wonder if someone is destined to spend eternity in hell, separated from God, due to your failure? It is ironic. You may have been afraid of a bad response. Yet no negative response could create anguish like that caused by possibly taking away someone's chance of eternal life.

Are you still reluctant to share Christ? Help is available for you. Most churches have Gospel-sharing tracts and programs. Both will build your confidence.

Action: Consider the difference in the joy of leading a person to Christ with the shame of letting Jesus down. Pray for God to place before you daily an opportunity to share the Gospel, to give you boldness to act, and for the Holy Spirit to guide you and give you the words to use.

Scripture Meditation: Matthew 28:19–20: "'Go therefore and make disciples of all the nations, baptizing them in the name of the Father and of the Son and of the Holy Spirit, teaching them to observe all things that I have commanded you; and lo, I am with you always, even to the end of the age.'"

RUN HARD! DO NOT CRAWL!

We believe in Jesus. He is our Lord and Savior. He placed before us the race of life. It is no ordinary race. We run the race only once. It begins with our receipt of salvation and ends with our physical death. The prize is greater than our imagination. It is Heaven. So, how well are we running our race?

Never give up. Run harder to persevere. We can do it. Faith in the Lord is our fuel that sustains us during the race. The race, though, is still very difficult at times.

Sometimes we stumble. Satan tricks us and leads us astray into sin. Overindulgence in our secular needs is also heavy baggage. The stumbling blocks for some are larger than those of others. No matter. We can run with stamina the race that the Lord has placed before us. (See Hebrews 12:1 below.) We can overcome the traps, as did the heavenly witnesses, by casting aside every stumbling block, sin, and such that entangles each of us.

The heavenly witnesses include a Who's Who of the Bible and throngs of other saints in Heaven. They endured to the finish line while overcoming all kinds of traps. They are great examples. David is probably saying, "I persevered through faith in the Lord. So can you." Is that Abraham waving us on? There is Sarah smiling. Do you see Moses? He wants to pat us on the back. They are magnificent inspirations.

There is Jesus, the foundation of our faith, who obediently endured His race to the cross. (See Hebrews 12:2 below.) Jesus is with us. He took our sin away. He helps us hurdle every stumbling block. He is the greatest witness. Jesus can make our run of life considerably easier—that is, if we call on Him.

Do not crawl or stroll in your race. Run hard.

Action: Pray for remembrance of the perseverance and great faith of the heroes in the Bible when you stumble. Stay focused on Jesus each day and ask Him to lead you through your race of life. Thank God for all He has provided through Jesus.

Scripture Meditation: Hebrews 12:1–2: "Therefore we also, since we are surrounded by so great a cloud of witnesses, let us lay aside every weight, and the sin which so easily ensnares us, and let us run with endurance the race that is set before us, looking unto Jesus, the author and finisher of our faith, who for the joy that was set before Him endured the cross, despising the shame, and has sat down at the right hand of the throne of God."

STOP ABUSING YOUR FREEDOM

Consider this. You told a little white lie. Did you think the sin was too minor to get God's attention? Think again. What about the time you fell for your neighbor's spouse? Did you convince yourself just one time is a failure God will overlook? Think again. Do you remember when you were late getting a report to your boss? You said that the report required more time than anticipated, but the truth was you had been slacking off. You believed God would not mind because you were tired. Think again.

You say, "There are worldly problems and temptations flying all around us every day. God says we are free. I, like other Christians, use my freedom to get through the things the world throws at me. Sometimes I have to use my freedom to exercise worldly solutions. God understands." God understands that you have sinned against Him.

God did say Christians are free. Paul wrote that God has called all believers to be free. But there is a catch. God understands sin, but He disapproves of sinning. God, through Paul, made this clear that God commands us to not use our freedom to indulge in the sinful ways of the world. (See Galatians 5:13 below.) God does not approve of any sin, large or small. Sinning to satisfy our own fleshy desires is an abuse of the freedom we received from God. There also is good news though.

The problems are correctible. God provided a way for us to avoid abusing our freedom. Rather than wrongfully using our freedom from God, we should serve one another with love. God actually commands that we love everyone as much as we love ourselves. (See Galatians 5:13–14 below.)

Each worldly temptation or problem places us at a fork in our path. One way is Satan's way—sin. The other way is God's way—serving through love. Which path will you take? We each must choose for ourselves.

Action: Commit to stop abusing your freedom. When you are tempted to use your freedom wrongfully, look around and go serve someone humbly as an act of love. Pray for the Holy Spirit to guide you in being alert to fulfilling God's will while using your freedom.

Scripture Meditation: Galatians 5:13–14: "You, my brothers and sisters, were called to be free. But do not use your freedom to indulge the flesh; rather, serve one another humbly in love. For the entire law is fulfilled in keeping this one command: 'Love your neighbor as yourself.'"

MY CONDUCT REFLECTS ...

You probably have seen some Christians turn themselves into a public spectacle. I have, and it was embarrassing each time. One such incident occurred in a restaurant.

After receiving their food, a married couple decided her barbeque was overcooked. The man quickly and loudly berated the waitress till she was fighting back tears. He then tore into the manager. Later, the couple bowed their heads to offer thanks to God for their meal. The other customers had watched. Probably some of the patrons were not believers. I wonder what they now think of Christians.

The man was obnoxious. Do those unbelievers now think Jesus is obnoxious? Probably. Likewise, if we use foul language, would they think our Lord is foul mouthed? Probably. If we steal, would they think Jesus is a thief? Probably. This type of conduct certainly does not glorify God.

Do we forget that nonbelievers observe what we say and how we act? Every unchristian act we Christians commit reflects negatively on Jesus. This behavior also disobeys Jesus, is sinful, and damages our relationship with God. The behavior is the opposite of how Jesus commanded us to behave. He said that good works should be our witness to all others so God would be glorified. (See Matthew 5:16 below.) We are to let our light shine.

Letting our light shine is similar to living in a glass bowl. It provides continuous opportunities to showcase the grace, goodness and righteousness of Jesus. When we are patient, nonbelievers believe He is patient. We remain calm. They think Jesus is calm. We display love. They think He loves. We show compassion. They think Jesus is compassionate. You get the idea. Our glass bowl allows light to be a witness that continuously plants seeds of the good news of Jesus. Some of the seeds will open doors, allowing the Gospel to be explained. Some seeds will close doors, shutting out the light.

We must realize that our conduct will always reflect the grace, righteousness, and holiness of Jesus or the evil, dishonesty, and immorality of Satan. We cannot be part-time disciples of Jesus. He is not a part-time Lord. Does your conduct imitate Jesus or Satan?

Action: Be ever mindful that your conduct will reflect either the light of Jesus or the darkness of Satan. Pray often for the Holy Spirit to guide you in your daily conduct and that it reflects the light of our Lord. Praise God for allowing you to reflect the light of Jesus.

Scripture Meditation: Matthew 5:16: "'Let your light so shine before men, that they may see your good works and glorify your Father in heaven.'"

LOOKING FOR A SAFE HAVEN?

Most of us have a safe haven where we feel more secure and confident. It may be a person, a place, or both. This began when we were children. We felt safe in our homes. The presence of our parents created an even greater haven. As adults, we sometimes use a certain room in our home as a safe haven. Sometimes a husband and wife use each other for a mutual safe haven. There are other havens that provide secure feelings. Still, there is a much greater safe haven available to us, if we seek it.

Where is this great haven? This haven is available to all Christians, and it is near to all. This great haven is in the shadow of our God, and it is each believer's fortress. (See Psalm 91:1–2 below.) No other haven is stronger or safer. Each believer can enter God's safe haven by trusting in Him.

Are your worldly foes closing in on you? Trust God and His Word. Have you been injured? Trust God and His Word. Is sickness upon you? Trust God and His Word. Are problems becoming too much for you? You guessed it—trust God and His Word.

As you trust God, He will deliver you from the dangerous traps, serious illnesses, and evil. (See Psalm 91:3 below.) Your trials and tribulations are no match for God. He will protect and care for you. God will cover you with His wings, under which you will be safe, and His Word will be your defensive shield. (See Psalm 91:4 below.) Just as the eaglets' fears and anxieties dissipate when the mighty eagle covers them with his wings, your fears and anxieties will melt into feelings of confidence and safety when covered by God's wings.

Just think what an awesome trade God provides. We give Him our trust. He gives us the best and safest of all safe places.

Action: When problems strike, always trust God to deliver and protect you in His safe haven. Let Him be your shield. In prayer, praise God for allowing you into His safe place. Ask Him for opportunities to share what He has done for you.

Scripture Meditation: Psalm 91:1–4: "He who dwells in the secret place of the Most High shall abide under the shadow of the Almighty. I will say of the Lord, 'He is my refuge and my fortress; My God, in Him I will trust.' Surely He shall deliver you from the snare of the fowler and from the perilous pestilence. He shall cover you with His feathers, and under His wings you shall take refuge; His truth shall be your shield and buckler."

I AM LEANING ON ...

No doubt we all have had some days when we felt everything seemed to be falling apart. Maybe it was small problems striking simultaneously. Or it could have been our boss thought we let him down. Perhaps we received a devastating medical diagnosis. Even worse, we may have lost a loved one. Who or where do we turn to for help and support?

Do you first turn to your spouse? Maybe you go to your closest friend. These individuals love you and provide great support. Greater support and love is available though.

Jesus and the Holy Spirit love us more than anyone's ability to love. We should turn to Him first. Jesus is always there. As our High Priest, He intercedes for us, and He leads and takes care of everyone who becomes a child of God through Him. (See Hebrews 7:25 below.)

Like Jesus, the Holy Spirit is always ready. The Holy Spirit assists us in overcoming our weaknesses, especially our inability to rightly communicate our prayers. The Holy Spirit clarifies our prayers with groanings that humans cannot understand. He also intercedes for us to conform our will to the will of God. (See Romans 8:26–27 below.)

God has provided the best source of assistance, relief, and encouragement that exists—His Son, Jesus, and the Son's agent, the Holy Spirit. When a trial hits us, prayer should be our 911 call. The power of Jesus is unleashed and intercedes on our behalf. Sometimes we stammer in prayer. We might not know what to say. But the Holy Spirit intercedes and brings clarity to your prayer through groanings to God.

Jesus is ready. The Holy Spirit is ready. Lean on them. They will assist and support you.

Action: Train yourself to pray to God immediately when you first need help and support. Ask for what you need. Thank and praise Him for allowing Jesus and the Holy Spirit to fill your needs.

Scripture Meditation: Hebrews 7:25: "Therefore He is also able to save to the uttermost those who come to God through Him, since He always lives to make intercession for them." Romans 8:26–27: "Likewise the Spirit also helps in our weaknesses. For we do not know what we should pray for as we ought, but the Spirit Himself makes intercession for us with groanings which cannot be uttered. Now He who searches the hearts knows what the mind of the Spirit is, because He makes intercession for the saints according to the will of God."

THE RUBBER HITS THE ROAD

Suppose this is your story. Your life is wonderful and happy. Worshipping God is a great joy. You participate in several ministries of your church. The mutual love between you and your family is evident. Your career continues to be successful. Then it happens.

You suddenly have a heart attack. Your life has taken a devastating turn. You now are disabled with a heavily damaged heart. Your bright future is a lost dream. Your faith is under pressure. The rubber has hit the road. How will you react?

Has your dire situation made you angry toward Jesus? Has your faith in Him become a doubting trust? Or is your faith in Jesus holding firm? Stand fast. God will continue to help you make your life worthy and able to obey His call. He also will give to you the power to achieve everything that your faith leads you to become involved in during your life. Then your Lord and Savior, Christ Jesus, will be glorified because of your living testimony of His righteousness. God will also honor you along with Jesus. (See 1 Thessalonians 1:11–12 [NLT] below.) This occurs when your focus is on the Lord rather than your problems.

Tribulations provide opportunities for God to demonstrate His work to the world. The greater the problem the greater is His work. The trials also reveal what kind of person everyone is. What are you—a why-me person or a faithful servant worthy of God's calling? Your strong faith will provide a compelling witness to nonbelievers during trials and tragedies. They care more about what you do than what you say.

God is ready to use your adversity to deepen your faith and trust, broaden your love, increase your witnessing power, and fill you with comfort in your trial. Are you ready?

Action: Pray for the Holy Spirit to guide you in standing firm in your faith. Trust in God and His Word, regardless of your situation. Praise God for His Word and His faithfulness to His Word. Thank Him for using you to be a living testimony of His power, love, and grace.

Scripture Meditation: Second Thessalonians 1:11–12 (NLT): "So we keep on praying for you, asking our God to enable you to live a life worthy of his call. May he give you the power to accomplish all the good things your faith prompts you to do. Then the name of our Lord Jesus will be honored because of the way you live, and you will be honored along with him. This is all made possible because of the grace of our God and Lord, Jesus Christ."

YEARNING FOR GOD'S GLORY

If you were told that you must choose to spend the rest of your life in sunlight or darkness, which would you select? Surely most would pick daylight. We seem to have an inherent preference for the daytime.

As children, we feared the darkness because we could not see what might be lurking in the dark. Our young and middle-age years brought awareness that most of our work is better accomplished in light. Senior citizens find that aging eyes make the difficulty of seeing in the dark much worse. We also know that darkness brings more wrongdoing than daylight.

We try to lessen the perils of darkness by installing lights in most inside places and many outside places. Lightbulbs help, but no number or strength of bulbs can match the sunlight. It will be a lot different and immensely better in Heaven.

Most of us know of the wonderful changes we will see in Heaven. No more tears. No more sickness or injuries. No disagreements. No more deaths. No hate. And on and on. Do you know there will be no sun or moon nor any darkness for the best of reasons? There will be no need for Heaven to have a sun or moon. It was revealed to John that Heaven will be eternally illuminated by God's glory. (See Revelation 21:23 below.) Yes. God's glory will be your light, and He will be your eternal glory. (See Isaiah 60:19 [NLT] below.)

No one can see God's face on earth and live. But upon entering Heaven, we will be glorified. We will see His face for the first time. (See Revelation 22:4 below.) Come, Jesus, and take us to Heaven. He will be our glory, and we shall be able to face Him forever.

We yearn for God's glory. We can hardly wait for the day that we will see God in all of His glory, and He will be our glory. Are you along with us, yearning for God's glory?

Action: Pray for the Holy Spirit to lead you to focus on the heavenly prize of God's glory as you race through your daily life. Yearn for Him. Persevere. At every setback, think of God's glory awaiting you.

Scripture Meditation: Revelation 21:23: "The city had no need of the sun or of the moon to shine in it, for the glory of God illuminated it. The Lamb is its light." Isaiah 60:19 (NLT): "'No longer will you need the sun to shine by day, nor the moon to give its light by night, for the Lord your God will be your everlasting light, and your God will be your glory.'" Revelation 22:4: "They shall see His face, and His name shall be on their foreheads."

GO AND TELL

The one thing with which all Christians will agree is that Jesus's recorded words are very important, but which ones are the most important? Surely, Jesus's last statements made before returning to Heaven are His most important. Two reasons: 1) Jesus was about to leave the earth without knowing when He would return; and 2) Jesus came to save the world. As Jesus's disciples, Christians should assist Him in His mission.

So, what were Jesus's most important words? He said that we are to go across the land to the end of the earth, spreading the Gospel and baptizing and making disciples of the new believers. (See Acts 1:8 and Matthew 28:19 below.) We are told to spread the great news of Jesus—the Gospel. This involves more than waiting for a nonbeliever to cross our path. We are to be Jesus's witnesses and go and tell as commanded by Him.

To obey, we must be intentional in spreading the Gospel. Going and telling could mean we only need to step next door to see a neighbor or go halfway around the world. Regardless, we must obey.

You may think your next-door neighbors are not believers. Many times, you see their kids playing when you and your family are leaving for church. You say, "It would be nice if our neighbors went to church." Have you told them about Jesus? Have you invited them to church? Jesus's command to go applies to all believers, not just some. Go and tell.

We need to have a sense of urgency about spreading the Gospel. Once an individual breathes his or her final breath, all opportunities to accept Jesus as Lord and Savior are lost. The present time is the best time to spread the Gospel, because no one knows when death will occur. Your neighbor could unexpectedly die. There no longer would be a chance for him or her to enter Heaven. So, go and tell now.

Action: Ask God daily where you should go and tell about Jesus. Obey, whether He sends you next door or across the globe. Some will accept the Gospel. Some will not. Celebrate with those who accept Jesus. Pray for those who do not.

Scripture Meditation: Acts 1:8: "'But you shall receive power when the Holy Spirit has come upon you; and you shall be witnesses to Me in Jerusalem, and in all Judea and Samaria, and to the end of the earth.'" Matthew 28:19: "'Go therefore and make disciples of all the nations, baptizing them in the name of the Father and of the Son and of the Holy Spirit.'"

HEALING THE UNHEALTHY

A visiting preacher said in a sermon that most Christian churches do a super job of discipling, nurturing, and caring for their members through various ministries. This is probably true of the church(es) where you have been a member. But before you stick your chest out on behalf of your church, he raised an additional point.

The preacher continued by explaining that only a few of those churches have matched their excellent task of discipling members with great evangelism and mission work outside the walls of the church. Ouch! We do a better job of healing the healthy (saved people) than we do of healing the unhealthy (lost people). But why is this true?

Churches seem to promote evangelism and missions. Their staff members seem to share the Gospel with a lot of people. So, what is the problem? Did you not notice the missing ingredient? Friend, the problem is you and I and the other church members. We are Jesus's disciples. We are supposed to be carrying on His work.

Jesus defined our work by explaining that the healthy or believers do not need a doctor (Jesus), but the sick or unbelievers need to be healed by hearing the Gospel. Jesus said that He did not come for those who believe in Him, but He came to heal the sinners to repentance. (See Matthew 9:12–13 below.) Jesus came to heal the spiritually unhealthy. Now, we as His followers are His tools in healing the unhealthy. How often do you share the good news of Jesus? Is it a lot each year? How about sometimes? Is it rarely? Never? We all need to step up to the plate and stay there.

We have no real excuses. God will equip us. Our churches will assist Him with various evangelizing ministries. And the unhealthy are everywhere. In our country, there are more people than ever who need Jesus's healing. Jesus called us all to be His nurse practitioners. Will you say yes? The unhealthy need healing. Do not leave them to Satan.

Action: Commit to spreading the Gospel. Pray to Jesus, asking for guidance in determining what process He wants you to use in locating the lost. Look for the opportunities Jesus places before you to share the good news of Him with others. Praise God for allowing you to assist in healing the unhealthy.

Scripture Meditation: Matthew 9:12–13: "When Jesus heard that, He said to them, 'Those who are well have no need of a physician, but those who are sick. But go and learn what this means: "I desire mercy and not sacrifice." For I did not come to call the righteous, but sinners, to repentance.'"

EYES OF UNDERSTANDING

Are you a believer who thinks living the Christian life involves two things: 1) learning all you can about God, and 2) being a good person? If so, you've left out the most important ingredient—the understanding of what you learn about God. This is how we get to know God, not just knowing about Him. Atheists know about God, but they do not know Him.

Paul prayed for Christians to receive the true understanding of their prior revelations about God. Paul asked God to give to them wisdom, knowledge, and understanding within their hearts. Then they would know their eternal salvation within God's glory and their inheritance of being eternal children of God. (See Ephesians 1:17–18 below.)

God intends for us to know Him fully through our understanding eyes. We are His children. God will give us the insight to grow in Him. We began with the knowledge of Jesus at the time of our salvation. This work continues until completion at our resurrection and entrance into Heaven. These are the riches of the glory of our inheritance.

Paul also said that Christians would receive God's great power, which is the same power He used to resurrect Jesus from the dead and return Jesus to His heavenly place—the right hand of God. (See Ephesians 1:19–20 below.) Hallelujah! God gives to every believer His magnificent power, the same power He used to resurrect Jesus. What more could we need?

We must realize that God has given us all the power we need to fulfill His calling for us as revealed through our eyes of understanding. This power and enlightenment enable us to trust and obey Him.

Action: Pray that God will reveal His calling for you, how to be like Jesus, and for insight into the makeup of His inheritance for you on earth and in Heaven. Praise and thank God for the wisdom and revelation in knowing Him and for giving you His power.

Scripture Meditation: Ephesians 1:17–20: "That the God of our Lord Jesus Christ, the Father of glory, may give to you the spirit of wisdom and revelation in the knowledge of Him, the eyes of your understanding being enlightened; that you may know what is the hope of His calling, what are the riches of the glory of His inheritance in the saints, and what is the exceeding greatness of His power toward us who believe, according to the working of His mighty power which He worked in Christ when He raised Him from the dead and seated Him at His right hand in the heavenly places ..."

FEELING JESUS'S PRESENCE

Jesus is always with us—a simple, straightforward fact. We often think of Him as far away but willing to come when we call upon Him. Yet He is with us every second of every day. Jesus takes no vacation or sick leave. He does not punch a clock. Jesus knows when we are awake or asleep. He knows what we are doing and thinking. Jesus even knows the number of hairs on our head.

Often, we think we carry on our daily lives without Jesus. We are wrong. He is there in every phase of our lives. Jesus is our unseen companion. The problem is that in parts of our daily living, we ignore Jesus, but ignoring Him does not remove His presence.

Jesus promised us, as His disciples, that He would always be with us. (See Matthew 28:20 below.) We cannot see the sun during the dawning of a new day, and we cannot physically see Jesus. Yet He is there.

When a new day dawns, we see rays of the sun streaming through trees and lighting God's creation around us. We cannot yet see the sun, but we know that it is there. Each sunbeam that glistens on the morning dew gives us comfort that the darkness of night will again be removed. So it is with Jesus. We cannot see Him, but He is with us.

Knowing Jesus is always with us is indeed a great comfort. He is our Lord. Jesus gives us peace and comfort. He guides us along the righteous path. He provides for us. We can rejoice in Jesus. His presence is complete with great joy as He leads us along of path of life. (See Psalm 16:11 below.) Jesus is everything we need. We should want for nothing, for He is always with you and me.

Jesus's constant presence is not only a promise; it is a fact. Do you feel His presence? You can if you focus on Him throughout each day.

Action: Pray for the Holy Spirit to guide you in focusing on Jesus and His love each day. Heed the Holy Spirit's reminders that Jesus is near, waiting to hear from you in all phases of your life. Enjoy Jesus's peace, comfort, and joy as He assists you with your daily living.

Scripture Meditation: Matthew 28:20: "'Teaching them to observe all things that I have commanded you; and lo, I am with you always, even to the end of the age.' Amen." Psalm 16:11: "You will show me the path of life; in Your presence is fullness of joy; at Your right hand are pleasures forevermore."

WHAT INHERITANCE ARE YOU SEEKING?

At times, we look forward to inheriting things of value. These things might be valuable in financial terms. Or some of them might only be valuable as keepsakes, relics, or memory joggers. But anything we inherit from a family member, friend, or other person is time limited. The inheritance will rust, fall apart, be used up, or wear out.

There is a more valuable and far better inheritance available for all believers in Jesus Christ as their Lord and Savior. This inheritance is in Jesus and is provided through Him in conjunction with the will of God. (See Ephesians 1:11 below.)

Our inheritance in Jesus is comprised of everything related to our salvation and can be summarized in four words—eternal life in Heaven. This is what makes the inheritance so great, marvelous, and desirable. It is perfect in every way, as He is perfect. This is unlike any other inheritance. Nothing on earth is perfect, including earthly inheritances.

It just gets better and better. No part of the inheritance of Jesus will perish. Nothing! Contrast this with earthly inheritances, which will completely perish. We may inherit a house, but it will deteriorate into nothing at some point. Earthly inheritances are imperfect, perishable, and unreliable. Jesus's inheritance is perfect, imperishable, and guaranteed to be unchangeable.

Your earthly inheritance is not guaranteed. You may have been told what you can expect to inherit, but that is no guarantee. The will could be changed to alter or withdraw your inheritance. Our heavenly Father has guaranteed our inheritance in Jesus. The gift of the Holy Spirit to each believer is a seal of the promised guarantee, and Jesus will glorify God by escorting us to our inheritance in Heaven. (See Ephesians 1:13–14 see below.) Our reserved home in Heaven is guaranteed. Will Heaven be the inheritance that you seek?

Action: Seek an inheritance in Jesus. Self-evaluate to ensure your belief in Jesus is real and not imagined. Accept Jesus as your Lord and Savior if you have not previously done so. Take comfort in your inheritance from Jesus, which He has prepared for you.

Scripture Meditation: Ephesians 1:11, 13–14: "In Him also we have obtained an inheritance, being predestined according to the purpose of Him who works all things according to the counsel of His will, In Him you also trusted, after you heard the word of truth, the gospel of your salvation; in whom also, having believed, you were sealed with the Holy Spirit of promise, who is the guarantee of our inheritance until the redemption of the purchased possession, to the praise of His glory."

MY BEST FRIEND IS ...

We all have friends. We share a reciprocating affection and personal regard with our friends. We support them. They support us. When we have problems, our friends are there for us. We trust and rely on one another. It is fun being around them. Friends are valuable assets.

We are closer to some friends than others. Among our close friends, there is usually one we consider to be a best friend. Yet those who believe in Christ Jesus as our Lord share Him as a friend who is greater than even a best friend.

You say, "I do not think of the Lord in social terms." Why not? Jesus is both your Lord and greatest friend. He said that we are His friends. (See John 15:14–15 below.) Not only did Jesus declare that we are friends, He also told us why. Jesus has revealed to us all that He learned from God the Father. This is what best friends do.

A best friend shares important information. Jesus does that. A best friend is willing to die for his friends. (See John 15:13 below.) Jesus has already done that. A best friend helps his friends whenever he can. Jesus has done, is doing, and will continue to do that. A best friend is restricted to doing what is possible. Jesus can do even more. A best friend is limited by his inherent human traits and characteristics. Jesus is not limited. A best friend is bound by his capabilities. Jesus is not bound by anything.

We should be thankful for all of our friends. Yet we should be ever mindful that Jesus is our greatest and best friend. Jesus will not force His friendship upon us, because He is the ultimate gentleman. Jesus is always waiting nearby for us to experience His love, mercy, and grace. Will you allow Jesus to be your best friend?

Action: Express thankfulness for your friends loving you. In prayer, thank Jesus for including you as one of His friends and joyfully accept His friendship. In all the days to come, let your greatest friend and best friend guide your steps and fill your every need. Note how your steps will be livelier as your joy and confidence grow in Jesus.

Scripture Meditation: John 15: 13–15: "Greater love has no one than this, than to lay down one's life for his friends. You are My friends if you do whatever I command you. No longer do I call you servants, for a servant does not know what his master is doing; but I have called you friends, for all things that I heard from My Father I have made known to you."

STOP TAKING HIS GRACE FOR GRANTED

Grace is generally considered to be the undeserved and excessive love of God shed upon humankind. No definition captures the endless nature of God's grace. There are no limits, and there are examples galore of God's grace in the Bible. None are greater than Jesus saying that He will lay down His life for His followers. (See John 10:15 below.) Our Lord, Christ Jesus, willingly gave His life for us. So, why do so many Christians refer to His sacrifice in unemotional, shallow ways? Are we now taking Jesus's death for granted?

Jesus laid down His life for us in a horrific way, including extreme emotional stress, torturous pain, and agony of being separated from God. His death demonstrates the limitless nature of God's grace.

Jesus's suffering actually began just before His arrest. He was praying while under emotional stress so great that He sweated blood. Then the soldiers came to arrest Him. With His power, Jesus could have walked away. But He didn't. While being tried, Jesus's face and head were beaten, battered, and bruised. He could have walked away. But He didn't. After being tried, Jesus was scourged—beaten to near death. He was left with strips of skin and muscle hanging from His body. Jesus could have walked away. But He didn't.

While walking, stumbling, and falling on the way to Golgotha, Jesus was again battered. Arriving there, he was nailed to a cross. For several hours, He suffered in ways we cannot imagine. Jesus's pain and agony included cramping muscles that caused relentless deep pain, burning nerves that had been torn, intermittent partial asphyxiation, paralyzed muscles, horrible chest pains, and dehydration. Jesus's last words came in agonizing whispers. Then He died. Jesus could have hopped down and walked away. But He didn't.

We must remember that Jesus endured a horrifying and painful torture for us. He did it so we all could have redemption from our sins and be forgiven through His marvelous grace. (See Ephesians 1:7 below.) This is true grace being fueled by God's love that surpasses our understanding. Never, ever take His grace for granted.

Action: Pray for the Holy Spirit to make you ever mindful of the manner of Jesus's death and why He willingly suffered through it. This will make you more humble and thankful for Jesus's sacrifice. Then you will be less prone to take His grace for granted.

Scripture Meditation: John 10:15: "As the Father knows Me, even so I know the Father; and I lay down My life for the sheep." Ephesians 1:7: "In Him we have redemption through His blood, the forgiveness of sins, according to the riches of His grace."

WHOM DO WE LOVE?

Let's evaluate our love for others. Make a list of everyone you love. Is your list becoming so long you cannot complete it? If so, pat yourself on your back. But do not pat too much. There is another list we need to build.

Now let's list everyone we know but did not include in our first list. These are the folks we do not love. They represent where we have work to do. Jesus told us to love all others as we love ourselves. (See Matthew 22:39 below.) This is not a suggestion from Jesus. He commanded us to love everyone, and He did not give any exceptions to His command.

All those people we try to avoid are not excepted. The know-it-all. The one-upper. The bragger. The suspicious one. We could go on and on, but you get the idea. We all know people who make it very difficult to love them. Yet it does not excuse us from obeying Jesus's command.

It is imperative that we work to obey Jesus. If we do not love others, we do not know God, since He is love. (See 1 John 4:8 below.) Ouch! This verse hurts. Did it hit you hard also? We must love everyone, regardless of how he or she acts in our presence.

Love is the common thread between us and everyone else. The Bible tells us that we fulfill the law by loving one another. (See Romans 13:8 below.) God is serious about us loving others.

Forget the difficulty some people cause. We need to ensure God is our role model. We know He loves us mightily. Again, God is love, and as long as we believe in Him, trust in Him, obey Him, and love Him, He will abide in us. (See 1 John 4:16 below.) The more we abide in God, the more loving we become. As we become more like God, we become a better witness for Him.

Action: Abide in God and love everyone. Pray for the Holy Spirit to guide you in transforming your heart into a greater loving heart. Ask the Spirit to convict you when you fail to love someone. Bask in the love of God while loving others.

Scripture Meditation: Matthew 22:39: "And the second is like it: 'You shall love your neighbor as yourself.'" First John 4:8, 16: "He who does not love does not know God, for God is love. And we have known and believed the love that God has for us. God is love, and he who abides in love abides in God, and God in him." Romans 13:8: "Owe no one anything except to love one another, for he who loves another has fulfilled the law."

ARE YOU PLAYING GOD?

If someone asked each one of us, "Have you ever played God?" we all would likely answer with a resounding no. If so, we all need to rethink our answer by examining our past. Who among us can say, "I have not exercised revenge against someone who hurt me physically or mentally"? If you still are thinking, *No*, have you wished that the person who harmed you be hurt in some way? This is indirect retribution rather than direct.

When we exact or call for revenge, we are usurping God's authority—playing God. This is an affront to Him. God declared that all vengeance is His, not ours. (See Romans 12:19 below.) Think about it. Our seeking retribution results in two things: 1) we anger God by appropriating His authority; 2) we please Satan because we are in effect mimicking his evil work—playing God. God is God, and we are not.

God, being the great and wonderful Lord He is, described how we should react to being harmed. We should do the opposite to our enemies when they harm us—be loving and be good to them. (See Romans 12:20 below.) God says we are to replace our desire for vengeance by filling the offender's needs. Did a neighbor steal from you? Give him or her something to eat and drink. You have to admit this is the last thing he or she would expect. Still, this is what our Lord expects from us.

God commands us to be like Christ by forgiving one another while being nice and warmhearted toward one another. (See Ephesians 4:32 below.) Did someone offend you? React with kindness and forgiveness. Watch as the hardness melts away.

When we are harmed, we can please God by reacting in His declared way. Or, we can offend the Lord by reacting in Satan's way. Which reaction will you display?

Action: Be intentional in reacting to harm or hurt according to the will of God. Pray for the Holy Spirit to guide you in always having a loving and forgiving reaction to harmful things against you. Savor the comfort and peace of being in God's will.

Scripture Meditation: Romans 12:19–20: "Beloved, do not avenge yourselves, but rather give place to wrath; for it is written, 'Vengeance is Mine, I will repay,' says the Lord. Therefore 'If your enemy is hungry, feed him; if he is thirsty, give him a drink; for in so doing you will heap coals of fire on his head.'" Ephesians 4:32: "And be kind to one another, tenderhearted, forgiving one another, even as God in Christ forgave you."

DO YOU BOAST?

Many people have said that nobody likes a braggart. There is both worldly and biblical truth in this statement when the braggart is boasting about himself or herself. The worldview usually considers bragging to be a display of arrogance. The biblical view is predicated upon why we are boasting and what we are boasting about.

Bragging on ourselves displeases God. It is a sin. God's Word says that we should not brag on ourselves, and any bragging on us should come from a stranger. (See Proverbs 27:2 below.) We should not promote ourselves before others. If we deserve praise, it will come from other people without our promotion. Also, God sees our boasting of self as claiming the Holy Spirit's work. Self-boasting is sinful in multiple ways, and it has no value. (See 2 Corinthians 10:18 [NLT] below.)

So, why are we wasting our time boasting on ourselves? It matters little. It is sinful and displeasing to God. It belittles the Holy Spirit. Yet, we can still boast by changing the focus of our bragging. God told us that the only boasting we should do is about knowing Him. (See Jeremiah 9:24 [NLT] below.) But how should we brag on the Lord?

Boast to others that God created the world and us. Share the Gospel with nonbelievers. Tell others of His love, mercy, and grace. Brag about what the Lord has done for us. Boast about God's never-ending love, holiness, and justice and that these things elate us. (Again, see Jeremiah 9:24 [NLT].)

As we desire to brag, let us all ensure that our boasting follows the commands of our Lord. We need to be ever mindful that all of our bragging should be boasting in God.

Action: Pray for the mental strength to avoid bragging on yourself. Ask for assistance in persevering as you seek opportunities to boast in the Lord. Also, ask that your boasting in God will glorify Him.

Scripture Meditation: Proverbs 27:2: "Let another man praise you, and not your own mouth; a stranger, and not your own lips." Second Corinthians 10:18 (NLT): "When people commend themselves, it doesn't count for much. The important thing is for the Lord to commend them." Jeremiah 9:24 (NLT): "But those who wish to boast should boast in this alone: that they truly know me and understand that I am the Lord who demonstrates unfailing love and who brings justice and righteousness to the earth, and that I delight in these things. I, the Lord, have spoken!"

READING AND PRAYING

How often do you pray and read the Word of God? Has your praying become little more than reciting a personal wish list mostly composed of things you do not truly need? These are important questions that need to be answered through self-evaluation.

Reading God's Word and praying fervently are the sources of spiritual power provided by God, to be used while serving and pleasing others. Remember, we serve God by serving others. While serving, we have some valuable resources available.

Are you helping someone who thinks his job or task is too big for him? Read about Moses. His life is a great witness of patience and overcoming shortcomings. Know someone struggling with keeping the faith? Read about David slaying Goliath. Learn and gain hope from the scripture. The scriptures are God's Word and are there for our learning and inspiration. (See Romans 15:4 below.) Learning and gaining hope from the scriptures places all believers on the same page in working to serve others.

Fervent prayer includes praying for individuals, for groups, and for God's will to be done. God wants us to come together in fulfilling His will. So, we pray for one another to accomplish the will of God in the name of our Lord and Savior, Jesus Christ. (See Romans 15:5–6 below.) Unity brings success in serving the Lord, demonstrates our obedience and faith, and glorifies God.

You must be alert and intentional. Satan knows our reading and praying will defeat him. He will pull out all the stops. His lies and tricks will be more cunning. He is determined to keep you from reading and absorbing scripture and having a fervent prayer time with our Lord. Yet the power you get from prayer and scripture will allow you to overcome the evil one. Are you ready to read and pray daily?

Action: Persevere in having a daily time for studying God's Word and praying to Him. Include time for God to speak to you. Pray for the Holy Spirit to help you keep your quiet-time schedule. Praise and thank God for the spiritual power you receive. Be bold in telling Satan to get lost. Enjoy the presence of God your quality quiet time will facilitate.

Scripture Meditation: Romans 15:4–6: "For whatever things were written before were written for our learning, that we through the patience and comfort of the Scriptures might have hope. Now may the God of patience and comfort grant you to be like-minded toward one another, according to Christ Jesus, that you may with one mind and one mouth glorify the God and Father of our Lord Jesus Christ."

WHO PROVIDES YOUR STRENGTH?

As Christians, we often say that we trust in Jesus, but do we always trust Him? This is an important question to ponder. Sometimes we habitually say we trust in Jesus rather than meaningfully. The Bible teaches us to trust in Jesus in all things. Yet do we?

Do you consult with Jesus in your business decisions? He is a great partner. Does Jesus guide you through each day? He is willing. Do you trust Jesus only in the most trying of circumstances, while trusting just yourself in the easier times? Who do you look to for protection? I could go on and on. But you get the idea.

We should trust in God in all circumstances. Then each of us could say, "The Lord protects me, makes me strong, and helps me when I put my trust in Him." (See Psalm 28:7 below.) The more we trust Him, the stronger we become. He is our never-ending source of strength.

We all have different circumstances. Yet when we truly trust Jesus, He will make our life-path travel as steady as the feet of a deer. (See Habakkuk 3:19 below.) Jesus will make us as sure-footed as the deer that scales mountains as He leads us through our circumstances in both the difficult and easy times. We get true strength from Jesus, not the world.

Trust Jesus. Make Him the source of your strength. He will make you strong because He loves you. Want another reason? Jesus is your salvation. (See Isaiah 12:2 below.) Jesus is all you need. You should desire to respond as the psalmist did. Let your heart rejoice and praise Him in a mighty way with singing. (See Psalm 28:7 below.) Wrap all this together, and you will become a brighter beacon for Him.

Do you trust Jesus to be your sole source of strength in all circumstances?

Action: In prayer, ask for guidance for yourself in developing greater and greater trust in Jesus to be your source of strength. Rejoice in Him. Praise Him for being your strength and sustainer. Relax in your expanded joy of life.

Scripture Meditation: Psalm 28:7: "The Lord is my strength and my shield; my heart trusted in Him, and I am helped; therefore my heart greatly rejoices, and with my song I will praise Him." Habakkuk 3:19: "The Lord God is my strength; He will make my feet like deer's feet, and He will make me walk on my high hills." Isaiah 12:2: "'Behold, God is my salvation, I will trust and not be afraid; "For Yah [Yahweh], the Lord, is my strength and song; He also has become my salvation."'"

HOW IS YOUR HEART?

Maybe you have experienced times when your heart felt heavy, whether a little or a lot. But you are at a loss as to why. This seems to make the heart heavier. You are sad. The spring in your step is dwindling. The feeling makes you edgy. Your fuse may be getting shorter.

You keep thinking, *Something is wrong with me.* Maybe you do not remember committing a sin that caused the Holy Spirit to be tugging at your heart. Or you may be contemplating some action or event without knowing that it is contrary to God's will. Again, the Holy Spirit is tugging. But whatever the reason, God knows.

Call out to God. He will answer. God said that He would answer you if you call upon Him. (See Jeremiah 33:3 below.) You are God's child. He will help you. I hear you saying that you do not know what to ask of Him because you do not know why you have a heavy heart.

God will identify the problem for you. Ask the Lord to look into your heart, know what is bothering you, and let you know if you have sinned against Him. (See Psalm 139:23–24 below.) We are imperfect. We can offend God without realizing it. Get right with God by obeying Him and asking Him for forgiveness.

Yes, God will forgive you. He will also display His love for you by rejoicing over you with song. (See Zephaniah 3:17 below.) Wow! You go to God with a heavy heart, and He instills the proper solution while showing His mercy and love as He rejoices over you with singing.

Your heavy heart has now been transformed to a joyful heart. You are stepping lively. Your smile radiates happiness. And you know God is near because you can feel His love again.

Action: Pray to God. Ask Him to reveal the reason for your heavy heart, and seek forgiveness for any offense against Him. Obey Him. Rejoice with God by praising Him for transforming your heart. Enjoy your closeness to God.

Scripture Meditation: Jeremiah 33:3: "'Call to Me, and I will answer you, and show you great and mighty things, which you do not know.'" Psalm 139:23–24: "Search me, O God, and know my heart; test me and know my anxious thoughts. Point out anything in me that offends you, and lead me along the path of everlasting life." Zephaniah 3:17: "'The Lord your God in your midst, the Mighty One, will save; He will rejoice over you with gladness, He will quiet you with His love, He will rejoice over you with singing.'"

I SINNED BY ...

When you enter the presence of God and talk to Him in prayer, in what manner do you discuss your sin with Him? Do you talk to God about specific sins you committed? Or do you simply acknowledge that you're a sinner in a general sense?

I'm guessing you have told God during one or more of your quiet times that you are a sinner without mentioning a particular sin. I am also guessing these quiet times did not glorify God. He will not allow you to get by with generalization of your sin. He wants you to understand fully the nature of your sins. His presence demands it.

Isaiah discovered how the presence of God compelled him to acknowledge his specific sin rather than some broad and general statement of his being a sinner. When he entered the presence of God and saw Him, he was shaken and fearful because he had sinned verbally against God. (See Isaiah 6:5 below.)

The same is true for us today. Meeting God one-on-one will fully occur only when we surrender to the conviction of our sin. It creates a repentant heart. This is true for all believers, from the occasional sinner to the worst of sinners.

It is very difficult at times to be before our Lord and confessing our sins. All of our sins are sins against Him, whether the world considers them to be large or small. Admitting this to God makes us uncomfortable. However, this is good. Our fearful reluctance is evidence that we feel the Lord's presence.

While in God's presence, confess your specific sins even though naming specific sins is difficult to do. Through His grace and mercy, He will forgive you just as He forgave Isaiah. After confessing his sin, Isaiah said an angel told him that the Lord had forgiven him by removing his sin and purged his wrongdoing. (See Isaiah 6:7 below.)

Action: Meet with the Lord in daily prayer and listen to the Holy Spirit's conviction of your sin. Confess your sin. Be specific and sincere with your repentance. Enjoy knowing God purged your sin. Feel His peace as you converse with Him. Be alert to all God reveals to you. Praise Him for His mercy and revelations.

Scripture Meditation: Isaiah 6:5, 7: "So I said: 'Woe is me, for I am undone! Because I am a man of unclean lips, and I dwell in the midst of a people of unclean lips; for my eyes have seen the King, the Lord of hosts.' And he touched my mouth with it, and said: 'Behold, this has touched your lips; your iniquity is taken away, and your sin purged.'"

WHAT EXCITES YOU?

A Christian should never explain the Gospel to anyone without some excitement in their face and voice. Suppose you are a nonbeliever in Jesus. A Christian wanting to share the Gospel with you approaches. You notice the furrowed brow and the slight frown, which project unhappiness. You also notice the monotone voice, which indicates a mundane chore. How would you react? You would probably think, *I don't want to be like him. His Jesus must be unhappy.*

Contrast the man with a lady who is bubbling over with joy as she presents the Gospel to you. Her smile draws your attention to her words. She exudes excitement as she makes each point. She radiates a joyful compassion as she talks about her Jesus. Now, I'm guessing you would think that this Jesus must be something. He died for all of us. He creates joy, excitement, and compassion. He must be a loving God. *I want what she has.*

Believers should be more excited about Jesus. We would be more effective. And we do have a great reason to be exuberant.

We all are sinners. (See Romans 3:23 below.) God condemned all sinners to death. (See Ezekiel 18:20 below.) But God revoked the death decree for believers in Jesus. Because of God's great love for us, He sent His only Son to die as payment for the penalties of our sins so we could have eternal life, if we believe in Jesus. (See John 3:16 below.) We get excited when a physical life is saved. We should be even more exuberant when telling others about Jesus. He saves souls.

As a believer, there is no greater reason for excitement than assisting God in redirecting individuals' lives from eternal damnation to walking with God in Heaven. Don't bottle up your exuberance. Let it showcase a loving God.

Action: Pray for the Holy Spirit to remind you continually of the reason for spreading the Gospel. Be intentional in telling others about Jesus. Allow your evangelizing to reenergize your excitement level. Praise God for each opportunity for you to share the news of Jesus.

Scripture Meditation: Romans 3:23: "For all have sinned and fall short of the glory of God." Ezekiel 18:20: "The soul who sins shall die. The son shall not bear the guilt of the father, nor the father bear the guilt of the son. The righteousness of the righteous shall be upon himself, and the wickedness of the wicked shall be upon himself." John 3:16: "For God so loved the world that He gave His only begotten Son, that whoever believes in Him should not perish but have everlasting life."

WHY ME, LORD?

Why me, Lord? This is a question many believers sometimes ask of God. But why? Asking the question is an affront to God. It questions His will and sovereignty. This question seems to arise most when blessings are flowing our way. We seem to ask the question out of guilt because the blessings were not earned or deserved.

It is ironic that many believers do not raise the question when receiving the greatest blessing of all, their salvation. Yet it is asked later, after receiving additional blessings. We need to stop asking the question. God loves each of us; He delights in us; He revels in us with song; and He comforts us with His love. (See Zephaniah 3:17 below.) Can you imagine God rejoicing and singing over you? What an amazing truth.

God's rejoicing over us demonstrates a love for us so strong that He sent His only Son to die for us so that we could have eternal life. (See John 3:16 below.) This is how much God loves every person ever born and to be born.

God's love for us runs very deep. So, He will bless us richly. Remember, He gave up His only Son for us, so He will surely give us everything that we need for further sanctification. (See Romans 8:32 below.)

Do you understand? God freely blesses us and gives us all things for two reasons: 1) His love for us; and 2) our belief in the Lord. That's it. It has nothing to do with our earning or deserving anything. It is that simple.

We have two choices when God blesses us. We can ask, "Why me, Lord?" and aggrieve God, or we can accept what He gives us the way it is given—through love. Which will you choose?

Action: Anytime "Why me, Lord?" pops into your mind, replace it with the image of God rejoicing over you. In prayer, praise and thank Him for His loving you. Pray also for the Holy Spirit to remind you of any lapses in keeping the thought of God's love in the forefront of your mind. Enjoy your walk with the Lord.

Scripture Meditation: Zephaniah 3:17: "The Lord your God in your midst, the Mighty One, will save; He will rejoice over you with gladness, He will quiet you with His love, He will rejoice over you with singing." John 3:16: "For God so loved the world that He gave His only begotten Son, that whoever believes in Him should not perish but have everlasting life." Romans 8:32: "He who did not spare His own Son, but delivered Him up for us all, how shall He not with Him also freely give us all things?"

ARE YOU TRULY HAPPY?

You believe in Jesus, your Lord and Savior. You regularly attend your church's Sunday school and Sunday-morning worship service. The joy of your Christian brothers and sisters is evident to you. But their joyfulness appears to be at a much higher level than yours. You feel that your contentment has holes in it. What is wrong?

Do you realize that Christ Jesus is in you? Jesus is not just in you. God wants you to realize that Jesus lives in you and is your gateway to Heaven. Yes! Jesus does live in you, and He is your guaranteed entrance into glory. Your heavenly place is reserved. You are eternally linked to God and Jesus. But this is only the beginning.

We were not created to just to hang out day-to-day in a state of blessedness because we hold a ticket to Heaven. Jesus did not live on earth this way. While here, He held His return ticket to Heaven, but He still served people. God commanded us to be servants also, for He knows us and wants us to be like Jesus. (See Romans 8:29 [NLT] below.) Striving to be Christlike comforts us, draws us closer to God, and fills any holes in our contentment. Be obedient to God in being Christlike.

"How?" you ask. Use what you learned to spread the Gospel and make disciples. (See Colossians 1:28 [NLT] below.) Sharing Christ with others is a must. Someone shared Him with you. Also, look around to see how other Christians are exercising their servant hearts. Join some of them in serving others through love. Finally, listen as you serve. God will give to you some specific things to do for Him. He will reward your obedience.

Which path will you take, the path of a passive and discontented Christian or the path of the contented Christian who is obedient to God by becoming Christlike? It is your choice.

Action: Thank God for allowing Christ to live in you. Pray for the Holy Spirit to guide you in seeking opportunities to share the good news of Jesus and in learning to become a servant. Also, ask for continuing strength to be obedient to God. Enjoy the comfort of being obedient to the Lord. Praise God for your salvation.

Scripture Meditation: Romans 8:29 (NLT): "For God knew his people in advance, and he chose them to become like his Son, so that his Son would be the firstborn among many brothers and sisters." Colossians 1:28 (NLT): "So we tell others about Christ, warning everyone and teaching everyone with all the wisdom God has given us. We want to present them to God, perfect in their relationship to Christ."

BE A DO-GOODER

Have any nonbelievers criticized you by referring to you as a do-gooder? If so, how did it make you feel? Did it make you angry or embarrass you? Or did you silently say, "Yes. My witness was good."

It is quite common for nonbelievers to call Christians do-gooders. There is nothing wrong with the label. This is who we should be. It shows we are walking the walk and talking the talk. It means our do-gooder ways are a good witness for Jesus Christ. Doing good is a natural and obedient response to our faith.

God commanded us to avoid wrongdoing in favor of doing good, which reflects our godliness. (See 3 John 1:11 below.) Being a do-gooder reveals our obedience to Him. We follow the Lord, so His good ways become our good ways as we obey Him. The Lord is pleased when our obedient actions glorify Him. (See 1 John 5:3 below.)

We have the capacity to obey, for as Christians, we are under the guidance of the Holy Spirit. The Spirit will assist us in staying on the path of increasing faith and obedient behavior. Our decisions will become godly decisions. The Lord will be honored and glorified. So, let them label us as do-gooders. We should wear it as a badge of honor within our hearts. We also should feel an inner peace due to our obedience to the Lord.

At the same time, we must be careful that our avoidance of wrongdoing includes all evil things. Obviously, we do not obey the Lord when we do evil. This means we are not walking as we talk. A hypocrisy label now replaces our do-gooder label. Our witness goes from good to bad. The Lord is displeased because we disobeyed Him.

We must decide whether we will do good or evil. Will we each be a do-gooder or a hypocrite? This is good versus evil. But you cannot choose for me. Nor can I decide for you. Which label will you strive to achieve—do-gooder or hypocrite?

Action: In prayer, seek assistance for strength to persevere in striving to do good as commanded by God. Listen to the guidance of the Holy Spirit. Use Jesus as the model for godly behavior. Praise God for the privilege of being a good witness for Him.

Scripture Meditation: Third John 1:11: "Beloved, do not imitate what is evil, but what is good. He who does good is of God, but he who does evil has not seen God." First John 5:3: "For this is the love of God, that we keep His commandments. And His commandments are not burdensome."

FOUNTAIN OR DRAIN?

In today's world, most of us are around a lot of people. Some of the people are drawn to us. Most are just flowing by us, whether in small or large numbers. This creates a question: what type of witness are we projecting to those who flow by us?

Before answering, liken the flow of people to the flow of water. As water flows by, some of the water goes into a fountain. Fountains are designed to disperse water in a controlled, powerful way, be beautiful to the human eye, and project a peaceful and comfortable feeling to onlookers. Now, consider that some of the water flows to and through a drain. A drain is the gateway to a dark, dirty, smelly place. Yet some people are drawn to drains by their curiosity to see what is on the other side. So, is our witness to the people flowing by us like that of a fountain or a drain?

As followers of Jesus, our testimony is Jesus's light for the world. Our light is a reflection of Jesus and His love, peace, and comfort. He draws people in a controlled, powerful way. Jesus says that our actions are to do likewise. Being like Jesus is like a fountain. We should let our light reflect all the God-ordained things that we do and ensure our behavior glorify Him. (See Matthew 5:16 below.)

If our light does not shine, we are filled with darkness like the drain. Darkness is the shadow of death—the second death, a spiritual death. Satan holds the power over darkness. If we say we are walking with God while disobeying Him, we are following darkness. This means we are lying by not being truthful. (See 1 John 1:6 below.) Wow! Obedience is the Lord's light, and disobedience is Satan's darkness. Know the difference.

What will you be? Will you be a fountain by letting your light illuminate the path to Jesus and eternal life? Or will you be a drain, attracting others to follow darkness into eternal damnation? It is your choice. Will you be a fountain or a drain?

Action: Be a fountain. Let your light shine brightly to show others the way to Jesus so that His blood can cleanse their sins. Pray for assistance in making your light brighter and brighter as you walk closer and closer with God.

Scripture Meditation: Matthew 5:16: "Let your light so shine before men, that they may see your good works and glorify your Father in heaven." First John 1:6: "If we say that we have fellowship with Him, and walk in darkness, we lie and do not practice the truth."

WHY GIVE THANKS TO THE LORD?

You may think that today's topic is not necessary. You, like most Christians, thank the Lord regularly, but is your thanksgiving heartfelt or just a tradition? So, the topic title, "Why Give Thanks to the Lord?" is a question all believers need to answer.

We need to search our hearts for the answer. Has our thanksgiving to the Lord become a routine and perfunctory procedure? If so, maybe we have forgotten the greatness of God's love for us. Paul reminds us that the Lord has a great love with which He loves us. (See Ephesians 2:4 below.)

God continues to show His wonderful love for us through His mercy and grace. Both are rich and everlasting and enable us to bring glory to God through thanksgiving. (See 2 Corinthians 4:15 below.) Every blessing we receive is rooted in God's mercy and grace, which are fueled by His marvelous love for us.

The greatest blessing from God is that He sacrificed His only Son to death so that we all could have eternal life. (See John 3:16 below.) God allowed Jesus, who was without sin, to be crucified on a cross as payment for our sins. Dying on a cross is one of the most horrendous, torturous, and agonizing deaths known to man. Yet God arranged it to benefit everyone who believes in Jesus. This is true love.

Even more stunning is that Jesus had the power to walk away without suffering such a horrendous death. He chose to stay the course. He knew His sacrifice would provide a way for us to be cleansed from sin and make us worthy to enter Heaven.

Why should God care about us? We constantly sin against Him. Yet God loves us, and He proved it.

Reflecting on what God has done should humble us and create an eagerness in us to thank Him. Are you willing to begin this type of reflection?

Action: Reflect on Jesus's suffering on the cross. Let the image humble you and remind you of His love, mercy, and grace. Let humility replace routine words of thanks to God.

Scripture Meditation: Ephesians 2:4: "But God, who is rich in mercy, because of His great love with which He loved us." Second Corinthians 4:15: "For all things are for your sakes, that grace, having spread through the many, may cause thanksgiving to abound to the glory of God." John 3:16: "For God so loved the world that He gave His only begotten Son, that whoever believes in Him should not perish but have everlasting life."

GENTLENESS + LOVE = CHRISTLIKE

Have you ever observed another believer being overcome with a sin? What did you do, if anything? Sadly, for most of us, the answer to the second question would probably be nothing. However, doing nothing is sinful.

God's Word directs us to gently and lovingly help other believers who are sinning to get back onto God's righteous path. (See Galatians 6:1 [NLT] below.) It is important for us to approach the person(s) gently and humbly for correction purposes. We cannot be judgmental. We should be loving, for we are commanded to love all others as ourselves. (See Mark 12:31 below.)

Our self-interjection must start with forethought so that we will not trip over the same temptations and make the same mistakes. Also, we must choose our words carefully before we approach the individual.

So, how do we correctly approach someone to assist him or her to return to the correct path of life? We should show respect by being gentle and loving with our words. This method is biblical and will be successful. Gentle words build up, while a harsh tongue tears down. (See Proverbs 15:4 below.) Never be rude or judgmental. Harsh words make the person either bow up his or her back and get defensive instead of listening or withdraw from your presence and avoid you.

We must act though. Obedience to our Lord demands it. We should not fool ourselves into believing we are too important to help others. (See Galatians 6:3 [NLT] below.) It is obedience versus disobedience.

Will you be obedient to God and aid a fellow believer who becomes caught up in sin? You can by gently and humbly helping that person get back onto the right path.

Action: Be intentional in being obedient to God in assisting anyone overcome by sin to return to the right path of life. In prayer, ask for the Holy Spirit to guide you in being gentle, loving, and respectful in your efforts. Take comfort in knowing you have obeyed the Lord.

Scripture Meditation: Galatians 6:1, 3 (NLT): "Dear brothers and sisters, if another believer is overcome by some sin, you who are godly should gently and humbly help that person back onto the right path. And be careful not to fall into the same temptation yourself. If you think you are too important to help someone, you are only fooling yourself. You are not that important." Mark 12:31: "'And the second, like it, is this: "You shall love your neighbor as yourself." There is no other commandment greater than these.'" Proverb 15:4: "Gentle words are a tree of life; a deceitful tongue crushes the spirit."

DO YOU WANT TO GLORIFY JESUS?

We are living in troubling times for Christians. Nonbelievers seem to be having more success in keeping anything related to Christianity away from public view or hearing. They do not like Jesus. Many of them seem to enjoy insulting us or treating us unfairly. Why? It is because we believe in Jesus and follow Him. This is the only reason. So, how are we to react to this wrongful treatment?

Through Paul, God told us how to react. Expect the bad treatment and do not think of your being persecuted as bad luck or some strange event. (See 1 Peter 4:12 below.) It does not just happen by circumstance or coincidence. God allowed it to happen. He is sovereign. God will use it for your good. He is molding you for His work.

We should be happy in our suffering because we love Jesus. (See 1 Peter 4:13 below.) We are partners with Jesus in being persecuted for righteousness. Rejoice in the trial, for we know in the future when Jesus comes we will be elated in His glory. God will transform our suffering into glory at the proper time. So, rejoice!

When you are persecuted and suffer for the name of Christ, you will be richly blessed, and the Holy Spirit will be with you. (See 1 Peter 4:14 below.) God will give you the strength to endure the persecution, and as you persevere, Christ Jesus will be glorified.

Our persecution for following Jesus will continue in some form. Expect it. Accept it. Rejoice in it. It will result in good for you now and in Heaven. The tribulations will glorify Jesus. In your suffering, you will be blessed by His glory, giving you strength to persevere.

Action: Stand fast for Jesus in the face of persecutions. Pray for continued strength to accept and rejoice in sufferings so you may bring glory to our Lord, Jesus the Christ. Praise God for leading you and for allowing you to partner with Jesus in facing trials and tribulations created by nonbelievers.

Scripture Meditation: First Peter 4:12–14: "Beloved, do not think it strange concerning the fiery trial which is to try you, as though some strange thing happened to you; but rejoice to the extent that you partake of Christ's sufferings, that when His glory is revealed, you may also be glad with exceeding joy. If you are reproached for the name of Christ, blessed are you, for the Spirit of glory and of God rests upon you. On their part He is blasphemed, but on your part He is glorified."

WHO IS WITH YOU?

Who do you think about the most? Is it your spouse? Spouses certainly should be in your daily thoughts. Your children? They too deserve your thoughts. Unmarried? Maybe your parents occupy your mind each day. Make a list of those you think about most. Arrange the names descending from whom you think of the most each day.

Did God make your list? If so, did He top the list? God deserves top billing. As great as your family and friends are, none are with you always. But God is. You cannot see Him, but He is there in your heart. Your faith in the Lord allows you to feel His presence. Can you feel His presence?

Not only is God with you, but also He will not leave you. Jesus Himself said that He is with you till the end of time. (See Matthew 28:20 below.) He is *always* with you. Rejoice in the peace and comfort of His presence. He is there with you now. You cannot flee from Him. But why would you want to go anywhere without Him? No one can match Jesus's love for you, and He is with you to help you in any way that you may need Him.

Having trouble with decision-making? Call on the Lord. Family falling apart? Call on Him. Having difficulty coping in the business world? Let God take your hand and lead you through the trials. Trust Him. Interact with Him. Be aware of His presence.

Don't be like Jacob, who awoke from sleeping and could feel that the Lord had been with him without his knowing it. (See Genesis 28:16 below.) Do not overlook the presence of God. Feel God's existence by communing with Him.

God is not just with you. He is for you. (See Romans 8:31 below.) God is the ultimate protector, so who could ever be against you? What else could you possibly need? He can both protect you and provide for you.

Action: Pray that the Holy Spirit will make you ever mindful of God's presence. Communicate with God through prayer every day. Enjoy His presence. Never forget God is with you always. Praise Him for the comfort of His presence.

Scripture Meditation: Matthew 28:20: "'Teaching them to observe all things that I have commanded you; and lo, I am with you always, even to the end of the age.' Amen." Genesis 28:16: "Then Jacob awoke from his sleep and said, 'Surely the Lord is in this place, and I did not know it.'" Romans 8:31: "What then shall we say to these things? If God is for us, who can be against us?"

HIS BROKEN HEART

Jesus set aside His deity to come into this world as fully man. Jesus experienced the same emotions as we have, both the good and bad. He felt joy. He felt sorrow. He felt pain. He felt disappointment. Jesus even dreaded the last part of His earthly mission. He again would be rejected, breaking His heart.

Jesus's entire time on earth was filled with one rejection after another, one broken heart each time. It started with His birth. With Jesus's birth imminent, He was rejected because there was no room for Him anywhere. (See Luke 2:7 below.) Then throughout Jesus's ministry, most of the religious leaders rejected His teachings.

Jesus's final earthly rejection undoubtedly caused the worst broken heart for Him. He had come to save the people of the world, not to condemn them. (See John 3:17 below.) Yet the world rejected and condemned Him. Instead of accepting Him, they screamed for Him to be crucified. (See Matthew 27:22 below.) Jesus came into and left the world with a broken heart.

Have you broken Jesus's heart? You might say, "No, I have accepted Him as my Savior." Great! But think again. Are you fully obeying Jesus? Don't forget the sins you committed. Each one is an act of disobedience that breaks Jesus's heart because He loves you more than you can imagine.

You do sometimes break Jesus's heart. Sadly, we all do. None of us are perfect. But we must stop using our imperfection as an excuse. Any excuse hinders our yearning to not break Jesus's heart. We must act on, not hinder, our yearning.

Are you ready to raise the level of your obedience to Jesus's ways and commands? You can. Be sincere and intentional in your will to develop more obedience. Jesus knows your heart. He will strengthen you in your drive to not break His heart.

Action: Be intentional in wanting to be more obedient. In prayer, ask Jesus to give you strength to persevere in striving to be obedient to His commands and ways. As your obedience rises, take comfort in knowing you are following the will of God. Praise God for sending His Son to save the world.

Scripture Meditation: Luke 2:7: "And she brought forth her firstborn Son, and wrapped Him in swaddling cloths, and laid Him in a manger, because there was no room for them in the inn." John 3:17: "For God did not send His Son into the world to condemn the world, but that the world through Him might be saved." Matthew 27:22: "Pilate said to them, 'What then shall I do with Jesus who is called Christ?' They all said to him, 'Let Him be crucified!'"

WHERE IS OUR AMAZEMENT?

Do we no longer remember that Jesus's power has no limits? Granted, it is hard to wrap our minds around the fact of limitless power. The world tells us everything falls within boundaries. The worldview seems logical. Yet it is wrong.

Could it be that the worldview has quashed our amazement at the awesome power of our Savior? Maybe. Something has put a hiatus on our awe of Jesus's power. We no longer seem to be excited about His miracles.

Maybe it is complacency. Have we talked about Jesus's miracles so much that His power seems commonplace? I hope not. His power is a lot of things but certainly not a common variety. It is so much more. His power is unlimited, but we may be limiting the use of it.

Our loss of amazement often prevents us from calling on Jesus to help us when we have a need for a miracle. This failure also does not allow Jesus to use us to glorify God. So, we must rediscover our awe of what Jesus can and will accomplish through His might.

Imagine the awesome power needed to raise the dead. Jesus did that. In one circumstance, He told a weeping widow whose only son had died that she did not need to cry. Then He addressed the dead son. Jesus commanded the young man to get up, and the dead man arose and began speaking. (See Luke 7:14–15 below.) Do you find this to be amazing, or are you nonchalant?

Jesus raised the dead young man by commanding that he arise. Surely this kind of power amazes you, as it shows that Jesus's might is so great that it cannot be measured. Your reaction should be awestruck, like that of the witnesses to Jesus's miracle. They feared and glorified God because they knew He was there with them. (See Luke 7:16 below.) We too could be amazed if we call upon Him.

Action: Pray for a deeper understanding of Jesus, His power, and how He applies it to meet our needs in a way that glorifies God. Call upon Jesus when you need Him. Praise Jesus for His assistance to you and for using your circumstances to glorify God.

Scripture Meditation: Luke 7:14–16: "Then He came and touched the open coffin, and those who carried him stood still. And He said, 'Young man, I say to you, arise.' So he who was dead sat up and began to speak. And He presented him to his mother. Then fear came upon all, and they glorified God, saying, 'A great prophet has risen up among us'; and, 'God has visited His people.'"

WILL JESUS REALLY FORGIVE ME?

Have you ever wondered whether Jesus will forgive or has forgiven you for a certain sin? You may have committed some act that you think is so bad and offensive to Jesus that there is no way His blood can cover the sin. Or maybe you habitually repeated a sin, causing you to fear that the habitual nature of the sin will prevent you from receiving forgiveness. Perhaps you offended Jesus by pretending not to be His follower while among nonbelievers.

Could it possibly be that your fear of not being forgiven arises from your listening to Satan rather than Jesus? Satan is always trying to convince you that Jesus will not forgive certain sins, but the devil cannot be trusted.

Remember, Jesus, through His grace and His blood, *will forgive* you of your sin(s). (See Ephesians 1:7 below.) Note that there are no exceptions listed. Redemption and forgiveness are available. Turn to Jesus to purify your heart through forgiveness. Ignore Satan.

Still have doubts? Jesus demonstrated how serious He is about forgiveness. Jesus was carried to Calvary, placed on a cross, and crucified, and while hanging there, He asked God the Father to forgive those who were responsible for His crucifixion. (See Luke 23:33–34 below.) Do you realize for whom Jesus sought forgiveness?

When Jesus asked God to forgive them, the word "them" included a lot of people. He was referring to the arresting soldiers, the Jews who screamed, "Crucify Him!" and those who beat Him unmercifully until strips of skin and flesh were hanging from His body. Also included were those who spit on and mocked Jesus, the soldiers who tied the crossbar portion of the cross along His shoulders and beat Him on the way to Calvary, those who nailed His hands and legs to the cross, and all those who mocked Him hanging there.

Jesus is serious about forgiveness. He forgave everyone who had anything to do with His crucifixion and death. He will forgive you for your sins, regardless of your fears.

Action: Ignore Satan and pray for Jesus to forgive you for any sins that you have not sought forgiveness for. Praise Him for forgiving you, and relax in His comfort and peace.

Scripture Meditation: Ephesians 1:7: "In Him we have redemption through His blood, the forgiveness of sins, according to the riches of His grace." Luke 23:33–34 "And when they had come to the place called Calvary, there they crucified Him, and the criminals, one on the right hand and the other on the left. Then Jesus said, 'Father, forgive them, for they do not know what they do.' And they divided His garments and cast lots."

STOP BEING SELFISH

Are you selfish? Be honest. Most, if not all, of us are. The only real difference between us is the amount of selfishness we have. Some have a higher level, while others have a lower level. This commonality of selfishness seems to worsen in societies like we are experiencing today—the *me* society.

We are bombarded daily with ads and articles through television, radio, blogs, and social media that turn our attention toward ourselves. Even many of our governmental programs seem to encourage us to think of ourselves first. With so many things leading us toward more selfishness, how can we reduce and eliminate our personal selfish ways?

We should start by reminding ourselves how God views selfish activity. God commands us to avoid doing anything through selfishness but to regard others as better than ourselves. (See Philippians 2:3 below.) Wow! God's view is not complicated. He is telling us to not be selfish but to respect everyone more than we regard ourselves. We must be obedient.

Remember the beggar you see close to your office. Respect and regard him highly. He deserves it. He is a man who was created in God's image. (See Genesis 1:27 below.) We all need to respect everyone.

God's Word also tells us to protect the interests of others as well as our own interests. (See Philippians 2:4 below.) While taking care of yourself, help others who need it. This eradicates selfishness.

A minister once explained that the closing of his prayers with the sign of the cross helps ward off selfishness and pride. He said that the touching of his forehead and chest makes a capital I. The gesture of touching first one shoulder and then the other cuts the I in half.

Cutting our I in half is a worthy goal in ridding ourselves of selfishness. Let us all vow to cut our I in half through our interactions with others.

Action: Remind yourself each day that the person you see in the mirror is selfish. When each selfish thought or action arises, turn to Jesus. Pray for help in avoiding selfish thoughts and acts, and ask Him to place opportunities before you to help others.

Scripture Meditation: Philippians 2:3–4: "Let nothing be done through selfish ambition or conceit, but in lowliness of mind let each esteem others better than himself. Let each of you look out not only for his own interests, but also for the interests of others." Genesis 1:27: "So God created man in His own image; in the image of God He created him; male and female He created them."

WHY BE STRESSED OUT?

Stress is common in our society. Our culture breeds it. At work, we are urged to work faster and be more productive. We also think that we must chase a greater lifestyle—a newer auto, a bigger house, stylish clothes. These things are intertwined with concerns about a health problem, the loss of a loved one, the latest trouble caused by one of the kids, and such. Demands placed on us and ever-mounting problems make us want to throw up our hands and say, "I give up."

Most do not give up, but their shoulders bend under the weight of stress. Help is available though. But many either do not know this or fail to ask. Rest and worry-free days seem to be only a dream for them.

Jesus stands ready to relieve your stress. Jesus said that He would give us relief if we are stressed out from work and responsibilities. (See Matthew 11:28 below.) Before you say that stress is a human problem rather than a spiritual one, think again.

Jesus has been there, done that. In Mark, chapters 6 and 7, you can read where in a single day Jesus experienced the loss of a relative, John the Baptist; He suffered from the large masses of people trying to get physically close to Him; He welcomed the triumphant return of His missionary disciples; and His life was threatened. All of this occurred in one chaotic day. But Jesus did not get stressed out. He went to the mountain to be alone and to pray.

Paul explained that God commands us to not be anxious over anything. But turn the situation(s) over to Him in prayer. Then your mind and heart will be put at ease and rest by His peace, through Jesus the Christ. (See Philippians 4:6–7 below.) Jesus wants to help you relieve your stress.

Are you relying on Jesus for stress relief, or are you trying to shoulder your stress alone? Jesus will give peace and comfort to you if you ask Him.

Action: To relieve or avoid stress, pray for Jesus to give you His peace and rest in all circumstances. Thank Him and praise Him for His love and mercy in giving comfort to you.

Scripture Meditation: Matthew 11:28: "Come to Me, all you who labor and are heavy laden, and I will give you rest." Philippians 4:6–7: "Be anxious for nothing, but in everything by prayer and supplication, with thanksgiving, let your requests be made known to God; and the peace of God, which surpasses all understanding, will guard your hearts and minds through Christ Jesus."

IS YOUR LOVE LIMITED?

How would you answer the question in today's title? Before you answer though, I challenge you to be broad-minded in your self-evaluation. For example, you may feel that you have an unlimited love for your spouse or child. Yet you may not accept some annoying habit(s) of one or the other. This limits your love for your loved one(s).

Oh, it would be great if true love were akin to shopping in a store. We could place in our cart the things we like and cast aside the things we dislike. Just chew on this for a while.

We could easily choose our child being the school football hero but ignore the typical teenage know-it-all section. We would be happy to cart our spouse's dimpled smile while rejecting his or her medical problems.

And then there are our careers. Most of us would select that promotion for the higher pay. Yet we would most likely turn our back on the section containing all the problems associated with more responsibility.

We could go on and on. But I think you get the point. True love is not limited and protects, has faith in, hopes for, and is patient with all things. (See 1 Corinthians 13:7 below.) Protecting and being patient in *all things* can be one tall order. Still, the word *all* means all.

When shopping for love, we must put everything in our cart—the good and bad. Why? Love is a positive action—a gracious application of patience, elation toward truthfulness, and a heartfelt generous attitude toward others. Love is not being arrogant or envious. Love never faults others, angers, makes demands, or revels in evil things. (See 1 Corinthians. 13:4–6 below.)

Now, what is your answer to "Is your love limited?" I'm guessing your answer, like mine, will identify limits to your love. Are you willing to eliminate the limits by accepting them? Eliminating the limits to your love will enhance your daily joy and nearness to Jesus.

Action: Pray for the Holy Spirit's guidance in ridding yourself of any limits to your love. Be intentional in using the Spirit's assistance. Be thankful and praise God for allowing you to become closer to Him.

Scripture Meditation: First Corinthians 13:4–7: "Love suffers long and is kind; love does not envy; love does not parade itself, is not puffed up; does not behave rudely, does not seek its own, is not provoked, thinks no evil; does not rejoice in iniquity, but rejoices in the truth; bears all things, believes all things, hopes all things, endures all things."

STOP BEING DISTRACTED BY ...

Distractions are major occurrences in our lives. Most have a negative impact. Some are preventable. Others are not. Sadly, our spiritual life is also hit with distractions affecting our walk with our Lord. The event of Martha welcoming Jesus and some of His followers into her home for dinner is an example.

Martha's sister, Mary, was also there. But she was not helping Martha serve the guests. Instead, Mary sat at the feet of Jesus to absorb what He was saying. So, Martha was distracted by the hostess duties and asked Jesus to order Mary to assist her with the hostess chores. (See Luke 10:40 [NLT] below.) Do you see Martha's distraction with routine chores?

Jesus told Martha that she was worrying over details, while Mary had found the only thing worth worrying about. (See 10:41–42 [NLT] below.) Martha and Mary had two distinctly different attitudes. Martha was distracted by the details of serving guests. Mary ignored the distraction and was worshipping Jesus. Are you able to overcome distractions in order to worship Jesus? Do not be too quick to answer.

Consider why you knew how long the preacher's sermon was last Sunday. Were you worried about a crowd getting to your favorite restaurant first? Or were you concerned about the roast in your oven at home? Maybe you skipped church so that your child could play in a sporting event. You may be involved is so many ministries that each one has become a distraction to the others. Maybe you are so determined to get an early start to your daily responsibilities that you have stopped having daily quiet time with the Lord. Do you get the point? It is easy to be distracted like Martha. Jesus teaches us to be like Mary by placing a top priority on worshipping Him.

Are you a Martha or a Mary?

Action: Focus on worshipping Jesus. In prayer, ask that the Holy Spirit convict you every time you are about to be distracted from worshipping our Lord. Enjoy the peace and comfort of living within the will of God.

Scripture Meditation: Luke 10:40–42 (NLT): "But Martha was distracted by the big dinner she was preparing. She came to Jesus and said, 'Lord, doesn't it seem unfair to you that my sister just sits here while I do all the work? Tell her to come and help me.' But the Lord said to her, 'My dear Martha, you are worried and upset over all these details! There is only one thing worth being concerned about. Mary has discovered it, and it will not be taken away from her.'"

AH, A PERFECT WORLD

How many times have you dealt with bad situations, events, or feelings? It is probably impossible to know the number. Sometimes, bad occurrences happen to you. Other times, awful episodes that befall others also affect you.

Perhaps you lost a loved one. Or maybe your heart is heavy because your child is struggling in school. Your tears are flowing because of your spouse's job loss. You are in shock because you just learned your cancer could neither be controlled nor cured. Or, are your deteriorating finances placing bankruptcy on the horizon? Perhaps it could be one of a thousand things. But rejoice. Far, far better times are ahead. Heaven is waiting for you—that is, if you are a Christian.

God has a place reserved for all Christians in Heaven, with all its splendor, wonder, and greatness. When we arrive there, we will find that earthly things such as crying, pain, sorrow, and death do not exist. (See Revelation 21:4 below.) Can you imagine a perfect world?

In Heaven, there will be no illness, sadness, trial, pain, fear, disharmony, or death. Heaven will contain unimaginable beauty. Every person in Heaven will be a friend. Think of the Garden of Eden where everything was once perfect. God will hit the reset button. For He said that He would make everything new. (See Revelation 21:5 below.) We will be part of total perfection. Yet there is much more to this perfect world.

God will be with us, and we will reign with Him. This reign will be eternal, not time limited. God said that in the eternal time, the saints (God's people) would have the kingdom and rule for all eternity. (See Daniel 7:18 [NLT] below.) You, I, and all other believers will reign with God. Are you ready for Heaven? Your reserved place awaits you.

Action: Pray for the Holy Spirit to remind you of the reality of Heaven and its perfection. Praise God for His grace and for reserving a place for you in Heaven. Not a believer? Accept Jesus as your Lord and Savior. Know the eternal bliss will then be yours.

Scripture Meditation: Revelation 21:4–5: "'And God will wipe away every tear from their eyes; there shall be no more death, nor sorrow, nor crying. There shall be no more pain, for the former things have passed away.' Then He who sat on the throne said, 'Behold, I make all things new.' And He said to me, 'Write, for these words are true and faithful.'" Daniel 7:18 (NLT): "'But in the end, the holy people of the Most High will be given the kingdom, and they will rule forever and ever.'"

STOP TRYING TO FOOL GOD

We all have probably done it—committing what the worldview considers a small sin. There are no big or small sins. All sins result from disobedience to the Lord. All sins, regardless of how the world classifies them, are sins against God. Yet all, if not most, of us keep falling into the trap of thinking this small thing is too inconsequential for God to notice. He has to be extremely busy running His kingdom.

I can almost hear you saying, "I would never do such a thing." Think again. What were those curse words you expressed to yourself when a business competitor undercut the renewal of a contract you had with a client? Did you think the expression was not a sin? Or were you trying to sneak the sin by God?

Was that you criticizing our government leaders instead of praying for them? Did you really make those cash contributions you listed as deductions on your tax forms? Have you effectively said, "Don't look, God, while I sneak a peek at the porn pictures on the Internet"? Surely, you get the point. You are like the rest of us. We have tried to fool God. And we always failed.

We all need to accept the truth about God. Try as we may, we are not able to fool Him. God knows everything. (See 1 John 3:20 below.) Not most things. But all things! He knows all of our thoughts, words uttered, and actions. God is also keenly aware of the status of our hearts. He knows whether our thoughts, words, and actions emanate from pure or tainted hearts.

Do not let Satan trick you into thinking God cannot possibly know everything. Jesus said that He has counted the number of hairs growing on your head. (See Matthew 10:30 below.) Think about it. God knows the exact number of hairs in your head. How could he not know everything? God does know everything. Believe it. Accept it. When we try to fool Him, the only one fooled is our self. And Satan is smiling at our disobedience.

Action: Stop trying to fool God. Pray for the Holy Spirit to guide you in making your heart more pure by convicting you of any sinful thought, word, or action. Ask God for forgiveness. Also, ask Him for strength in building your obedience to Him. Praise the Lord for being your true and living God.

Scripture Meditation: First John 3:20: "For if our heart condemns us, God is greater than our heart, and knows all things." Matthew 10:30: "But the very hairs of your head are all numbered."

DOES YOUR SERVICE PLEASE GOD?

Think about your service to God and how you came to get involved in that specific service or ministry. Did you select it, or did God? It is important that you know. The success or lack of success of your service just might depend on your answer.

Many believers choose their service to our Lord for the wrong reason(s). Some pick a ministry hoping it will make them stand out among their fellow Christians. Some view their selection as a stepping-stone to being named to a lay leadership position. Others simply want their choice to allow them to be regarded as a better Christian than certain friends. Personal enjoyment might also be a reason. There are other self-serving reasons, but these and the four listed reflect self-righteousness. God is unlikely to ordain the work, which leaves failure lurking on the horizon.

Avoid any possible failure. Identify the spiritual gift God gave you through the Holy Spirit. Use the gift by joining a ministry in which God leads you to participate. Rely on God, because He will perfect your way, and He is the source of your power and strength. (See 2 Samuel 22:33 below.)

As you take part in a God-approved ministry, pay close attention to your work. (See Galatians 6:4 below.) You must ensure you are within the will of God before helping others through the ministry. Then you will achieve satisfaction for doing a good job for God, and there will no reason to compare yourself with anyone. Do not boast unless you boast in God for working through you.

Each of us is responsible for our own conduct. So be mindful to be careful in making your daily decisions and elections so that you will not stumble in your spiritual growth. (See 2 Peter 1:10 below.) Now can you say that your service to God complies with His will?

Action: Pray for the Holy Spirit to lead you in evaluating your current and future service to God to determine if all of your work is or will be the work for which God called you. Praise and thank Him for affording you the privilege of having Him working through you.

Scripture Meditation: Second Samuel 22:33: "God is my strength and power, and He makes my way perfect." Galatians 6:4: "Pay careful attention to your own work, for then you will get the satisfaction of a job well done, and you won't need to compare yourself to anyone else." Second Peter 1:10: "Therefore, brethren, be even more diligent to make your call and election sure, for if you do these things you will never stumble."

DIAL UP GOD

There is an excellent reason to dial up God in prayer. He will listen to you. Guaranteed! Pray to God, for He will hear you. (See Psalm 4:3 below.) So, why not consult Him concerning all things?

Do you think God is too busy to have time for you? He has more time than you can even imagine. Maybe you think your need is too small to get God's attention. Think again. Jesus said that you will receive whatever you ask for if you faithfully believe you will receive it. (See Matthew 21:22 below.) Jesus was serious in His remarks. Do you believe Him?

You say, "I fear God might not take me seriously." Oh, He takes you seriously. Need proof? He sent His Son to die on the cross so that you could be saved from your sins. Oh yeah, God is really serious about you. Believe it.

God listens to everyone. He hears you, your family members, your neighbors, your friends, and anyone else who calls Him. It may be the guy operating the homeless shelter. Or it may be the wino who is trying to pull himself out of the gutter. Still again, it could be a family member dialing up God for help. It could be the murderer who is seeking the Lord's mercy and forgiveness. Maybe it is a friend who is experiencing marital problems and needs God's guidance. I could go on and on, but you get the idea.

Isn't it great and wonderful to have a living Lord who listens to you, me, and everyone else? We should be ecstatic. And it gets even better. God listens, and He answers in whatever way is best for us.

While sharing a written prayer with us, David implored the Lord to hear him, stated that God comforted him while in trouble, and asked for mercy. (See Psalm 4:1 below.) Know and believe that our Lord wants to hear from all of us. He listens. Then He answers. No request is too big or too small.

Action: Stand firm in believing and knowing that God listens to and acts on your prayers. Pray to the Lord to help you keep Him in your mind so you will approach Him as each circumstance arises. Be comforted by knowing He listens to your petitions.

Scripture Meditation: Psalm 4:1, 3: "Hear me when I call, O God of my righteousness! You have relieved me in my distress; have mercy on me, and hear my prayer. But know that the Lord has set apart for Himself him who is godly; the Lord will hear when I call to Him." Matthew 21:22: "'And whatever things you ask in prayer, believing, you will receive.'"

GOD SAVED ME BECAUSE ...

Have you ever taken time to reflect on the question "Why did God save me?" Most believers would probably answer with the most recognized verse in the Bible—John 3:16 (see below). God sacrificed His only Son to death so that we all could have eternal life. He did this because of His love for the world, and we are part of the world. So God loves us. This is definitely true, but think about this truth a little longer and a little deeper.

Before going further, though, note that none of us were saved because we are simply good, decent people who do a lot of good things for other folks. With that fact out of the way, continue your reflecting.

God desires for us to bring glory to Him. Also true. Keep digging. God is sovereign. Absolutely correct. Keep going. God, a paragon of justice, paid the price for our sin. Very accurate. Yet there is more.

There are several good reasons for our being saved by God. But one reason just seems to be even more personal and individualistic. King David said that God delighted in him. (See Psalm 18:19 below.) Wow! Think about it. God also delights in you. He is elated with you, and His joy in you is permanent.

He will not cast you aside. He keeps you because He delights in you in special, intimate ways. First, know that God is in your presence, and He will calm you with His love. Then—now read closely—He will joyfully rejoice over you in song. (See Zephaniah 3:17 below.) Can you grasp the full meaning of His delight in you?

The Lord your God, the God of all Heaven and earth, can move and calm the waters, shake the mountains, and stir and still the wind. Yet this same God has a great, everlasting joy in you. He rejoices over you with joy and singing. What else could we ever need or want?

Action: Be ever mindful that God had, has, and will always have a wonderful delight in you. Revel in the knowledge of God's joy in you. In humbleness, praise and thank Him for loving you and rejoicing over you with gladness and singing.

Scripture Meditation: John 3:16: "For God so loved the world that He gave His only begotten Son, that whoever believes in Him should not perish but have everlasting life." Psalm 18:19: "He also brought me out into a broad place; He delivered me because He delighted in me." Zephaniah 3:17: "'The Lord your God in your midst, the Mighty One, will save; He will rejoice over you with gladness, He will quiet you with His love, He will rejoice over you with singing.'"

LOVE YOUR ENEMIES. SAY WHAT?

Most of us are guilty at times of giving lip service to the thought of loving our enemies. But saying, "I love my enemies," does not make it true if the thought is not emanating from our hearts. We must learn to truly love our enemies. It is a commandment of God.

Jesus said that we are to love our enemies. (See Matthew 5:44 below.) Some say Jesus's comment was simply emphasizing His statement of loving your neighbors. Most others say, "Not true." Jesus meant what He said. And He demonstrated that He meant it.

There were a lot of enemies involved in the kangaroo trials of Jesus, His being tortured, and His death on the cross. Some spat on Jesus. Others beat Him unmercifully. Government and religious leaders falsely accused Him and convicted Him. They mocked Him. They hung Him on a cross to die a slow, painful death. Jesus reacted by praying for all of them.

In Jesus's prayer, He asked God the Father to forgive those involved in His crucifixion. (See Luke 23:34 below.) Jesus's act is a paragon of loving one's enemies. You are a follower of Jesus. Imitate Him by loving your enemies.

You might be thinking, *It is too hard to love my enemies. The mental scars are too painful and numerous. And I am not Jesus. I do not have His mental or physical strength.* Sometimes Jesus became exasperated. One instance involved His disciples. They had disappointed and irritated Jesus due to their misunderstanding parts of His teachings. So, how much more would His enemies hurt Him? Yet He forgave both groups—His disciples and His enemies. Strive to be like Jesus. Forgive friends and enemies alike.

Forgiving one's enemies is certainly not easy. It is downright tough. But God is tougher. He told us how to obey His command when Jesus said that we are to be good to and love those who hate, use, or persecute us, and pray for them. (See Matthew 5:44 below.) Are you ready and willing to obey?

Action: Pray for the wisdom and strength to properly love your enemies. Also pray for those who have mentally or physically hurt you. Praise the Lord as you begin to see some transformation of your enemies into more likable individuals and as your heart becomes more loving.

Scripture Meditation: Matthew 5:44: "But I say to you, love your enemies, bless those who curse you, do good to those who hate you, and pray for those who spitefully use you and persecute you." Luke 23:34: "Then Jesus said, 'Father, forgive them, for they do not know what they do.'"

IS YOUR HEART SPIRITUAL?

How often do you think about your Lord and Savior, Jesus? Do not include the times when you are in church. Is it daily, weekly, rarely, or you just do not know? Self-evaluate. But be honest with yourself. The more you think of Jesus, the more spiritual your heart is.

As believers, we are disciples of Jesus. He displayed a spiritual heart while walking on earth. His heart was shaped by His indwelling relationship with God the Father. Jesus said that He and the Father were in each other. (See John 14:11 [NLT] below.) Likewise, you and Jesus should be in each other.

Jesus relied on His intimate relationship with God the Father to steer Him each day. He explained that He could not do anything except what the Father had taught and shown to Him. Think of your mind-set. Is it like that of Jesus? It can be. Jesus told us how.

Jesus said that if we would live according to His Word, we would be his disciples. (See John 8:31 below.) Jesus is the perfect role model. By abiding in His Word, we learn to adhere to His ways, thoughts, words, and actions. We become better disciples. The more we become better disciples, the more we become like Jesus. The more we become like Jesus, the more we glorify God.

Does your self-evaluation indicate you need to be more like Jesus, but you still do not know how? Just do what Jesus did. Do you need to make some decisions? Consult God through prayer. Jesus did. Do you desire to strengthen your obedience and faith? Worship God. Jesus did. And He worshipped God regularly. Do you want to maintain Jesus's commands in your mind? Memorize Bible verses. Jesus did. He did it routinely. You can also do all of these things.

Grade the level of spirituality within your heart by using your self-evaluation as a guide. Use a scale of one to ten, with ten being a heart like that of Jesus. Are you willing to make your heart more like Jesus?

Action: Be intentional. Lean on Jesus in all areas of your life. Pray for guidance, strength, and perseverance in developing a Christlike heart and mind. Relax and enjoy being in the will of the Lord, and let your light be a testimony to others.

Scripture Meditation: John 14:11 (NLT): "'Just believe that I am in the Father and the Father is in me. Or at least believe because of the work you have seen me do.'" John 8:31: "Then Jesus said to those Jews who believed Him, 'If you abide in My word, you are My disciples indeed.'"

TEMPTED? DEAL WITH IT!

Someone once referred to temptation as a scourge of humankind. This description is likely true. But why? Is it our failure to overcome temptation that gives it success? Do we fail because of who tempts us? Does Satan or God tempt us?

Surely we all agree that Satan is a wily thing. He is always trying to deceive us through trickery. Yet, deception and trickery are not the same as temptation. Both can lead to temptations. Satan is our worst enemy and does tempt us. Yet he is not our only tempter.

Does God tempt us? Not according to James. (See James 1:13 below.) God does not tempt anyone. This is not to say God, in His sovereignty, is not able to prevent us from being tempted. He can and probably does at times. It depends on His divine purposes. Hmmm … Who else could tempt us?

We have not searched one place—the mirror. Another tempter is that good-looking person staring back at us. James said that we tempt ourselves when we allow our inherent worldly desires to cause us to stumble. (See James 1:14 below.) Good grief. We tempt our self. We are our second worst enemy.

But there is great news. Our God is a faithful God. He will neither tempt us nor allow us to be tempted beyond what we can endure. Also, God gives an escape route for temptations. (See 1 Corinthians 10:13 below.) The Holy Spirit will lead us to the escape route, if we let Him. Thanks to His limitations on temptation, we can overcome each one. So, the ball is in our court.

We can fall to the tempting, which is sinning against God. Or we can lean on Him and overcome the temptation. Two paths. One leads to sin. The other demonstrates faith in God and rejects temptation. Which path will you choose?

Action: Pray for the strength to avoid letting worldly desires become temptations. Stand up and overcome each temptation, whether self-imposed or not. Praise God for His faithfulness. Enjoy the surety of His faithfulness.

Scripture Meditation: James 1:13–14: "Let no one say when he is tempted, 'I am tempted by God'; for God cannot be tempted by evil, nor does He Himself tempt anyone. But each one is tempted when he is drawn away by his own desires and enticed." First Corinthians 10:13: "No temptation has overtaken you except such as is common to man; but God is faithful, who will not allow you to be tempted beyond what you are able, but with the temptation will also make the way of escape, that you may be able to bear it."

ARE YOU IN A HOLDING PATTERN?

Christians possess a ticket to Heaven. Our entry through the front door is guaranteed by God's grace. But the day of entering Heaven is not yet here. So, what should we be doing until then?

We need to be carrying out the will of God. Not just sometimes but all the time. God has a purpose for us. Identify His purpose and obey His will. God works in us to equip us with the ability and power to complete His will. (See Philippians 2:13 [NLT] below.) So, why are we not always doing His will?

Some are so thrilled to be Heaven bound they end up going into a holding pattern. They are waiting for Jesus to call them. Many of these attend church and feel blessed for their destiny but do little else. This is not God's desire for anyone.

There are many excuses made for marking time instead of acting on God's will. One is that His will seems elusive. Another is, *I am not qualified.* One other is lack of time. A newer one is, *I might offend someone.* The list goes on and on. The Lord has heard them all. His grace trumps every excuse, but we seem to shortchange God's grace.

We tend to limit God's grace to its role in our salvation. It is so much more. It sustains everything we do in our walk with the Lord. After our salvation, He continues to shed His grace upon us. (See 2 Corinthians 9:8 below.) And there is more good news.

We can be confident that God's grace will help us to overcome every excuse and obstacle. His grace enables us to have or obtain everything we would need to do the work He has chosen for us. (Again, see 2 Corinthians 9:8 below.) God gives us more grace than needed to carry out His perfect will. We all can say, "Hello, grace. Goodbye, excuses."

Will you act through God's marvelous grace and fulfill His plan for you? Or will you maintain a holding pattern? It is your choice.

Action: Pray for the Holy Spirit to direct you in being vigilant regarding God's plan for you. Accept His continuous grace in fulfilling His will. If you are not a Christian, experience God's grace by accepting Jesus as your Lord and by walking with Him after that.

Scripture Meditation: Philippians 2:13 (NLT): "For God is working in you, giving you the desire and the power to do what pleases him." Second Corinthians 9:8: "And God is able to make all grace abound toward you, that you, always having all sufficiency in all things, may have an abundance for every good work."

HAPPINESS IS FOUND IN ...

Have you ever wondered why people spend enormous amounts of money, time, and effort to be happy? None of us know the total value of all the resources expended. It doesn't take a rocket scientist though to understand the amount of money spent is mind-boggling. Yet the joy found is a worldly happiness and is at best temporary.

So, what do we do when our happiness wanes? Usually, we seek other joys to replace lost happiness. Then the new joy withers away. It is a vicious, never-ending cycle. Nothing changes. And strangely, happiness obtained with a lot of resources does not seem to last much longer than those gained from less assets.

There is nothing inherently wrong with temporary happiness in so far as it is kept in the proper perspective and is not overprioritized. Still, this gaiety is temporary.

Some individuals even take one or more years away from their education or career so they can be happy. You must admit, their need to find themselves begs a question. Who do they see in the mirror each day?

There is a much greater way to seek happiness. And this way has unlimited benefits. The joy will not fizzle out. It is permanent. Everyone can afford this joy. No one has to work for it. Still the provider of this joy wants you to have it. And it is easy to find this gleeful path. Dust off your Bible to get started on the happy road.

Ask Jesus to teach you His decrees in your Bible. (See Psalm 119:33 [NLT] below.) Jesus will lead you to them through the Holy Spirit. He also will assist you with the decrees. Ask Him to give you the ability to understand and have the heartfelt desire to obey His decrees. (See Psalm 119:34 [NLT] below.)

Your obedience to God's Word will allow you to gleefully travel along the path of God's commands. (See Psalm 119:35 [NLT] below.) As you walk along God's path, you are in His will. There is no greater happiness on earth than that found in obeying God's commands.

Action: Immerse yourself in God's Word. Pray for wisdom to understand His decrees, the strength to obey His instructions, and the faith to put His decrees into practice. Revel in the resulting happiness, which will not melt away.

Scripture Meditation: Psalm 119:33–35 (NLT): "Teach me your decrees, O Lord; I will keep them to the end. Give me understanding and I will obey your instructions; I will put them into practice with all my heart. Make me walk along the path of your commands, for that is where my happiness is found."

HAVE YOU CHANGED?

Have you changed? Interesting question. Ponder it. Remember that great feeling when you accepted Christ as your Lord and Savior? Then you repented and sought forgiveness for your sins. All was set right between you and God. Are you right with Him now though? If not, something changed. It has to be you, because God never changes.

Even God said that He does not change. (See Malachi 3:6 below.) You, like me, have sinned since you repented, for no one is perfect. So, we have changed. Not for the good but for the bad With each postsalvation sin, we change by turning the wrong way—away from God. But we can correct our errors by righting our ship. It is God's will. He told us to return to Him.

Returning to God is a command. He said that we turned away from Him through sin, but if we go back to Him, He will return to us. (See Malachi 3:7 below.) Repent of your additional sins and be drawn nearer to God.

I can almost hear you thinking, *But what sins? I have strived to not sin.* Do not fool yourself. What about that temper-driven outburst toward your spouse? Do you recall those inappropriate sexual thoughts you had about a coworker? Remember that little boy hungrily staring at you? Did you help him? How about that waitress you angrily berated for getting your lunch mates' food orders wrong? Have you forgotten those cuss words you muttered or shouted when someone cut you off in the morning rush hour? I could go on and on. But surely you get the point.

All the situations I asked about are but a few of many possible sins against God. Each sin pushes one away from God. The more one sins, the farther away from God one is shoved, which damages one's personal relationship with Him.

God wants and commands you return to Him. He will forgive you. Will you obey Him?

Action: In prayer, ask the Holy Spirit to convict you of any sins you have committed and for which you have not sought forgiveness. Repent and ask God to forgive you for these sins. Enjoy the contentment of being closer to God.

Scripture Meditation: Malachi 3:6–7: "'For I am the Lord, I do not change; therefore you are not consumed, O sons of Jacob. Yet from the days of your fathers you have gone away from My ordinances and have not kept them. Return to Me, and I will return to you,' says the Lord of hosts. 'But you said, In what way shall we return?'"

CHILD OF HELL OR CHILD OF GOD?

Every person born into this world will leave it as a child of hell or child of God. That's it. There are no other options. Every child of hell is destined for eternal damnation in hell—infinite misery. Every child of God is headed to eternal life with our Lord—infinite bliss. Oh, some will tell you there are other post death possibilities. They are wrong, dead wrong! Don't bet your soul on what they say. Compare the two real options instead.

A child of hell (also called son of hell, child of the devil, and son of perdition) is one who does not believe in Christ Jesus. The title points to his destiny of eternal separation from God in never ending damnation. Imagine the misery. It never stops.

A child of God is also called son of God. Anyone led by the Holy Spirit is a child of God through belief in Jesus Christ. (See Romans 8:14 [NLT] and Galatians 3:26 [NLT] below.) The title, child of God, also points to an established destiny, which is eternal life with our Lord in Heaven. There will be no more sadness, tears, stress, illness, injuries, or any other bad thing. Nothing but heavenly bliss.

Are you a child of hell or a child of God? If you say child of God, do your actions reflect your belief in Jesus and His Word or that of a pretender? Remember, your actions will influence others. Be honest.

Don't be like the Pharisees in the Bible. Pretenders' actions are not Godlike. Their sins lead others to be children of hell. Anyone causing someone to become a child of hell is actually turning the novice into twice the child of hell as he or she is. (See Matthew 23:15 [NLT] below.) Wow. Pretenders are children of hell, and those they influence are twice as sinful.

A child of God helps Jesus extend His kingdom in Heaven. A child of hell helps Satan build his fiefdom in hell. Which child will you be?

Action: Be a child of God. Accept Jesus as your Lord and Savior, if you have not yet done so. Pray for the Holy Spirit to guide you in being obedient to God. Praise God for accepting you as His child.

Scripture Meditation: Romans 8:14 (NLT): "For all who are led by the Spirit of God are children of God." Galatians 3:26 (NLT): "For you are all children of God through faith in Christ Jesus." Matthew 23:15 (NLT): "'What sorrow awaits you teachers of religious law and you Pharisees. Hypocrites! For you cross land and sea to make one convert, and then you turn that person into twice the child of hell you yourselves are!'"

TO WHOM ARE YOU LISTENING?

Accepting Christ Jesus as your Lord and Savior comes with responsibilities. One is that we should follow Him as His disciple. Sounds simple, doesn't it? It should, but it isn't.

Consider what Paul said about following Jesus. He said that the roots of our lives should be in Jesus, and we could learn from His Word so our faith will be strong. (See Colossians 2:7 [NLT] below.) This is what maturing as a Christian is about, strengthening our faith by learning and living in God's truths as we build our lives in Jesus. The more we stay in Him, the stronger our faith becomes. But this comes with a constant danger—false teaching.

Paul warned that Satan, his minions, and misguided human thinking can overtake us with untrue but great-sounding assurances of empty theories. (See Colossians 2:8 [NLT] below.) False teachings can be difficult to identify.

False teachers are all around us. Some are on television masquerading as God's servants. Some have infiltrated local churches. Some are even pretending to be traveling evangelists. All are proficient at mixing false ideas with accurate truths to make their teaching appear legitimate.

Yet God provides us with discernment. Develop it. Study Jesus's teachings in God's Word. Jesus has used His might as being over all rulers and authorities to make us complete through Him. (See Colossians 2:10 [NLT] below.) We should use Jesus's teachings to apply our discernment to recognize false teachers.

There are competing philosophies battling for our acceptance. One is false teaching presented through trickery. The other side is God's truths presented by Jesus, who lives in the fullness of God. Ignore the false teaching and follow Jesus to get God's truths. Are you practicing your God-given discernment?

Action: Learn God's truths from Jesus. Pray for wisdom in developing discernment to identify and ignore false teachers and their teachings. Also, ask that God be glorified through your shunning of false prophets. Do not be afraid to discuss your suspicion of any false teaching with those you know to be true followers of Jesus.

Scripture Meditation: Colossians 2:7–8, 10 (NLT): "Let your roots grow down into him [Jesus], and let your lives be built on him. Then your faith will grow strong in the truth you were taught, and you will overflow with thankfulness. Don't let anyone capture you with empty philosophies and high-sounding nonsense that come from human thinking and from the spiritual powers of this world, rather than from Christ. So you also are complete through your union with Christ, who is the head over every ruler and authority."

ARE YOU LOVING WITH HUMILITY?

Jesus placed a high priority on loving others—just under loving God with all our being. He said that this important love commandment is to love everyone as we love ourselves. (See Matthew 22:39 below.)

Some have a difficult time understanding how they can love others as they love themselves. Let Jesus be your mentor. He gave us an example of how to train ourselves to love others. (See John 13:15 below.) Jesus served others with a humility-laced love by washing the feet of eleven of His original disciples. He did this so we would know to do the same. (See John 13:14 below.) This is Jesus's pattern for us to love everyone with humility.

Jesus's example sets a high standard. The washing of feet for someone in Jesus's day was usually reserved for the lowliest of servants. It was a dirty job. Yet Jesus did it.

Think about it. Jesus is the King of kings and the Lord of lords. He created Heaven and earth. Jesus set the stars in the sky. His hands dug the Grand Canyon. Yet He humbly went to His knees and washed the feet of His disciples. This is an example of humility at its finest. Are you following Jesus's precedent?

Think before you say yes. There is a homeless person you may sometimes see. He or she can barely walk and probably has not eaten lately. The person's odor screams for a bath. You give the person money so he or she can get some food and maybe a bath. The person may or may not be appreciative. Does your action fit within the standard Jesus created? Probably not. So, what should you do?

Let the Holy Spirit guide you. This may lead to several things. See that the person gets a bath and clean clothes. Carry the individual to eat with you. Obtain personal information that you could use to assist him/her in landing a job. The sky is the limit when acting through love with humility. Are you willing to humble yourself and act?

Action: Obey Jesus. Pray for the Holy Spirit to guide you in every opportunity to love through humility. Look for the opportunities around you. Act. Then bask in the joy and comfort that results from obeying Jesus.

Scripture Meditation: Matthew 22:39: "'And the second is like it: "You shall love your neighbor as yourself."'" John 13:14–15 "'If I then, your Lord and Teacher, have washed your feet, you also ought to wash one another's feet. For I have given you an example, that you should do as I have done to you.'"

WORKING ON YOUR ASSIGNMENT

Did you know that Jesus has given every Christian an assignment? He even gave each of us the same assignment. Not just some Christians but all! In prayer, Jesus said to God the Father, "Like You sent Me to save the world, I have sent My disciples to go throughout the world." (See John 17:18 below.) Jesus sent them, His disciples. Now we are His disciples. The torch has been passed to us.

The torch is carrying on the work Jesus started. He said that He came to save the world. (See John 12:47 below.) Jesus later confirmed our torch bearing just before ascending back to Heaven. He said that we would be His witnesses throughout the entire world. (See Acts 1:8 below.)

We have our assignment. Call it a mission or marching orders if you like. Jesus told us to go and tell nonbelievers the good news of His willingly dying on the cross to pay the price for our sins. Through God's grace, anyone can obtain his or her free salvation by believing in and having faith in Jesus. The price of sin has been paid.

Jesus said to go and tell. This might involve walking across the street. Or going across town. It might require going to another city, state, or nation. You may even need to go halfway around the world. It could involve any combination of destinations. Just do your assignment.

You, like me, might say you do not have time. You have time to maintain a near par average golf game. Is that dinner you are preparing more important than the fact that a couple of your neighbors are currently destined for hell? Could it be the unexpected money you received was God's way of funding a mission trip abroad for you?

Are you working on your assignment?

Action: Obey Jesus. Pray for the Holy Spirit to guide you through your assignment from Jesus. Let God direct you when and where you will go and spread the good news of Jesus. Make His will a top priority in your life. Thank God for using you in His perfect will.

Scripture Meditation: John 17:18: "'As You sent Me into the world, I also have sent them into the world.'" John 12:47: "'And if anyone hears My words and does not believe, I do not judge him; for I did not come to judge the world but to save the world.'" Acts 1:8: "'But you shall receive power when the Holy Spirit has come upon you; and you shall be witnesses to Me in Jerusalem, and in all Judea and Samaria, and to the end of the earth.'"

SEARCHING FOR SAFETY?

It is our nature to desire safety whether or not we are in imminent danger. We spend a lot of money providing security devices and processes for ourselves and loved ones. This is being a responsible citizen. But none are completely fail-safe.

Things happen that puncture our man-made safety net. So what do we do? We probably spend more money for better security items. Maybe we are looking in the wrong places for the top-of-the-line security.

The Lord has the best safety system. It is available to us free of charge. God's promises are our armor of protection, and His promises cover us as protective wings. (See Psalm 91:4 [NLT] below.) So, why do we not always call upon Him?

We leave home into rush hour traffic in an automobile with the latest safety features—all part of the price we paid for the vehicle. Yet we ignore God's top-rated and free protection plan. Likewise, at home, we have smoke alarms, carbon dioxide alarms, and burglar alarm systems. But we still have God riding the bench on the sideline. We should allow Him in the protection game. His plan is impeccable.

All the benefits of God's policy are rock solid because He is faithful to His word. Just ask Daniel of Bible fame. The king had Daniel thrown in the lions' den for worshipping God. The king tried to excuse his action by telling Daniel that he was so faithful to his God, He would save him. (See Daniel 6:16 below.) The king was correct. God intervened and saved Daniel.

Daniel was locked in the lions' den overnight. Not a tooth or paw touched Daniel. God sent an angel to protect him. Daniel was released without a scratch. God protected Daniel, and He stands ready to keep you safe. You can trust the Lord to keep you safe. Or you can keep Him on the bench. It is your call. God will not force you to use His safety net. What will be your decision?

Action: Ensure your security. Depend upon the Lord. Pray, asking God to protect you in your daily endeavors with His wings and faithful promises. Praise and thank God for protecting you. Enjoy the peace and comfort of His protection.

Scripture Meditation: Psalm 91:4 (NLT): "He will cover you with his feathers. He will shelter you with his wings. His faithful promises are your armor and protection." Daniel 6:16: "So the king gave the command, and they brought Daniel and cast him into the den of lions. But the king spoke, saying to Daniel, 'Your God, whom you serve continually, He will deliver you.'"

ARE YOU AND GOD INSEPARABLE?

Few Christians think about being inseparable from God when they are dressed up, wearing clean clothes, sporting combed hair, and marching to church with their head held high. These times mostly evoke thoughts like, *All is well in my world*, or, *I am marching to Zion*. If that is you, you greet everyone happily. But what about other days when you are not feeling so spiritual?

You may have a grudge against a coworker for making you look bad before your boss. You may have moody days when you snarl at most everyone you see. Then there are times when your thoughts belong in the gutter rather than in your head. All kinds of people, powers, and events wrongfully influence our minds, hearts, and actions. Often we fall prey to temptations. Then the evil one happily leads us away from God.

But the Bible tells us that we can defeat all these bad things through our Lord and Savior, Christ Jesus. (See Romans 8:37 below.) Ignore Satan, and trust Jesus. His love cements us to God. There is absolutely nothing spiritual or physical or anything created that is able to separate us from God's love, which is in Christ Jesus our Lord. (See Romans 8:38–39 below.) Strong words. But they are great and strong words that give us much comfort.

How great is our God! Nothing separates us from Him. Absolutely nothing in all creation, including the powers of hell, is able to separate us from God's love, which is revealed through Jesus, our Lord and Savior. His love, mercy, and forgiveness trump our sins.

Unfortunately, none of this applies to you if you have not accepted God's free gift of salvation. God's Son, Jesus, is our redeemer. He paid the price for our sins. Redeem your salvation today by accepting Jesus as your Lord and Savior.

If you are a believer, trust in God and ignore the evil one. You and God are inseparable.

Action: For Christians: Pray for strength to overcome the evil forces with the mindset that you and God are inseparable. For non-Christians: Accept Jesus as your Lord and Savior. Enjoy the blessings of being inseparable from God.

Scripture Meditation: Romans 8:37–39: "Yet in all these things we are more than conquerors through Him who loved us. For I am persuaded that neither death nor life, nor angels nor principalities nor powers, nor things present nor things to come, nor height nor depth, nor any other created thing, shall be able to separate us from the love of God which is in Christ Jesus our Lord."

GOD IS ALWAYS WITH US

Do you truly believe that God is with us always? This is not a trick question. You either believe it or you don't. There is no middle ground. He is or He isn't. In Psalm 23:4 below, David said that God is with him. Some say that David did not include the word always, but he did not say sometimes either. And Lord Jesus confirmed his words. Jesus said that we could be certain that He is always with us forever—now, every day until our physical death, and for all eternity. (See Matthew 28:20 below.) We are never without Him.

Do you sometimes act as though God is not with you? Did you think God was not looking over your shoulder when you berated your spouse? Where do you think God was when you were telling that dirty joke? Do you remember the filthy movies you privately watched? Did you believe your privacy excluded God? Even your most secret unspoken thoughts can portray nonbelief that God is always with you.

Maybe you had some inappropriate thoughts concerning a neighbor's spouse. How many times have you silently taken the Lord's name in vain while in a state of anger? Keeping your thoughts within yourself does not make them appropriate.

No one can hide any private thoughts, spoken words, or actions from God. And no one should try. His continuous presence with us means His goodness and mercy are where we are every day of our lives. (See Psalm 23:6 below.) If we could hide things from God's presence, it follows that we would also be hiding from His goodness and mercy. This is a terrible consequence. Avoid it. Believe you cannot hide from God's presence or sovereignty. And you will be blessed by His closeness.

Yes, God is always with you. Believe it. Think like it. Act like it.

Action: Know that God is always with you. Pray for the Holy Spirit to make you mindful of His presence. Let your thoughts and actions portray God's approval. Enjoy the joy and comfort of God's blessings brought by His closeness.

Scripture Meditation: Psalm 23:4, 6: "Yea, though I walk through the valley of the shadow of death, I will fear no evil; for You are with me; Your rod and Your staff, they comfort me. Surely goodness and mercy shall follow me all the days of my life; and I will dwell in the house of the Lord forever." Matthew 28:20: "'Teach these new disciples to obey all the commands I have given you. And be sure of this: I am with you always, even to the end of the age.'"

HOW MANY IDOLS DO YOU HAVE?

Idolatry is alive and well. So, today's topic is a real and important question. In most instances, today's idols are much different from the idols in the Old Testament. In those days, idols were usually made for worship purposes. Now, most idolatry is subtle, as many idols were not created for worship purposes.

The subtle idols are usually not things made with hands. They are personal characteristics and desires and cultural customs. Most have a rightful place in our world. But they were not intended to be idols. They were born out of the three lusts of the world—two cravings and pride. The cravings are for physical pleasure and things we see, while pride is in our assets and successes. (See 1 John 2:16 [NLT] below.) But you say, "I am a Christian. My God is the living God." Think about your words.

Do you consult with social media more than you consult with Jesus? Does the time you spend increasing your income tower over the time you commune with God? Did you cut back your tithe so that you could buy a newer or bigger house? Are you continually thinking of ways to increase your physical pleasure? Get the point?

Anything (including cultural customs, items, and deeds) that we place ahead of our Lord is an idol. Social customs, money, possessions, physical pleasures, and food are just some of the things that many in our society turn into idols. None were created to be idols. Some are necessary. All have good purposes as long as they are subservient to God.

Consider how our Lord feels about idols. Remember that an idol is a false god. Our God said that no other god shall be placed above Him. (See Exodus 20:3 below.) This is the first of the Ten Commandments. God's declaration was precise. His words left no room for misinterpretation. Having a false god or gods is a sin again the true God—our God. He is sovereign.

Now, how many idols do you have? And what are you going to do about them?

Action: Self-evaluate. Pray for the Holy Spirit to guide you in identifying any idols you may have. Also ask for strength, guidance, and perseverance in moving God up to His rightful place in your mind and heart—above all else. Depend wholly upon God.

Scripture Meditation: First John 2:16 (NLT): "For the world offers only a craving for physical pleasure, a craving for everything we see, and pride in our achievements and possessions. These are not from the Father, but are from this world." Exodus 20:3: "'You shall have no other gods before Me.'"

IS IT WELL WITH YOUR SOUL?

Everyone has suffered or will suffer a devastating loss of a loved one. The degree of pain felt varies among individuals. The relationship of the person to the loved one is also a factor. The way one deals with the agony is determined by the spiritual health of our souls.

On November 22, 1873, Horatio Spafford sent his wife and all four daughters to England by ship. The ship was struck by another ship, and all of the Spafford daughters were lost. Mrs. Spafford survived and made it to England. Horatio then set sail for England. While aboard the ship, Spafford penned the lyrics to the famous hymn, "It Is Well with My Soul."

The lyrics of Mr. Spafford's song speak of having peace and comfort during any trial or tribulation that he faced. Also, the song clearly credits Christ Jesus for providing the peace that comforted his soul.

Mr. Spafford used his faith to rely on the God's promises of peace. (See John 14:27 below.) We should never worry or be saddened or angered over life's circumstances. Jesus will give us peace. The peace within Spafford enabled him to overcome the deep hurt of losing his daughters. So he wrote "It Is Well with My Soul." Sadly, everyone does not rely of God's promise of peace.

A man died suddenly at the early age of fifty-seven. His spouse's broken heart caused a deep depression. His son was devastated and blamed God for the loss of his dad and his mom's depression. The son's hurt led him from Jesus. For three years, he tried to find a joy to relieve his hurt and anger. It didn't work, as he looked in all the wrong places. Finally, he turned back to God. Jesus filled him with His peace, and his renewed faith allowed him to defeat his anger and hurting. Now all is well with his soul.

Both Mr. Stafford and the man's son suffered from mental anguish and had the same decision to consider. Each could rely on Jesus's promise of His peace or seek comfort through worldly ways. Stafford wisely looked to Jesus. The son foolishly sought the world.

When tragedies strike you, do you look to Jesus or the world to comfort your soul?

Action: Pray for the peace of Jesus when you face a problem, trial, or tribulation. Praise the Lord and thank Him for His peace and comfort. Then let others see Jesus in you.

Scripture Meditation: John 14:27: "Peace I leave with you, My peace I give to you; not as the world gives do I give to you. Let not your heart be troubled, neither let it be afraid."

GOD IS FOR YOU! CHA-CHING!

Have you been going through a lot of bad days lately? Maybe coworkers are mentally harassing you. Or those sales contracts you thought you landed never materialized. Perhaps someone short-circuited that promotion you thought would easily be yours. Your enemies seem to be coming out of the woodwork.

Your struggle with your enemies is worsened by the sudden outbreak of medical issues in your life. A friend told you, "If you did not have bad luck, you would not have any luck at all." You've even begun to question God.

"God, why are these things happening to me? I was racing through a great career path and enjoying wonderful health. Then everything changed! God, I cannot feel your assistance or presence." Did you ask Him for help? He is on your side. He is for you.

Lean on God's Word. He stands ready to assist you. Cry out to Him in faith. Like David, you will know that your enemies will fail and turn back because God is on your side. (See Psalm 56:9 below.) God is for you. Believe it and seek His help.

Yes, God is on your side. And you are assured of this truth because God has sealed His written support in His hands. (See Isaiah 49:16 below.) Think about it. Chew on it. The God who parted the Red Sea, set the stars in the sky, and offered us the free gift of salvation is for you. In fact, He is so much for you He has written your name on the palms of His hands. Surely this raises your comfort level to much greater heights.

What is the meaning of God being for us and sealing His support in His hands? Paul said that when God is for us, no one can be against us. (See Romans 8:31 below.) God's power and sovereignty cannot be matched.

Will you face your enemies with or without God? Choose God and receive victory with peace and comfort. Ignore God and struggle with anxiety, stress, and unhappiness, while being alone.

Action: When an enemy attacks, call on God in prayer. Praise Him for being for you and ask Him to lead you through each battle. Give God the glory for each victory, whether in sight or not. Bask in your newfound peace and comfort.

Scripture Meditation: Psalm 56:9: "When I cry out to You, then my enemies will turn back; this I know, because God is for me." Isaiah 49:16: "See, I have inscribed you on the palms of My hands; your walls are continually before Me." Romans 8:31: "What then shall we say to these things? If God is for us, who can be against us?"

MY PRAYER LIFE STATUS IS ...

Reflect on your prayer life. Are you regularly communicating with the Lord? Sadly, most Christians do not. Yet prayer is one of the greatest privileges God has given to us. So, why is prayer underutilized? Is it a lack of faith in God, or in His answering prayer, or both?

God places a high priority on prayer. The Bible uses the words pray, prayer, and praying a total of 601 times altogether. God intends for us to pray to Him. It is our best way to communicate with Him. But God is the perfect gentleman. He will not force Himself upon us. The ball is in our court.

Yes, God is serious about prayer. He answers all prayer—yes, no, or He has something better for us. And each answer occurs according to God's perfect timing. So our faith in God's answering prayer must be lacking.

Jesus said that when we ask for things while praying, we will receive them if we believe we would receive them. (See Matthew 21:22 below.) Believing is having faith. Jesus also said that we can move mountains if we have faith that we can move them. (See Matthew 21:21 below.) Note that true faith does not include doubt. True faith and doubt cannot exist together.

Either we have total faith in God or we doubt His power. Do not listen to Satan. He will go the extra mile to convince you that God's power and mercy cannot fulfill our needs. Call Satan out for being a liar. God has unlimited power and mercy. Believe it. Have faith in it.

Think about this. God is our creator. He turned water into wine. He cured the sick. He healed the lame. He even raised some from the dead. The miracles go on and on. So, we cannot possibly present any prayer request to God that He is not able to fulfill. We just need a strong faith in our Lord. Then we can pray with confidence in all circumstances.

Action: Engage God. Pray for His guidance in all daily circumstances. Also, ask for perseverance in developing a strong faith in your prayers being answered according to His will and timing. Know that all answers will be what is best for you.

Scripture Meditation: Matthew 21:21–22: "So Jesus answered and said to them, 'Assuredly, I say to you, if you have faith and do not doubt, you will not only do what was done to the fig tree, but also if you say to this mountain, "Be removed and be cast into the sea," it will be done. And whatever things you ask in prayer, believing, you will receive.'"

FOLLOW JESUS EVERYWHERE

Christians often say that we follow Jesus. We say this because we are His disciples. Jesus said, "If you want to be My disciples, you have to stop your worldly ways, be prepared to sacrifice all for Me, and follow Me." (See Matthew 16:24 below.) Are we truly doing as Jesus says?

To completely follow Jesus, a disciple must put aside worldly ways and desires and substitute total commitment to happily obeying Jesus's commands. Oh man! The total commitment part is a big stumbling block.

It is easy being committed to following Jesus during the good and peaceful times and places. But following Him into dangerous and unsavory places really strains total commitment. Sometimes Jesus's followers have to suffer physically or mentally or both. They may be mocked, slandered, or spit on. Physical harm, including death, could occur. And personal worldly gains may be sacrificed. Some sinners are the worst of the worst.

Be mindful that when you take up your cross and follow Jesus as He commanded, your obedience could be difficult to maintain. There will be strong temptations to turn your back to Him, especially when Jesus may lead you to unsavory places where sin rules.

Jesus will go to the sinners regardless of where they are. He said that those who faithfully believe in God are not in danger, so He came to save the lost. (See Mark 2:17 below.) Jesus will fulfill His calling—go, find, and save the lost. His disciples must also fulfill their calling by doing as Jesus did.

Are you accompanying Jesus wherever He goes? If not, is your commitment to Him lacking? Maybe complacency has set in. Or it could be that you are fearful of harm or losing some of your worldly possessions. Or, your trust in Jesus might not be sufficient. Whatever may be holding you back can be overcome with Jesus's help. He is willing. Are you willing to allow Him to take your hand and assist you?

Action: In prayer, talk to Jesus, asking for forgiveness for failing to fully follow Him. Also ask the Holy Spirit to guide you in seeking Jesus's will for you. Substitute your worldly desires and ways for Jesus's will. Praise Him for the privilege of serving Him.

Scripture Meditation: Matthew 16:24: "Then Jesus said to His disciples, 'If anyone desires to come after Me, let him deny himself, and take up his cross, and follow Me.'" Mark 2:17: "When Jesus heard it, He said to them, 'Those who are well have no need of a physician, but those who are sick. I did not come to call the righteous, but sinners, to repentance.'"

WARDING OFF PERSECUTION

Christians within free countries of the world are experiencing more persecutions than in previous generations. This is true of physical and nonphysical persecution. So, would you react in fear? Would you flee? Would you hide? No, no, and no! Jesus's light intensifies when believers are under the gun. Let His light shine through you.

Peter the apostle once said that most people, including evil ones, do not have the desire to harm those who are doing good. Apparently, it hurts their conscience more. Yet some will still seek to harm you.

You may suffer for obeying Jesus as you work to carry out the will of God. (See 1 Peter 3:14–16 below.) Do not fear or worry over anyone's threats against you. Just continue to worship Christ as your Lord, while being respectful. God will reward you for your faith in the Lord.

So, instead of fearing persecution, worship the Lord continually from your heart. The more you worship, the greater witness you will be for Jesus. But do it Jesus's way by being meek and respectful. The results will amaze you.

You will be credited with blessings (rewards). And some of the would-be persecutors will be ashamed when they realize your being a disciple of Christ led to your good life. (See 1 Peter 3:16 below.) Your strong witness for Christ will help Him extend His kingdom. The comfort you will experience is a reward for obeying God.

What will you do when facing persecution? Will you whine while having a nervous fear? Cower down and do nothing? Or will you view each crisis as an opportunity to be witness for Jesus? Choose wisely. It is much better to suffer for obeying God and doing good than to suffer for committing evil acts. In facing persecution, will you be obedient or disobedient to the Lord?

Action: Boldly face persecution. With all your heart, worship Christ as Lord of your life. Ask the Holy Spirit to guide you in boldly witnessing for Jesus. Praise Him for using you.

Scripture Meditation: First Peter 3:14–16: "But even if you suffer for doing what is right, God will reward you for it. So don't worry or be afraid of their threats. Instead, you must worship Christ as Lord of your life. And if someone asks about your hope as a believer, always be ready to explain it. But do this in a gentle and respectful way. Keep your conscience clear. Then if people speak against you, they will be ashamed when they see what a good life you live because you belong to Christ."

STOP BEING LONG-FACED

Christians who go around sporting long faces are not projecting the light of Jesus. Yet many do. They have created an oxymoron—long-faced Christians. This is not God's will for us. Christians should be a group of blessed, happy folks. So, why the long faces?

Through a psalmist, God said that a person is blessed when he or she does not seek advice from sinners, refuses to walk on the unbeliever's path, and does not join in with the scornful. (See Psalm 1:1 below.) Christ's followers are rewarded when not being guided by nonbelievers, walking with sinners, or hanging out with those who have contempt for Christians. These activities are all part of a marching order for what not to do—disobey God.

Disobedience. Maybe, just maybe, that's it. Long-faced Christians must have been disobedient by acting ungodly. Those who act ungodly find they are like chaff that the wind blows away. (See Psalm 1:4 below.) Hmmm. Long-faced Christians might be experiencing the guilt of disobeying God. Surely they feel the Holy Spirit convicting them of their disobedience. They probably are feeling the effect of not being as close to God.

Christians should do the opposite—obey God. Each believer receives joy in the Word of God when he or she meditates on His Word. (See Psalm 1:2 below.) Obedience creates delight in the reward of blessedness. The psalmist also said that anyone living by God's Word will prosper and glorify Him. (See Psalm 1:3 below.) Obedience to God transforms long faces into brilliant smiles as blessings and joy build.

Which is better? Being guilt ridden, which filters out Jesus's light emanating through you, or feeling exuberant and blessed, while reflecting the wonders of Jesus's light? It is disobedience versus obedience. It is long faces or smiles. For which will you strive?

Choose wisely. The best choice is obedience and joy. Be happy in the Lord.

Action: Be intentional in meditating on God's Word daily. Pray for strength to persevere in obeying God. Say goodbye to any guilt. Enjoy the blessings of obedience to God.

Scripture Meditation: Psalm 1:1–4: "Blessed is the man who walks not in the counsel of the ungodly, nor stands in the path of sinners, nor sits in the seat of the scornful; But his delight is in the law of the Lord, and in His law he meditates day and night. He shall be like a tree planted by the rivers of water, that brings forth its fruit in its season, whose leaf also shall not wither; and whatever he does shall prosper. The ungodly are not so, but are like the chaff which the wind drives away."

SEEKING GOD CONTINUALLY?

We are good at seeking the Lord during tough times. King David was the same way. He wrote during one trial that his soul panted for God the way a deer pants for water. (See Psalm 42:1 below.) A deer depends upon flowing water for survival. David depended on God for survival. Who or what do you lean on for your survival?

It is easy to seek God when facing dire circumstances. You feel as though you are at your rope's end. Your means of supporting your family are eroding. Monthly bills are now more than your income. Maybe a loved one died. It could be your mind is fully occupied with your recently diagnosed Parkinson disease. Or it could be one or more of a myriad of things weighing your shoulders down.

The need for God keeps growing. David also said that his soul thirsts for the presence of God. (See Psalm 42:2 below.) Fortunately, God is easily found. Jesus said that anyone who thirsts should go to Him. (See John 7:37 below.) He will answer the 911 call. God will lead you through the trial and fill you with peace and comfort.

But why not also pant for God during the good times? He is always available. Jesus's statement about coming to Him has only one qualifier—a thirst for God. Your shoulders do not have to be stooped to the floor to have a yearning for God. A love for God will provide a strong desire for God all day, every day—that is, if you let it.

Think about it. A continuing desire for God could prevent some hard times from striking. When trials do hit, you will be prepared to march through them. Your joy will be greater during the good times. And your life will become a paragon of happiness.

Call it what you may: seeking God, panting for God, desiring God, thirsting for God, and so on. Just do it continually. The Lord will be pleased.

Action: Be intentional in thirsting for God each day. Pray for the Holy Spirit to guide you in satisfying your desire for God. Know He is always there. Rely on Him. Realize that your daily walk with the Lord is a testimony to others, especially unbelievers. Revel in your happiness.

Scripture Meditation: Psalms 42:1–2: "As the deer pants for the water brooks, so pants my soul for You, O God. My soul thirsts for God, for the living God. When shall I come and appear before God?" John 7:37: "On the last day, that great day of the feast, Jesus stood and cried out, saying, 'If anyone thirsts, let him come to Me and drink.'"

STOP BEING DISSATISFIED

A church member once expressed how nice it was to be contented with his life. He then spent the next five minutes talking about his dissatisfaction with his job. Now, was the man contented or dissatisfied? One cannot be both in the same circumstance.

Contentment breeds happiness. Dissatisfaction breeds unhappiness. One cannot be happy and unhappy at the same time. It must be one or the other. Paul said that he was not always happy. (See Philippians 4:11 below.)

Paul had sought fulfillment through persecution of Christians. Each act of persecution put him in a satisfied state that was temporary at best. Then he would become unhappy again. As a missionary for God, though, Paul found that obeying God creates contentment. (See 1 Timothy 6:6 below.) The contented missionary Paul was much happier that the dissatisfied persecutor Paul. Is your life like the dissatisfied Paul or the contented Paul?

Self-evaluate. Are you yearning for more income? Do you now think moving to another city or state will bring happiness? Are you longing for a new house or car? Or do you feel your day is not complete unless you are holding the latest digital gadget? Do you get the point? There are so many possessions you might desire to have or circumstances you want changed. Are yours arising from a need or dissatisfaction?

Is there anything you want to have so much that you feel you must have it? Has your dissatisfaction at not having it created an idol? Thirsting for material things has created many idols. Jesus said that none of us can serve two masters—God and an idol. (See Matthew 6:24 below.) Our loyalty would be split, and we would end up despising one or the other.

God will not put up with one who tries to serve two masters. And just think, one's idol worship started with being dissatisfied with something.

Action: Strive to be contented like Paul. Pray for strength, wisdom, and perseverance in learning to want what you have and desire to be where you are. Savor the joy of being contented. Let the happiness of your contentment be a testimony to unbelievers.

Scripture Meditation: Philippians 4:11: "Not that I speak in regard to need, for I have learned in whatever state I am, to be content." First Timothy 6:6: "Now godliness with contentment is great gain." Matthew 6:24: "'No one can serve two masters; for either he will hate the one and love the other, or else he will be loyal to the one and despise the other. You cannot serve God and mammon.'"

PRAY WITH FAITH

Christians often speak of answers to prayer with joy and surprise. God's answer to prayer should be joyous. But being surprised that He answered indicates a lack of faith in our Lord. All prayer is answered when we pray in faith. We must be more faithful.

Jesus taught that a deep faith in Him and His Word enables us to abide in Him and empowers us to pray with faith. (See John 15:7 below.) When we do pray with faith, all of our prayers will be answered in any of these ways—yes, no, or He has something better for us. Also, any answer may be delayed to better accomplish His purposes. This is why it is imperative that we wait on God. Being patient is part of praying in faith.

How long does God delay answers to prayers? No one knows. He is not constrained by our time. But we know that God's timing is perfect. We saw that in Jesus's birth on earth that came some four thousand years after God first promised a Savior. Yet Jesus came in the fullness of time and in the form of a new baby born unto a virgin. (See Galatians 4:4 below.) God's answers to prayers are never late or early. They arrive at the perfect time.

Sometimes we feel our affairs are too small or unimportant to bother God. We could not be more wrong. Paul told us that we should submit in prayer all our needs, with thanksgiving, to God. (See Philippians 4:6 below.) Do not try to limit God. Just submit everything to Him. Not only Is God able to handle all of our needs, He prefers that we make everything known to Him.

Three things result when we pray with faith. Our prayers are fruitful, God is glorified, and others see Jesus in us. And all three occur in His perfect timing. Still we sometimes fail to consult God about many things. Are you praying with faith?

Action: Abide in Christ. Read God's Word and pray to Him daily. Wait on Him to speak to you through His Word. Pray for the Holy Spirit to guide you through the process. You will enjoy having confidence that your prayers will all be heard and answered in His perfect time, will be fruitful, and will glorify God.

Scripture Meditation: John 15:7: "'If you abide in Me, and My words abide in you, you will ask what you desire, and it shall be done for you.'" Galatians 4:4: "But when the fullness of the time had come, God sent forth His Son, born of a woman, born under the law." Philippians 4:6: "Be anxious for nothing, but in everything by prayer and supplication, with thanksgiving, let your requests be made known to God."

GOODNESS OF GOD

We Christians enjoy saying, "God is good." An unknown person even coined the phrase, "God is good all the time, and all the time God is good." Both statements are great because both are correct and descriptive of God. But do you know that His goodness is an effective tool for us in fighting temptation?

Everyone has been tempted, is being tempted, and will continue to be tempted. Most of us struggle with temptations. The hard thing is the yield or don't yield part. Temptations do not harm us unless we yield to them, and we can use the goodness of God as a shield against yielding to temptation.

Every good and perfect thing is a gift from God, who is the creator of all that is good. (See James 1:17 below.) If it is good, it is from God. Granted we might not immediately realize the goodness in the blessing. God might test us so His goodness might be displayed. But through His goodness our needs will be met by His blessings.

Also, all good things come down from Heaven from an endless supply. His goodness will shower blessings upon us forever. It's true. The Bible says so. And His goodness never leads anyone astray. Anything that is not good comes from Satan. Beware. Whatever temptation he may offer, you do not need. God's goodness takes care of your needs. So, mentally review God's goodness. Then watch the devil and his cronies flee from you.

The best part of God's goodness is that He never changes. Instead of casting a shadow, He casts good things. (See James 1:17 again). God is sovereign and holy. His goodness cannot diminish. God is unable to improve Himself. He is already perfect. He will not change. Rely on His goodness.

Think for a moment. Consider your past sins that keep nagging you because you yielded to temptations. Those failures never would have happened if you had been mindful of the goodness of God. Remember King David's affair with Bathsheba. If David had been mindful of God's goodness, the sexual encounter would not have happened. Yet David learned from his mistake. Will you use God's goodness to shield temptations?

Action: Focus daily on God's goodness. Embed His goodness in your mind and heart. Pray to our Lord for assistance in learning to keep God's goodness uppermost in your mind. Praise Him for His being good all the time, and all the time being good.

Scripture Meditation: James 1:17: "Whatever is good and perfect is a gift coming down to us from God our Father, who created all the lights in the heavens. He never changes or casts a shifting shadow."

HOW DO YOU VIEW DISASTERS?

Could this be you? That phone call that every parent fears came late in the night. Your daughter was in a car accident. She is still being treated in the intensive care unit of the hospital. Her recovery will be long. Your continuous trips to be with her have taken you away from a lot of your work.

Your job is performance based. The less you work, the less income you earn. Your previously unstable financial condition now seems to be on the verge of collapse. How would you react? Would you think all is lost? Or would your faith have you eagerly awaiting the blessings God is going to create from your disasters?

God will do that, you know. He demonstrated it throughout the entire Bible. God even created His greatest blessing out of the world's greatest disaster. Jesus foretold it. He said that He would be betrayed into His enemies, who would kill Him. Then three days later, He would be resurrected from the grave. (See Matthew 17:22–23 below.)

God's only begotten Son, Jesus the Savior of the world, was murdered on a cross by the most horrendous and painful death ever devised by mankind—crucifixion. His followers fled and hid, because they thought all hope died with Jesus. But God had other ideas.

Just as Jesus said, God resurrected Him. He lives. This is God's greatest blessing to mankind. Jesus conquered death, so we can also overcome death and have eternal life, because our sins would be forgiven through Jesus's blood. That is, for all who believe in Christ Jesus. (See John 3:16 below.)

God converted the greatest disaster into the greatest blessing. So, just imagine what He can do with your trials and tribulations. Does your faith give you confidence that some blessings will be born out of your disasters? Or do you fear all is lost?

Action: Cry out to God in prayer, asking for peace, comfort, and assistance in dealing with the results of your latest disaster. Praise and thank Him for blessing you after each trial. Believe in and accept Christ as your Lord and Savior, if you are not a Christian.

Scripture Meditation: Matthew 17:22–23: "Now while they were staying in Galilee, Jesus said to them, 'The Son of Man is about to be betrayed into the hands of men, and they will kill Him, and the third day He will be raised up.' And they were exceedingly sorrowful." John 3:16: "For God so loved the world that He gave His only begotten Son, that whoever believes in Him should not perish but have everlasting life."

WHERE IS YOUR FOCUS?

As Christians, we are disciples of Jesus. He is not just our leader. He is our mentor. We should try to act like Jesus. The more we are like Him, the more obedient we are to the will of God.

I can almost hear you thinking, *Man, being like Jesus is difficult to do.* Have you tried, really tried, to focus on being like Jesus? Seek the will of God. Then focus on it. Not just temporarily. Keep your focus on His will. Jesus never wavered from God's will.

God's will for His Son, Jesus, was to find and save lost people by sacrificing His life for them. (See Luke 19:10 and Mark 10:45 below.) Jesus never lost sight of the cross from which He would hang one day. Oh, He had distractions. He taught those who would listen. There were the sick to be healed, and the hungry to be fed. Yet, Jesus kept His focus on that cross while awaiting God's perfect timing for Him to be nailed to it.

Are you relentlessly focused on God's will? You say, "I try to focus, but I am so busy fulfilling my responsibilities I lose sight of God's will." Is it your responsibility to be in the stadium watching your favorite team play? Or who requires you to view the just-released movie? Get the picture? You might need to reprioritize.

The entire will of God is different for each Christian. Yet a portion of His will for each one is the same—assisting Jesus in extending His kingdom. Jesus commanded all disciples to witness for Him by spreading the truths of Him throughout the entire world. (See Acts 1:8 below.)

So, is your focus on God's will or distractions? Continuous focus on His will is difficult. But we have assistance in obeying Jesus. He said that we would have the Holy Spirit to help us. (See Acts 1:8 below.) With the Holy Spirit helping you, there are no more excuses. So, look to your mentor.

Action: Pray for the Holy Spirit to guide you in placing God's will as your number one focus and for perseverance in maintaining your focus. Praise God for allowing Jesus to work through you.

Scripture Meditation: Luke 19:10: "'For the Son of Man has come to seek and to save that which was lost.'" Mark 10:45: "'For even the Son of Man did not come to be served, but to serve, and to give His life a ransom for many.'" Acts 1:8: "'But you shall receive power when the Holy Spirit has come upon you; and you shall be witnesses to Me in Jerusalem, and in all Judea and Samaria, and to the end of the earth.'"

BE PATIENT. WAIT ON GOD.

We all have heard it. Most of us have said it. Some now cringe when they hear it. So what is this *it*? The "it" referred to here has two meanings: 1) The statement, "God answered my prayer." 2) The statement, "God did not answer my prayer."

Number 1 is usually stated when one receives exactly what was asked of God. Number 2 is wrong. God did answer but in a way other than what was asked of Him.

God answers all prayers made in faith. Let me say it again—God answers all prayers made in faith. We know this because Jesus said so. He said that if we really believe that we will receive what we ask for in prayer, we will indeed receive it. (See Mark 11:24 below.)

Every faithfully offered prayer is answered. God may say yes to our prayer. This answer is easy to identify. All other answers are more difficult for us. For example, the perceived answer "no" may truly be no or may be that God has something better for us. Also, God may delay His answer for our greater benefit. We are not likely to realize a delayed answer may be forthcoming due to our impatience. We are not disciplined in waiting on God.

Are you able to wait on God for answers to your prayers, or do you assume that God's purposeful delay is a no answer? I hope you wait on the Lord for your prayer answers. God is faithful to His Word. He will answer your petitions. Remember Job of "patience of Job" fame?

Job hurt mightily. His suffering was much greater than we are likely to experience. He lost his children, possessions, and health. Even his wife stopped supporting him. Yet he was patient and waited on God to end his suffering. He was adamant. Job said that, as hard as it was to endure, he would wait on God to end the suffering. (See Job 14:14 below.)

Are you a Job? Probably not. There are few Jobs around. But you can greatly improve your patience. You can begin by yearning for more patience. You have a choice—more patience or status quo? Only you can decide. Act now.

Action: Read and meditate on God's Word, and then wait on Him. Pray for the Holy Spirit to help you in developing patience. Praise God for answering all of your prayers.

Scripture Meditation: Mark 11:24: "Therefore I say to you, whatever things you ask when you pray, believe that you receive them, and you will have them." Job 14:14: "If a man dies, shall he live again? All the days of my hard service I will wait, till my change comes."

HOW THANKFUL ARE YOU?

The Lord has richly blessed Americans in many ways. Our comfort level is so great it would shock earlier generations. Our homes far exceed our needs. We drive luxury autos for transportation. Some families have more cars than family members. We own so much clothing that it is difficult to decide what to wear each day. Our society throws away more food than some people groups will ever see. We enjoy being entertained so much that the money we spend on entertainment is greater than the economies of some countries.

We possess an array of convenience items. We can communicate instantly with people all around the world. Needed information is only a few smartphone or computer clicks away. These items are great, but we usually want to replace them with the latest and best. We think we have it made.

If we have it made, why is our society less joyful than previous generations? Reflect on it. The greatest blessings bring an everlasting joy when received with gratitude—thanksgiving—for God's provision of the blessings, material possessions. That must be it. We are losing our thankfulness for what God provides for us. Without thanksgiving to God, the joy of receiving the possessions is temporary and falls away like autumn leaves.

Being thankful to God pleases Him. A psalmist said that we should be thankful to the Lord and express our thanksgiving. (See Psalm 100:4 below.) God expects to hear our gratitude. It is part of serving Him. We should serve God with a thankful heart and with gladness. (See Psalm 100:2 below.)

Happily serving God through a spirit of thankfulness is a standard the Lord set for us. We should obey Him, for His truths last throughout every generation. (See Psalm 100:5 below.) God has showered us with His blessings. He deserves to have us serving Him with thankful and gleeful hearts.

Examine your heart. Do you look to God through the lens of thankfulness? Or have you become ho-hum about the provisions God has made for you?

Action: In prayer, gladly thank the Lord for all blessings you receive. Acknowledge to Him that you do not deserve His provisions. Gleefully praise God for His grace. Know that your joyful and thankful heart will assist the Lord in lighting the path for others to follow.

Scripture Meditation: Psalm 100:2, 4–5: "Serve the Lord with gladness; come before His presence with singing. Enter into His gates with thanksgiving, and into His courts with praise. Be thankful to Him, and bless His name. For the Lord is good; His mercy is everlasting, and His truth endures to all generations."

MY WORST ENEMY IS ...

Everyone has enemies. An enemy is anyone who is openly or covertly antagonistic toward you. You may not be aware of some of your enemies, but they still exist.

You are probably thinking, *So, what do I do about my enemies?* Paul said that God commanded us to be kind, caring, and forgiving toward one another. (See Ephesians 4:32 below.) Does this sound like an easy and simple solution? It's not. Being kind, caring, and forgiving is much more difficult than just not engaging in hostile, antagonistic, or revengeful action toward your enemies, according to Jesus.

Our Lord commanded us to love and pray for our enemies. (See Matthew 5:44 below.) Oh my. It is not so easy, is it? In order to be kind, caring, and forgiving, we have to love and pray for our enemies. Our obedience to Jesus begins by identifying our enemies where possible. Then we learn to love and pray for our known and unknown enemies.

Now, of all the enemies you identified, who is your worst enemy? Difficult choice? It is probably easier than you think. You may be like many others who do not have to look beyond their mirror to see their worst enemy. For some reason, many believers can forgive others but not themselves.

Many Christians mentally beat themselves up over past sins. They are ashamed of some past actions. They worry about others knowing about their sins. With these thoughts lingering in their minds, they just seem unable to forgive themselves as God has.

When God looks at them, He sees children without a blemish. When they look into a mirror, many see a sinner. Guess who is right? Paul said that Christ has forgiven them. (See Ephesians 4:32 below.) God forgave all their sins, not just some. Do you not fully trust God? Or maybe you do not understand that it is impossible for our sin to outperform God's grace. His grace is greater than all the collective sins of the world.

God cast all your sins to the wind. Can you do the same? Are you ready to be loving, kind, and forgiving while praying for yourself?

Action: Pray for strength and wisdom in forgiving and loving yourself. Praise God for His grace, love, and mercy in forgiving you.

Scripture Meditation: Ephesians 4:32: "And be kind to one another, tenderhearted, forgiving one another, even as God in Christ forgave you." Matthew 5:44: "But I say to you, love your enemies, bless those who curse you, do good to those who hate you, and pray for those who spitefully use you and persecute you."

CHANGES ARE ...

Changes are inevitable. They occur every day. Some are okay. Some are not. Some are good. Others are bad. Some are welcomed, while others are hated. Most create anxiety, if not stress. It seems as though the happier one may be, the more reluctant the individual is to change. Yet changes march on.

Our health changes. Job duties change. We change our residency. Relationships are altered. The government causes change. Technology changes at a rapid rate. Society and culture change. These are but a few examples. Every part of our lives is affected by change.

Most changes are unique. They evoke strong emotions. Many changes are temporary and will be replaced with still more changes. Possible results to change are often unknown before the change, causing fear or turmoil. Yet Christians are able to look to the never-changing one for calmness in a sea of never-ending changes.

Our God does not change. Never has. Never will. God said so. (See Malachi 3:6 below.) God is and will remain just as righteous, holy, merciful, powerful, and loving as He was at the beginning of time.

Our mighty God will protect us while we are in the throes of change. Believe it. He said that we would not be drained or eaten up by change. We will not be consumed. He will protect us. God said that He would take hold of us with His righteous right hand and lead, protect, and strengthen us. (See Isaiah 41:10 below.) All we have to do is take hold of His holy hand that He has extended to us. Think about it. From the time we accepted Jesus as our Lord and Savior, He has been available to assist and lead us through all of our anxiety, fear, and turmoil of change.

There is one future change that is common to all believers. Each Christian will experience the greatest change of all. It has no negative results, only great joy. Hunger for this change—the day each Christian's residency moves into eternal life with our Lord.

Action: Rely on the Lord to get you through the storms of change in your life. Pray that you will always be mindful of God's willingness to assist you. Take comfort in knowing you will experience the greatest change of all time—eternal life with the Lord.

Scripture Meditation: Malachi 3:6: "'For I am the Lord, I do not change; therefore you are not consumed, O sons of Jacob.'" Isaiah 41:10: "Fear not, for I am with you; be not dismayed, for I am your God. I will strengthen you, yes, I will help you, I will uphold you with My righteous right hand."

CAN YOU FATHOM TRUE PERFECTION?

We all have spoken of certain objects or events as perfect. He played a perfect ballgame. She gave a perfect performance. His PowerPoint presentation was just perfect. She developed into a perfect legislator. He is the perfect father. Most, if not all, of the time, we use the word perfect in an exaggerated sense.

There certainly will be no need to exaggerate in our life to come—eternal life with our Lord. Eternal life with God will be perfect because He said that there will not be any death, pain, tears, sorrow, or crying in Heaven. (See Revelation 21:4 below.) Christians will be leading a perfect life forever in Heaven. Our life will be perfection in the truest sense of the word.

Yet many Christians still have questions regarding our bodies. Some seem to believe that Christians will lead perfect lives while dwelling in imperfect bodies. God made it clear that our bodies will be changed.

The apostle Paul told us that we should be confident in knowing that Christ will transform our worn, mortal bodies into everlasting bodies like His. (See Philippians 3:21 [NLT] below.) Our bodies will be like Jesus's body, which is perfect.

Consider this. Your body will not be great. It will be better than great. It will be perfect. And your transformed body will remain great throughout eternity.

Your cancer-ridden body will be without a flaw. Your heart will never stop. There will no longer be a need for hip or knee replacements. Toothaches and dieting will be distant memories. Even ole Arthur (arthritis) will not make it to Heaven. As wretched as your body may be, never complain about it again. It is one resource Jesus will use to make you perfect. Can you imagine?

Action: In prayer, praise and thank God for the physical body you have. Ask for guidance in taking care of your body in the best possible way. When medical problems strike, pray for the Lord to guide the medical personnel who will treat you. Take comfort in the knowledge that your body is destined for perfection.

Scripture Meditation: Revelation 21:4: "'And God will wipe away every tear from their eyes; there shall be no more death, nor sorrow, nor crying. There shall be no more pain, for the former things have passed away.'" Philippians 3:21 (NLT): "He will take our weak mortal bodies and change them into glorious bodies like his own, using the same power with which he will bring everything under his control."

PRAISE AND THANK GOD, AND ...

Praying to God pleases Him. We ask for our personal needs to be met. Good. God expects it. But often we talk to God only about ourselves without much thought given to the needs of others. Intercessory prayer for individuals, groups, ministries, and such also delights God. And praising and thanking God definitely please Him.

Someone once said that praying to God is simple. We ask God. We receive. Others receive. We praise and thank Him. Regrettably, we often make our prayers even simpler by forgetting the praise and thank-you parts. This is contrary to God's Word.

Praising God is a sacrifice that should be continual. (See Hebrews 13:15 [NLT] below.) Continual means continual, not occasional. Did you praise God today for His holiness and righteousness? When did you last praise Him for His love, grace, mercy, and wisdom? The Lord uses His greatness to mold and protect us. Honor Him by praising Him continually.

Remember to thank God. The apostle Paul said that every time we make requests of God, we should include thanksgiving in our prayers. (See Philippians 4:6 below.) Did you thank God for your kids arriving home safely from school today? When your spouse drove into the driveway, did you thank Him for his/her return? Did you thank God for placing you where you could see that beautiful sunset?

You have so much for which to be thankful. You will learn this quickly if you try to compile a list of every blessing you have received from God. I'm betting your blessings are too numerous to count. Be obedient. Thank Him in every prayer.

Praising and thanking God will spur you to be good with others and to share with those in need. (See Hebrews 13:16 [NLT] below.) Praise Him. Thank Him. Do good. Share with the needy. All these please God and draw you closer to Him. Praising and thanking God can become a natural part of your daily life. Will you do it?

Action: Be obedient. Praise and thank God throughout each day. Do good and share with the needy. Praise and thank God for His grace in allowing you to assist Him in His work.

Scripture Meditation: Hebrews 13:15–16 (NLT): "Therefore, let us offer through Jesus a continual sacrifice of praise to God, proclaiming our allegiance to his name. And don't forget to do good and to share with those in need. These are the sacrifices that please God." Philippians 4:6: "Be anxious for nothing, but in everything by prayer and supplication, with thanksgiving, let your requests be made known to God."

IS YOUR SALVATION SECURE?

The apostle John, while quoting Jesus, said that God, because of His love, sacrificed His only Son so that all who believed in the Son could be saved unto eternal life. (See John 3:16 below.) Most Christians can paraphrase or quote this verse. All who believe in Christ are saved unto salvation. This ensures believers will go to Heaven to be with God. While awaiting our departure to Heaven, we become one with Jesus, who told us that if we abide in Him, He will abide in us. (See John 15:4 below.)

Many Christians question the reality of their salvation. Have you ever been curious about why? Probably the main reason for such doubting is the evil one, Satan. He works hard at tricking individuals into believing their salvation is not real. Those who fall for the trickery begin to doubt God's Word.

As Christians, we are destined for eternal life in Heaven. Until then, we are one with Jesus. So, why do we at times listen to Satan? Maybe, just maybe, it is our silence. Paul told us to confess our salvation to others. (See Romans 10:10 below.) We should always be ready to tell others of our relationship with Jesus. Silence opens the door for Satan to do his work. We need to be like a man named Frank.

Frank knew that his faith in Jesus made him and Jesus one. Frank explained, "If God should carry me to hell's gate and say to me, 'In you go, Frank. Here is where you deserve to be.' I would tell Him, 'I agree, Lord. But if you make me go to hell, Your only Son, Jesus, must go in with me. He and I are one, and we can never be separated.'" Wow. Frank's faith in Jesus is really strong.

Your doubting and silence would end if you possessed a faith in Jesus like Frank's. You are able to build upon your faith through the Lord. Will you let Him guide you in doing so?

Action: When doubt creeps in, quote or read to yourself God's word, especially John 3:16, John 15:4, and Romans 10:10. Pray for the Holy Spirit to lead you to opportunities to proclaim Jesus as Lord. Praise God for His grace. Thank Him for your salvation.

Scripture Meditation: John 3:16: "For God so loved the world that He gave His only begotten Son, that whoever believes in Him should not perish but have everlasting life." John 15:4: "Abide in Me, and I in you. As the branch cannot bear fruit of itself, unless it abides in the vine, neither can you, unless you abide in Me." Romans 10:10: "For with the heart one believes unto righteousness, and with the mouth confession is made unto salvation."

OH NO! I DENIED JESUS!

Keep the following question in your mind: "Have I denied Jesus since accepting Him as my Lord and Savior?" Reflect on the question. Your answer is important.

The apostle Peter, the stalwart among Jesus's famous twelve disciples, denied Jesus three times within a few hours. Fearing bodily harm, Peter said that he did not know Jesus. (See Matthew 26:74 below.) Peter failed by temporarily setting his cross aside. This should be a reminder to all Jesus's followers of the ever-present temptation to deny Him.

Instead of denying Jesus, we should deny ourselves. Jesus said that to follow Him, we must deny our self and take up our cross. (See Mark 8:34 below.) We are commanded to deny our worldly desires and follow Him through all the good and bad times. Our problem is those bad times. Carrying our cross requires sacrifices.

You may be thinking that you will not deny Jesus. Peter also thought that. Yet he denied Jesus. Are you like Peter? Don't answer too fast. Temptations to deny Jesus can be subtle.

Suppose your boss tells you on a Friday afternoon that you are needed to work all day on Saturday and Sunday due to some unexpected company needs. You panic. You tell your boss that you have a conflict due to your being a Sunday school teacher at church. He says you have to work. What will you do? Work or fulfill your commitment to Jesus? Choosing work is setting your cross aside for one day, just as Peter did.

Your son's elite soccer team coach scheduled an out-of-town game on a Sunday morning. Will you take your son to the game by being like Peter and temporarily setting your cross aside? If so, isn't your son learning that it is okay for him to set his cross aside?

Peter overcame his failure and became a great and faithful disciple. Will you mimic the Peter who failed or the Peter who later excelled at following Jesus? The decision is not always easy, but you must decide. Will you be faithful to the world or to Jesus?

Action: Pray for guidance in recognizing every temptation to lay down your cross and deny Jesus. Also ask for strength and perseverance in standing fast for the Lord against the temptations.

Scripture Meditation: Matthew 26:74: "Then he began to curse and swear, saying, 'I do not know the Man!'" Mark 8:34: "When He had called the people to Himself, with His disciples also, He said to them, 'Whoever desires to come after Me, let him deny himself, and take up his cross, and follow Me.'"

HOW GREAT IS THE LOVE OF GOD?

Christians very often use these terms—the love of God and God's love. But none fully understand the greatness of His love. There is no measuring stick to gauge God's love. It has no boundaries. This is proven by God's many demonstrations of His love.

Chances are you know the story of Adam and Eve—the first humans on earth. Eve and Adam were deceived into violating a key commandment of God. Their action created sin on earth. They had been forewarned that sin would result in death—spiritual separation from God. But Just before He ordered the two away, out of love, God provided some animal-skin clothing for Adam and Eve. (See Genesis 3:21 below.)

God knew the fig leaves worn by Adam and his wife were not sufficient. So, He properly clothed them before He banished them. God did this knowing their sin changed a perfect world to a sinful world. The Lord's disappointment was enough to despise Adam and Eve. Yet His love never wavered. He remained faithful, though, in disciplining them.

God lovingly gave mankind opportunities to live sinless throughout the entire Old Testament. Many, including Abraham, Jacob, Moses, David, and others, tried to abide by all of God's law. Everyone failed. Humans are simply not self-capable of avoiding all sin. The loving God, though, had a plan lying in wait.

God, because of His love, sacrificed His only Son so that all who believed in the Son could be saved unto eternal life and have their sins forgiven. (See John 3:16 below.) How amazing. He gave His Son to die on a cross—the most painful death ever devised—so that we could have eternal life with Him in Heaven.

Do you believe in Jesus? He is the Son of God. Jesus, though fully God, was born of a virgin, becoming fully human. He gave His human life for you on the cross. Jesus was resurrected from death so you could become sinless and have eternal life, *if you believe in Him*. This is a free offer from God. Do you believe in Jesus? Have you prayed for forgiveness of your sins?

Action: Believe in and accept Jesus as Lord. In prayer, tell God you believe the truth of Jesus. Ask God to forgive you for your sins. If you are already a Christian, praise God for what He has done for you.

Scripture Meditation: Genesis 3:21 (NLT): "And the Lord God made clothing from animal skins for Adam and his wife." John 3:16: "For God so loved the world that He gave His only begotten Son, that whoever believes in Him should not perish but have everlasting life."

STOP BEING WICKED

Nonbelievers sometimes mockingly refer to Christians as "Jesus fanatics." If you have been called a Jesus fanatic, wear the label proudly. It indicates your light is bright and projects the righteousness of Jesus.

Famous for his wisdom, Solomon said that righteousness is like a dawn ray that brightens until full sun. (See Proverbs 4:18 [NLT] below.) Our ability to shine the light of righteousness comes from being a Jesus fanatic. Jesus said that He is the light of the world, and His followers have the light of life and do not walk in darkness. (See John 8:12 below.) When we have this light of life, we are reflecting the righteousness of Jesus.

Jesus had a good reason for saying His followers do not walk in darkness. They avoid evil. Darkness is wickedness and causes us to stumble into sin. Hmm, walking in darkness projects wickedness and causes us to stumble. Righteousness and wickedness are opposing forces. As followers of Jesus, we should avoid all wickedness. Instead, we are to project righteousness by walking in Jesus's light.

Always project as much righteousness as possible, so the wickedness will be overcome. You can overcome continually by keeping your spiritual batteries charged. Equate your walk with the Lord to being a flashlight.

The better charge flashlight batteries have, the brighter the light. Likewise, the better your spiritual walk with the Lord is, the brighter your light shines, emanating greater righteousness. When flashlight batteries are not charged, the light dims until it no longer replaces darkness. Also, the further you get from walking with Jesus, the weaker your spiritual batteries become. Your light dissipates until you walk in wickedness.

Are you drifting away from Jesus into wickedness? Maybe your spiritual batteries need recharging. You cannot just sit around feeling blessed without feeding your spiritual life. You need to nurture your faith in the Lord. Are you ready?

Action: Each day, have quiet time with the Lord, reading His Word, praying, and listening to Him. While praying, ask for the strength to develop the discipline to overcome barriers that prevent you from having quiet times with God. Praise Him as your light brightens.

Scripture Meditation: Proverbs 4:18 (NLT): "The way of the righteous is like the first gleam of dawn, which shines ever brighter until the full light of day." John 8:12: "Then Jesus spoke to them again, saying, 'I am the light of the world. He who follows Me shall not walk in darkness, but have the light of life.'"

NEVER STOP MINISTERING

Imagine this picture. Jesus has been unmercifully beaten. Now, He is on the way to be crucified. Strips of His flesh and skin are hanging from Him. He is wearing a crown of thorns, which penetrate the skin of His head. Blood trickles into Jesus's eyes. He is so weak and fatigued that just being tired would be a great relief. Then something remarkable happens. Jesus keeps ministering to the people.

Many grief-stricken women are among those following Jesus as He struggles to complete His short walk. Though under a great duress, Jesus turns to the women and tells them that they should weep for their children and themselves, not Him. He then proceeds to foretell the future, dire woes and destruction of Jerusalem. (See Luke 23:28–30 below.) Still, Jesus's ministry work on earth is not yet done.

While hanging on the cross, Jesus asks that those responsible for His upcoming death be forgiven. (See Luke 23:34 below.) Jesus wants all who had any part in His upcoming death to be forgiven. The shame and horrific pain of the cross could not stop Jesus's ministry.

Before dying on the cross, one of two criminals being crucified with Jesus defends Him and asks to be remembered in Heaven. Jesus saves the man by telling him that he would be with Jesus in Heaven that same day (see Luke 23:43 below.)

Are you continuing to do God's work? The young and middle-aged may say, "But I no longer have time because of changes in my career." Did God ordain your leaving His work? The older folks may say, "I have gotten too old. I have one foot in the grave." Maybe you can use your other foot in proclaiming the good news of Jesus. Make no excuses. Be like Jesus. Minister to others during all circumstances.

Action: Pray for guidance and perseverance in being intentional in maintaining an awareness of opportunities to serve and minister to others. Act on each occasion. Praise God for each opportunity to serve Him.

Scripture Meditation: Luke 23:28–30: "But Jesus turned and said to them, 'Daughters of Jerusalem, don't weep for me, but weep for yourselves and for your children. For the days are coming when they will say, "Fortunate indeed are the women who are childless, the wombs that have not borne a child and the breasts that have never nursed." People will beg the mountains, "Fall on us," and plead with the hills, "Bury us."'" Luke 23:34: "Jesus said, 'Father, forgive them, for they don't know what they are doing.'" Luke 23:43: "And Jesus replied, 'I assure you, today you will be with me in paradise.'"

WHERE IS GOD?

Try something different today. Make a list of every place you went during the past week. After compiling your list, think about each place recorded. Are there any listed locations where you would not invite the Lord to go with you? Next, wherever you were, did you say or do anything that you would not do in God's presence?

Wherever you went and whatever you said or did, God was there. You did not see Him, but He was there. The Lord is always with you, me, and everyone else. God said that He is God, the Holy One with you. (See Hosea 11:9 below.) Yes, God is always with us.

Hundreds of years later, Jesus confirmed that He is always among us, not just in the present time but forever. (See Matthew 28:20 below.) Jesus was with us yesterday; He is with us today; and He will be with us tomorrow and forever more. There is no wiggle room for exceptions. Yep, the Lord is always with us. Count on it.

When you are in your car, God is also in there. At work? God is with you. When you stretch out in your recliner, He is on the sofa. At the baseball game? The Lord is the one who kept the line drive foul ball from hitting you in the head. He is always there to help you. This is the best part of His nearness.

You need help? The Lord is a prayer away. Pray to Him. His hand will extend to you before you finish uttering the words. Do you need wisdom to solve a problem? Ask God for some. He is right there with you. And He is for you. Rejoice in His presence. Do all this, and you will not carry God to the wrong places or say or do the wrong things.

You can feel hampered because the Lord is so near to you. Or you can be joyful and feel blessed that He is always close by to protect, help, and lead you. Which are you experiencing?

Action: In prayer, praise God for always being with you. Also ask the Holy Spirit to help you be aware of the Lord's continuing presence. Rejoice and enjoy the comfort of God being ever present.

Scripture Meditation: Hosea 11:9: "I will not execute the fierceness of My anger; I will not again destroy Ephraim. For I am God, and not man, the Holy One in your midst; and I will not come with terror." Matthew 28:20: "[Teach] them to observe all things that I have commanded you; and lo, I am with you always, even to the end of the age."

NEED A PICKER UPPER?

Have you had those days when you were feeling down in the dumps, and you did not know why? Maybe the reason is you wrecked your shiny new car. Or it could be you are grieving for your adult son who recently became unemployed. Or maybe the cause is you cannot forgive yourself for sinning against your family and God. Maybe you doubt some decision you recently made.

For whatever reason, you have the blues. The joy that you always so richly cherished is gone and now seems out of reach. You have trouble sleeping because the upcoming dawn will bring the same old gloom. You yearn for that once-possessed delight that kept a smile on your face. You are thinking, *What shall I do to overcome?*

Be mindful that assistance is just a short prayer away. The Almighty Lord God is there with you. He will aid you. He is ready. He is set. But before He will go, He waits on you to ask Him for help. God will not force Himself upon you. Nothing is so bad, severe, distressing, small, tiny, or unimportant that the Lord cannot rescue you. There is no circumstance that can prevent God from bringing relief to you. So, do not doubt that He is there for you. Pray for Him to restore your joy. King David did.

David cried out to God. He asked for mercy and assistance. (See Psalm 30:10 [NLT] below.) Imitate David. Call out to the Lord. Ask Him to hear you, have mercy on you, and help you. God's response to David was to take away his mourning and replace it with great joy. (See Psalm 30:11 [NLT] below.) What a blessing. The Lord will bless you also.

When God does bless you, do not just sit around in a state of blessedness. Continue to mimic David. He was graciously thankful for what the Lord did for him. (See Psalm 30:12 [NLT] below.)

When the blues strike, you can flounder with sadness, or you can request God to remove the gloom and clothe you with joy. It is your choice.

Action: Anytime gloom appears, pray to God and ask Him to replace the sadness with His peace and comfort, which produce joy. Thank the Lord for His response. Enjoy your happiness and radiate joy through your smile.

Scripture Meditation: Psalm 30:10–12 (NLT): "'Hear me, Lord, and have mercy on me. Help me, O Lord. You have turned my mourning into joyful dancing. You have taken away my clothes of mourning and clothed me with joy, that I might sing praises to you and not be silent. O Lord my God, I will give you thanks forever!'"

ARE YOU ON THE RIGHT PATH?

Suppose you take an exit from an interstate highway only to learn there is not an entrance for reentering the interstate at that location? Sick feelings rise up. You know you messed up. Anxiety sets in. You find a local two-lane road that will take you to the next interchange having an entrance ramp. You learn the local road has intermittent places, where only one lane of traffic is allowed due to roadwork. You check your watch. Time is ticking away. Now you realize you will be late for a job interview.

You had good intentions. You thought you could quickly leave and reenter the interstate. When you leave your intended path though, consequences occur—often bad. The same is true with your walk with the Lord.

God designed a personal path for each Christian. Like secular paths, we stray from God's paths. We are like sheep. We stray. We sometimes leave God's path for a worldly path. (See Isaiah 53:6 [NLT] below.) We will stray because of our mistakes, which are called sins. There is good news though. When we stray from God's ordained paths, we will not see any sign prohibiting us from reentering the paths He laid out for us.

Each path God designed includes an entrance ramp that can be used for both entering and reentering. It is the ramp of forgiveness. God will forgive our sins if we ask in faith. The price for our sins has been prepaid. Jesus paid the price for us when He died on the cross. This paved the way for us to reenter our godly path at the ramp of forgiveness.

God does more than just allow us to get back on track. He strengthens us and makes our feet as surefooted as a deer. (See Habakkuk 3:19 below.) He makes us surefooted through guiding and nurturing, which makes our walk with the Lord less mistake prone and helps us ward off temptations.

Will you select the path God planned for you or the path you designed?

Action: Ensure you are walking surefooted on the path designed by God for you. Lean on the Lord and His Word for guidance and nurturing. Pray for the Holy Spirit to convict you when you are about to stray. Praise God for your path. Revel in your walk with the Lord.

Scripture Meditation: Isaiah 53:6 (NLT): "All of us, like sheep, have strayed away. We have left God's paths to follow our own. Yet the Lord laid on him the sins of us all." Habakkuk 3:19: "The Sovereign Lord is my strength! He makes me as surefooted as a deer, able to tread upon the heights."

WHO SUSTAINS YOU?

Ask Christians, "Who is the Holy Spirit?" Many will only say they received the Holy Spirit when they accepted Christ Jesus as their Lord and Savior. This is true, but it does not answer the question.

Jesus said that God the Father will give to each believer a Helper, the Holy Spirit. The Spirit will live within all believers. (See John 14:16–17 below.) The Holy Spirit is the Spirit of truth and our Helper.

Every Christian has received the Holy Spirit. This is just what Christians need. We must ensure that we allow the Holy Spirit to guide our lives. Then we can avoid falling for the temptations that entrap us. (See Galatians 5:16 [NLT] below.) When we need help, we ask for guidance. Then we do the right thing and follow the Holy Spirit. Sounds simple, yet it isn't easy for all believers.

Some Christians must think the Holy Spirit is with them only to have a place to hang out. They never seek assistance from Him. Some other believers call upon the Helper only after they fall to temptations, botch planning, or fail after ignoring Him. Then there are the Christians who are ever aware of the Holy Spirit's presence. These are faithful in seeking His help and following the guidance of the Spirit.

Look around. You can easily spot the believers who are adept at following the Spirit's leading. They are the ones who have the fruits of the Holy Spirit—love, joy, peace, patience, kindness, goodness, faithfulness, gentleness, and self-control. (See Galatians 5:22–23 [NLT] below.) Their joy and good behavior reflect their Lord, Christ Jesus.

In which group are you? Those who 1) ignore the Holy Spirit, 2) are prone to seek the Helper only after failures, or 3) seek His assistance daily?

Action: Pray for the Holy Spirit to sustain you and guide you through your thoughts, plans, and actions each day. Thank God for giving the Helper to you.

Scripture Meditation: John 14:16–17: "And I will pray the Father, and He will give you another Helper, that He may abide with you forever—the Spirit of truth, whom the world cannot receive, because it neither sees Him nor knows Him; but you know Him, for He dwells with you and will be in you." Galatians 5:16, 22–23 (NLT): "So I say, let the Holy Spirit guide your lives. Then you won't be doing what your sinful nature craves. But the Holy Spirit produces this kind of fruit in our lives: love, joy, peace, patience, kindness, goodness, faithfulness, gentleness, and self-control ..."

GOD'S INDESCRIBABLE SACRIFICE

Throughout history, many have labeled Jesus's death on the cross as an indescribable sacrifice because of the heinous nature of a crucifixion. Being crucified was a horrendous way to die. Yet Jesus's sacrificial death was one part, albeit an important part, of multiple pieces to God's indescribable sacrifice.

The apostle John said that the Word has been with God forever and that the Word is God. (See John 1:1 below.) The Word is Jesus. So, Jesus was, still is, and will always be God. Jesus is one part of the triune God, not a separate being. John also said that all things were created through the Word. (See John 1:3 below.) Through Jesus, God made the universe and all its parts. God left His throne and came to earth as a man and sacrificial lamb. Why?

We know little about the characteristics of Heaven. John spoke of God's throne in the book of Revelation. Interpretations of John's words vary and conflict, but we can say the throne is holy and majestic, brilliant in color, and rich in splendor to the eye.

God had legions of angels at His beck and call. Saints continually worshipped Him. He was not bound by time. He was and is the creator of and Lord over everything. God's holiness, righteousness, grace, love, knowledge, wisdom, power, and faithfulness surpasses the understanding of humans. He traded His unequaled characteristics and the comfort of Heaven to become part of His own creation by becoming a man.

God became a man by being born of a virgin. He experienced all that you and I encounter in our lives. He hungered, wept, laughed, became angry, slept, blew his nose, suffered temptations, and went through trials. The difference between the God man (Jesus) and us is He did not succumb to any temptation. He never sinned. Yet He allowed himself to be nailed to a cross to die the most painful death known to humans, making Him a sacrificial lamb atoning for every sin committed by every person ever born into the world.

God left the glory of His throne, became a man, and allowed Himself to be sacrificed on the cross because He loves you, me, and all others.

Action: When you think of the Lord dying on the cross, also remember the sacrifices God made for you by leaving Heaven to become the man who would die on that cross. Praise God for His entire and indescribable sacrifice.

Scripture Meditation: John 1:1, 3: "In the beginning was the Word, and the Word was with God, and the Word was God. All things were made through Him, and without Him nothing was made that was made."

GOD'S MASTERPIECE—YOU

Have you ever wished to be or maybe wondered about being somebody else? Many people have. Some still do. Some even try to change themselves physically to appear like someone else. Why would anyone desire to be like anyone else?

King David said that he was a wonderful and marvelous product of our Creator, God. (See Psalm 139:14 below.) I can almost hear you thinking, *I am not like David. I am not handsome and I have a lifelong limp in my walk.* Think again. Paul (the short, bowlegged, and crooked-nosed apostle) said that we are all masterpieces created by the Almighty God through Jesus. (See Ephesians 2:10 [NLT].) Look in the mirror to see one of God's masterpieces.

God made you into a masterpiece so that you could be all that He planned for you. (See Ephesians 2:10 [NLT].) Before you were even born, God had an assignment for you—to do good works according to His will. And God did not leave you alone to complete your assigned task(s). God is at work in you and gives you the power to do His will. (See Philippians 2:13 [NLT].) How cool is this? God turns you into a masterpiece in order to do good things and gives you the desire and the power to do the work.

You are a masterpiece with power. God made you. There is no one like you. You are a one-of-a-kind, powerful masterpiece. There is no good reason to desire to be like someone else. You are disobedient to God if you want to be different from who you are. You are effectively telling God that His created masterpiece is not good enough. You think you can do better. Don't believe it.

You must decide: will you use your masterpiece status and do the will of God, or will you strive to be someone that you are not?

Action: Know, accept, and rejoice in the truth that you are God's masterpiece. Pray, asking for the Holy Spirit to continually guide you in using your God-given power to accomplish the good things the Lord desires for you to do. Praise and thank God for turning you into a masterpiece.

Scripture Meditation: Psalm 139:14: "I will praise You, for I am fearfully and wonderfully made; marvelous are Your works, and that my soul knows very well." Ephesians 2:10 (NLT): "For we are God's masterpiece. He has created us anew in Christ Jesus, so we can do the good things he planned for us long ago." Philippians 2:13 (NLT): "For God is working in you, giving you the desire and the power to do what pleases him."

REJOICE IN YOUR TROUBLES

Have you ever been around people who spend most of their time moaning and groaning about their problems? These folks seem to gravitate to one another. They seem to enjoy saying, "This weakness keeps me from doing ..." Or they say, "My problems prevent me from going ..." These people talk as if their troubles are worse than the difficulties of those around them. It seems they are trying to prove their suffering is the worst.

These individuals appear to find happiness in having their problems and wearing them as badges. The problem is their badge wearing is for the wrong reasons. There are good reasons though to rejoice in troubles. The apostle Paul learned this directly from the Lord.

The Lord told Paul that His grace will cover our needs, and His power will overcome our shortcomings. (See 2 Corinthians 12:9 [NLT].) Wow! All we need in times of trouble is Christ's grace. And the greater the problem, the better His power works. Paul wore his trials as a badge for the right reasons.

Paul also said that he boasts of his trials, which allows Jesus's power to work through him. He explained that he was happy to have his problems because he suffers for Christ. His weaknesses make him strong. (See 2 Corinthians 12:9–10 [NLT] below.) We also should be proud. Our troubles make us strong in Jesus, if we allow them. Then we are working with Christ through God's grace. (See 2 Corinthians 6:1 below.) There are no better reasons to wear our trials as badges.

The ball is in your court. Will you join with others in the moaning and groaning over your problems? Or will you gladly accept your troubles as badges of the power of Jesus and work with Him in pleasing God?

Action: Be obedient. Rejoice in your troubles. Accept Christ's strength that your trials will bring out and use His power while working with Him for God's purposes. Praise God for using your weaknesses and hurts to strengthen you.

Scripture Meditation: Second Corinthians 12:9–10 (NLT): "Each time he said, 'My grace is all you need. My power works best in weakness.' So now I am glad to boast about my weaknesses, so that the power of Christ can work through me. That's why I take pleasure in my weaknesses, and in the insults, hardships, persecutions, and troubles that I suffer for Christ. For when I am weak, then I am strong." Second Corinthians 6:1: "We then, as workers together with Him also plead with you not to receive the grace of God in vain."

OAK TREE OR SHRUB?

Do you remember the day you accepted Christ Jesus as your Lord and Savior? Some cannot remember because they were very young at the time the great event took place. Most Christians do remember though. Think of that day as Acceptance Day.

Through the Holy Spirit's guidance, you accepted Jesus as your Lord and Savior. Lord Jesus accepted you into His flock. You received a reservation to live eternally in Heaven with God. You were jubilant, because you became a disciple of Jesus. Hallelujah! Your walk with the Lord had begun.

You became like a tree living on the bank of a river and bearing fruit. (See Psalm 1:3 below.) You (like a tree) and others are righteous trees and were placed there by God for His glory. (See Isaiah 61:3 below.) Initially, a disciple begins as a small oak sprig. He or she finds joy in the Lord's truths and studies them. (See Psalm 1:2 below.) This allows the sprig to grow and become blessed with joy for not hanging out with the wicked, nor following their advice that displeases God. (See Psalm 1:1 below.)

Some disciples continue to obey the Lord, allowing them to achieve greater and greater growth until their sprigs become like older oaks—majestic, tall, and full of branches. They reflect righteousness, bringing glory to God. And, yes, they did fail along the way, but the failures became less and less.

Other disciples struggle to overcome their failures. They have wandered into sin and stopped growing. Their reflections of righteousness seem to be part-time at best. They seem to be more like a shrub than an oak tree. Which will you be: an oak tree or a shrub?

Action: Be an oak tree. Pray for guidance in organizing and maintaining a quiet time with the Lord each day. Follow and obey His Word. Keep a prayer journal. Bask in the joy of being in the will of God.

Scripture Meditation: Psalm 1:1–3 (NLT): Oh, the joys of those who do not follow the advice of the wicked or stand around with sinners, or join in with mockers. But they delight in the law of the Lord, meditating on it day and night. They are like trees planted along the riverbank, bearing fruit each season. Their leaves never wither, and they prosper in all they do." Isaiah 61:3: "To console those who mourn in Zion, to give them beauty for ashes, the oil of joy for mourning, the garment of praise for the spirit of heaviness; that they may be called trees of righteousness, the planting of the Lord, that He may be glorified."

IS YOUR FAITH STRONG OR WEAK?

All too often, many Christians go around complaining about the world in which we are living. They may be complaining because of a sickness or an injury. Sometimes they bemoan the existence of evil and mean people. They may constantly fret about damages arising out of acts of nature. The list of reasons is lengthy. Yet the reasons are not valid.

You, I, and every other Christian can overcome the very things complained about. Stunning statement? Yes, it is. Working with God always produces great results. The apostle John said that each believer could overcome the evil world through his or her faith. (See 1 John 5:4 [NLT] below.) Is your faith in God strong enough to overcome the world? It should be, and hopefully it is.

As a believer, you have a huge advantage over nonbelievers. Only the faithful who believe that Jesus is truly God's Son can overcome the world. (See 1 John 5:5 [NLT] below.) Truly believe that you can overcome the world, and you will. Jesus said that if you truly believe without a doubting heart, your overcoming the world could definitely occur. (See Mark 11:23 [NLT] below.)

Jesus confirmed you are able to overcome the world. Have faith in God. Believe it will happen. Have no doubts. It will happen. Are you ready to defeat the world?

Don't be overwhelmed by life's storms. Ditch the complaining. Trust God to team up with you. Let Him take you by the hand. God is more than willing to lead you. Then seek and achieve victory together.

You have a choice. Swim in the sea of sadness by complaining about the world? Or overcome it and bask in the joy of victory?

Action: Understand and believe that faith in God is a power that He wants you to possess. In prayer, ask for strength in walking alongside God in overcoming the world and its ways. Know that defeating the world results in your light beaming a calm and loving witness to the world. To unbelievers: you, too, can have the power of faith in God by accepting Jesus as your Lord and Savior.

Scripture Meditation: First John 5:4–5 (NLT): "For every child of God defeats this evil world, and we achieve this victory through our faith. And who can win this battle against the world? Only those who believe that Jesus is the Son of God." Mark 11:23 (NLT): "I tell you the truth, you can say to this mountain, 'May you be lifted up and thrown into the sea,' and it will happen. But you must really believe it will happen and have no doubt in your heart."

NEVER GIVE UP ON GOD

Does this sound familiar? You turn over a problem to God. Then you wait. And wait. And wait some more. Still no answer. You get frustrated. You begin to think an answer will not be coming. Now you are convinced it is your fault that God is holding back. So, you decide to resolve the matter yourself. Call this example what you may, but it is giving up on God.

Do not give up on God. Trust in Him. His timing is perfect. God's delay is for our good. Isaiah said that the Lord will wait so that He can graciously bless those who patiently wait. (See Isaiah 30:18 below.) God's delay is enabling His grace. Wow!

God waited four thousand years to send the Lord Jesus Christ after He promised He would do so. But Paul said Jesus came at the right time for His purpose. (See Galatians 4:4 below.) God is never late, never ahead of time, and never in a hurry. And today, God still uses perfect timing in His works.

A US soldier in Iraq had asked for prayers asking for an end to the continuous sandstorms and torrential rains that were keeping the troops from crossing the Euphrates River. The rain did not stop. Instead, the sandstorms and rain intensified. At some point, the strong wind and rain did finally stop. Then the soldier saw the riverbanks had eroded and was very surprised.

The bank of the other side of the river was covered with hundreds of land mines. The intense storms had uncovered them. Scores of troops would have been killed if the storms had ceased before they caused the erosion. After the mines were exposed, they were easily cleared. God's perfect timing prevented a major tragedy. So, I believe those soldiers will never give up on God.

Will you trust in God's timing, wait on Him, and never give up? You will be greatly blessed if you wait.

Action: Trust God's timing, which is far better than yours. Pray for the power to persevere. Never give up. Thank God for using His timing instead of yours. As you wait, take comfort in knowing something better is coming your way. Praise God for His grace.

Scripture Meditation: Isaiah 30:18: "Therefore the Lord will wait, that He may be gracious to you; and therefore He will be exalted, that He may have mercy on you. For the Lord is a God of justice; blessed are all those who wait for Him." Galatians 4:4: "But when the fullness of the time had come, God sent forth His Son, born of a woman, born under the law."

ARE YOU HOLDING A TICKET TO HELL?

Ask individuals how they would answer God if He asked them, "Why should I let you into Heaven?" Too many of the answers would be akin to "I would tell Him all the good things I had done for my family and other people." Notice there is no mention of Jesus.

Also, one or more religions have been created for people believing that individuals can work their way into Heaven. Members of these religions sometimes refer to themselves as Christians, but they apparently have rejected parts of God's Word.

One of the most quoted verses in the Bible is John's quote of Jesus in John 3:16. Jesus said that God, because of His love, sacrificed His only Son so that all who believed in the Son could be saved unto eternal life. (See John 3:16 below.) Jesus did not mention good works. The verse only lists one requirement to receive God's gracious gift of eternal life—belief in Jesus.

There is no room for misinterpretation. God, through Paul, confirmed Jesus's statement. He said that you were saved by grace through faith as a gift from God rather than your works or anything else. (See Ephesians 2:8–9 below.) God intentionally created a system where our salvation is a gift from Him. It cannot be earned. All we have to do is accept it through belief (faith) in Jesus.

After accepting God's gift of salvation, we then become God's workmanship to do good works through Christ Jesus. As a disciple of Jesus, we then are commanded to do good works.

If you have not accepted God's free gift of salvation, a ticket to hell and eternal separation from God is reserved for you, regardless of your good works. *But* the ticket may be canceled by accepting Jesus through faith. Then you will be given a ticket to a new destination—Heaven and eternal life with God. Which ticket are you holding?

Action: If you have not accepted Jesus as your Lord and Savior, do so now. If you have accepted Him, tell others the good news of God's salvation gift that is offered to anyone through His grace. Praise God for loving you.

Scripture Meditation: Ephesians 2:8–9: "For by grace you have been saved through faith, and that not of yourselves; it is the gift of God, not of works, lest anyone should boast." John 3:16: "For God so loved the world that He gave His only begotten Son, that whoever believes in Him should not perish but have everlasting life."

HAVING TROUBLE BEING HUMBLE?

If we are honest with ourselves, we will admit that our humility is lower than where our Lord desires it to be. Probably for most of us, our attempts to be humble can best be described as dismal. Surely, the Lord dislikes our feeble stabs at humility.

I hear you saying, "I am humble. I assist other church members who need help. I cook meals for them, visit them, run errands for them, and such." Your loving service to fellow church members is great. But are you limiting your service to church members only?

Do you remember the homeless-looking man who crossed your path recently? He appeared to need a bath and was dressed in ragged and filthy clothes. Did you humble yourself to help him? He obviously needed assistance.

We are told to be humble and always consider others to be better than us. (See Philippians 2:3 [NLT] below.) The word "others" is not qualified or limited in any way. We are told—no, commanded—to consider everyone to be better than ourselves. Everyone means just that and includes those who the world considers to be undesirables. Paul was even more specific in telling us to place the interests of others above our own. (See Philippians 2:4 [NLT] below.) This is a tall order in our world. Jesus showed us the way though.

Lord Jesus humbly obeyed God and allowed His enemies to crucify Him on the cross unto death. (See Philippians 2:8 [NLT] below.) Jesus knew His humility would cause him to be mocked, hated, stripped of His clothing, and nailed to a cross, while hundreds watched as He suffered unequaled pain. How could Jesus muster up such humility? He could and did because His love for us enabled Him to view all of us as better than Himself.

We are disciples of Jesus. He is our mentor. It is unlikely that we will encounter as much to overcome in being humble as Jesus did. Still, we all should strive to follow Jesus's lead in loving everyone, which enables us to humble ourselves in serving others regardless of who they are.

Action: When you see a stranger, remind yourself that the person is better than you. Love him or her and humble yourself before them. Praise God for placing that person in your path. Help the person as much as you can.

Scripture Meditation: Philippians 2:3–4, 8 (NLT): "Don't be selfish; don't try to impress others. Be humble, thinking of others as better than yourselves. Don't look out only for your own interests, but take an interest in others, too. He humbled himself in obedience to God and died a criminal's death on a cross."

SEEN ANY ANGELS LATELY?

Angels are largely a misunderstood lot. They do exist though. God's Word tells us of assignments completed by angels in both the Old and New Testaments. They are probably as active today as they have ever been.

Many times, God had angels appear temporarily in the form of humans to carry out His purpose. There is a strong possibility that angels have at least assisted most if not all believers without the believers realizing it.

Did you just utter, "I doubt that an angel ever helped me"? Doubting the help of angels is the same as doubting the Lord, because He said through a psalmist that He will save and protect everyone who trusts and loves Him. (See Psalm 91:14 [NLT] below.) God uses angels to rescue and protect you. Trusting in the Lord means believing and knowing He will act, not just hoping and wishing.

The psalmist also told us how the Lord rescues and protects us. If we use God as our safe haven, no evil or plague will come close to us, because His angels will protect us. (See Psalm 91:9–11 [NLT] below.) The angels will even guide us by taking our hands so that we will not stumble. (See Psalm 91:12 [NLT] below). Wow! Bodyguards are available to us.

Yes, God often uses angels as tools in carrying out His will. We know this to be true because He said He would use angels, and He is faithful to His word. This is an important truth. If we doubt or do not believe that God sometimes uses angels to protect us, we could end up stealing His glory by giving ourselves credit for our protection. As Christians, we are all called to bring glory to God, not take any of His glory.

Remember, whenever a person you have never seen before helps you, he or she is an instrument of God and could be an angel disguised as a human.

Action: Pray for guidance in recognizing God's use of angels to assist and protect you. Thank God for His work for you, and give Him all the glory for His protection.

Scripture Meditation: Psalm 91:9–12, 14 (NLT): "If you make the Lord your refuge, if you make the Most High your shelter, no evil will conquer you; no plague will come near your home. For he will order his angels to protect you wherever you go. They will hold you up with their hands so you won't even hurt your foot on a stone. The Lord says, 'I will rescue those who love me. I will protect those who trust in my name.'"

THE JOY OF HAVING JESUS

What does your daily life disclose about you? Do your actions reveal a heart like that of a human or God? I'm guessing the amount of happiness you have over a sustained time is an indication of your answer to both questions.

Christians strive to have a heart like God. Paul reminded us that God's grace has been revealed to those who believe in Christ Jesus, and the coupling of our belief and God's grace brought salvation to us. Also, Paul told us to stop our evil and sinful living in favor of godly living so that we will be wise, righteous, and devoted to God. (See Titus 2:11–12 [NLT] below.) God reveals His grace through Jesus Christ, allowing us to be transformed from the unholy power of sin to godly living, which pleases and glorifies Him.

The more we live like our mentor, Jesus Christ, the more we please God. Our lives please Him because our actions reveal a heart like His. This godly living radiates a continuous happiness that only believers in Jesus experience.

Nonbelievers cannot understand the joy Christians exude. They are accustomed to sinful pleasures, which create only a temporary happiness that cannot be sustained. They try to rekindle their lost joy. Some have success, but it also is short-lived. Nonbelievers' joy creates a never-ending cycle—unhappiness to happiness, then back to unhappiness. The opposite is true of believers' happiness.

For Christians, our sustained joy is comforting while we wait in anticipation for that great day in the future when God's almighty glory will be revealed through the Second Coming of our Lord and Savior, Christ Jesus. (See Titus 2:13 [NLT] below.) Then our happiness will be even better. We will begin living with our Lord in complete bliss throughout eternity

Do you have a joyful heart that reveals Jesus in you?

Action: If you are in the happy-unhappy cycle, listen to the urging of the Holy Spirit and accept Jesus Christ as your Lord and Savior. If you are a Christian, praise God for using you to radiate His grace and the happiness of having Jesus as Lord and Savior.

Scripture Meditation: Titus 2:11–13 (NLT): "For the grace of God has been revealed, bringing salvation to all people. And we are instructed to turn from godless living and sinful pleasures. We should live in this evil world with wisdom, righteousness, and devotion to God, while we look forward with hope to that wonderful day when the glory of our great God and Savior, Jesus Christ, will be revealed."

NEED A SAFETY NET?

Most people insure themselves, their family members, and their possessions. Although insurance is good, it generally cannot be used until after problems and disasters occur. What we need is a safety net for our spiritual, mental, and physical well-being before and after trials hit.

A safety net is available to us. This net does not cost any money to obtain or to retain during the rest of our lives. No down payment. No monthly payment. No annual payment. We cannot purchase the net. Do not think this sounds too good to be true. It isn't.

The Lord will protect any believer who has a childlike faith in Him. (See Psalm 116:6 [NLT] below.) If our faith in the Lord is strong like that of a child, we can obtain His safety net. Humankind has proven that we are less likely to seek safety in Christ without a deep childlike faith.

Having a childlike faith will prompt us to pray for Jesus's safety net at the first hint of any trial. The psalmist said that he was about to be overcome by death, and he feared the grave. He was facing trouble and sorrow, so he asked for the Lord to save him. The Lord responded by saving him. (See Psalm 116:3–4, 6 [NLT] below). The Lord still responds to believers today.

You may be thinking that you do not deserve to be saved from your problems. Don't you remember how kind, loving, and merciful our God is? (See Psalm 116:5 [NLT] below.) Again, He will respond directly to you and have His angels watch over and protect you. (See Psalm 91:11 below.) Have faith in the Lord.

A childlike faith assures protection. How strong is your faith? Do you know that Jesus will protect you, or do you just hope that Jesus will provide safety for you?

Action: Develop a deeper faith in Jesus by absorbing God's Word daily. Pray for the Holy Spirit to assist you. Live by your faith in the Lord and seek God's safety net. Praise Him for His grace, love, and mercy. Revel in the Lord's safety.

Scripture Meditation: Psalm 116:3–6 (NLT): "Death wrapped its ropes around me; the terrors of the grave overtook me. I saw only trouble and sorrow. Then I called on the name of the Lord: 'Please, Lord, save me!' How kind the Lord is! How good he is! So merciful, this God of ours! The Lord protects those of childlike faith; I was facing death, and he saved me." Psalm 91:11: "For He shall give His angels charge over you, to keep you in all your ways."

STOP REDEFINING SIN

Today's topic is troublesome. Redefining sin into something acceptable is an age-old trick of Satan. Currently, his trickery is enjoying huge success because worldly wisdom has turned his trick into a regular practice. The results are unacceptable to God.

Premarital sex, adultery, same-sex marriages, and changing one's gender are all sins in the eyes of God. All of these activities have been redefined by so-called human wisdom to be acceptable events. So, what are we Christians to do as we are called upon to accept these sinful lifestyles? The answer is simple.

God, through Moses, said that a man shall leave his parents and be wed to his wife. Together they shall become one flesh. (See Genesis 2:24 below.) God created both man and woman to become one in both marriage and sexual activity. His only ordained marriage is between man and woman. The only ordained sexual activity is marital sex. Any other marriages or sex acts are not ordained and thus are sins.

Jesus confirmed what God the Father said about marriage. Jesus, while referring to Moses's writings, said that God made them (Adam and Eve) in the beginning, and He made Adam male and Eve female. Then Jesus said that the male and female shall become one flesh, so they would not be two but one. (See Matthew 19:4–5 below.)

Our Lord has commanded that we love everyone. This includes indulgers of all types of sin. We are to love the person but not the sinful lifestyle. We should not look down our nose at them in a judgmental sense. We should, though, tell them the good news of Jesus, invite them into our churches, and teach them how to be disciples of Jesus.

Do you love everyone regardless of his or her lifestyle while rejecting all sin?

Action: Reject redefinition of sins. Demonstrate your love for all people by sharing the Gospel with them and nurturing them into discipleship. Pray for the Holy Spirit to prepare receptive hearts in those to whom you will share the Gospel.

Scripture Meditation: Genesis 2:24: "Therefore a man shall leave his father and mother and be joined to his wife, and they shall become one flesh." Mathew 19:4–5: "And He answered and said to them, 'Have you not read that He who made them at the beginning "made them male and female,"' and said, 'For this reason a man shall leave his father and mother and be joined to his wife, and the two shall become one flesh?'"

IS YOUR BIBLE COVER DUSTY?

Do you know that Christians average only ten minutes a month reading God's Word? Either this statistic is pathetic or there is a huge number of speed-readers among Christians. We all probably know the statistic is indeed pathetic. It is also sad.

Think about ten minutes a month. That is two and a half minutes or 150 seconds per week. Most people spend more time than that looking at themselves in a mirror each day. No wonder so many Bibles are gathering places for dust. Is yours collecting dust?

Do you know that the less dusty your Bible is, the greater or higher your faith is? The more you read and digest God's Word, the greater your faith. The Lord both instructs you and communicates with you through His Word. The psalmist said, "God Himself had taught me His commands and truths, and now I hate disobedience." (See Psalm 119:102, 104 below.) It is really a simple process—reading God's Word teaches you to be obedient to His will and precepts. God even provided you with a Helper—the Holy Spirit.

Being obedient to God's ways benefits you through many blessings. The psalmist summarized the blessings in a good descriptive manner. He said that God's words are sweeter to him than honey, and the words light his path. (See Psalm 119:103, 105 below.) Obedience to God and His words bring a sweet comfort and peace and light your way.

Has your faith reached an altitude that produces obedience to the Lord and His Word? If not, maybe—just maybe—your Bible cover is dusty. There are two ways to remove the dust. You could clean the Bible cover and reshelf it to maintain a low-level faith, or you could wipe it clean, read it, and absorb it until your faith and obedience becomes sweeter than honey.

Which dusting process will you choose?

Action: Keep your Bible in a convenient place. Have a daily quiet time during which you read and consume God's Word. Also, listen to God as He speaks to you. Praise and thank God for making His Word available to you.

Scripture Meditation: Psalm 119:102–105: "I have not departed from Your judgments, for You Yourself have taught me. How sweet are Your words to my taste, sweeter than honey to my mouth! Through Your precepts I get understanding; therefore I hate every false way. Your word is a lamp to my feet and a light to my path."

WHERE IS YOUR FAITH PLACED?

We humans can be a mixed-up lot at times. We roll along each day thinking we are getting our lives in order. Then bam! Suddenly we encounter a roadblock. We have to stop. Our minds ponder the question, How can the roadblock be removed? This question prompts more questions.

Are we able to clear our chosen pathways of whatever roadblocks we face? Do we call friends to ask for assistance? If not, whom do we call for help? How much will the cost be? Can we see what is happening? Our analysis seems to be a logical process. Yet something appears to be missing. Where is God in this process?

Any barrier removal process should begin with God. He has an enormous track record in this area. A sea blocked Moses. God parted it. A wall of stone blocked Joshua. The Lord tore it down. A man was born blind. God removed the blindness. Jesus was put to death. The Lord brought Him back to life. The power of God can remove any obstacle or problem.

The apostle Paul said that our faith should be in God, not the wisdom of men. (See 1 Corinthians 2:5 below.) Our wisdom and that of our friends and professionals may rank high by world standards. Yet their collective wisdom and ours are no match for the wisdom of God, especially when applied through His power.

Why start without God when facing a roadblock? Do you have some doubt, albeit small, that God is both willing and able to guide you through any obstacle that may show up in your path? James said that when we pray for help, do so in faith without doubting. Doubts are unstable like things tossed around by the wind. (See James 1:6 below.) Your first call for assistance should be to the Lord, through faith in Him, with no doubts. Doubting has no place in true faith.

Where have you placed your faith? Is it in yourself and others, or is it in the mighty one—God?

Action: Pray for the guidance in being ever mindful of God's power and His faithfulness in applying His power. Strive to always call on God when you meet an obstacle of any kind. Praise God for His faithfulness in helping you overcome roadblocks.

Scripture Meditation: First Corinthians 2:5: "Your faith should not be in the wisdom of men but in the power of God." James 1:6: "But let him ask in faith, with no doubting, for he who doubts is like a wave of the sea driven and tossed by the wind."

DECISIONS, DECISIONS

Think about your ability to make choices. You received that ability from God when He created mankind. God created mankind in His own image and made them male and female. (See Genesis 1:27 below.) Humans being in the image of God includes the capability to make decisions. Many call it free will. Remember though, making choices should be done responsibly.

The first two members of mankind, Adam and Eve, were living in a perfect world. Then bam! They made a bad decision. They fell to temptation and disobeyed God by injecting sin into the previously perfect world. Adam, Eve, and the world were changed until the end of time comes.

Now the world is a sin-laden place. Some of our decisions will affect our destiny, whether in the short term, long term, or eternally. We choose our spouse, place of residence, and career, and we make other fate-determining choices. Many other decisions are less demanding.

We choose the brand of auto to purchase, the clothes we wear, the food we eat, the businesses from which we make purchases, what we read, our entertainment, plus a myriad of other decisions. The number of choices we make in a day, week, or year is astounding. Some decisions are hard or important or both, while some are easier or less important or both. Many of the decisions were bad ones. There is one decision though that will make up for all of our bad choices.

The choice of accepting or rejecting Jesus as one's Lord and Savior is the most important decision everyone will ever make. It is choosing between eternal life in Heaven with Jesus or separation from Him in hell.

Will you choose Jesus? He will not enter your life without your choosing Him. Jesus said that He will stand at the door and knock. If you hear Him and let Him in, He will join you for all eternity. (See Revelation 3:20 below.) He is waiting. Will you accept His free gift of eternal life and open the door?

Action: If you have accepted Jesus as your Lord and Savior, pray for the Holy Spirit to guide you in making your decisions each day. If you have not accepted Him, do it now through prayer. Revel in the joy, peace, and comfort of living with Jesus.

Scripture Meditation: Genesis 1:27: "So God created man in His own image; in the image of God He created him; male and female He created them." Revelation 3:20: "Behold, I stand at the door and knock. If anyone hears My voice and opens the door, I will come in to him and dine with him, and he with Me."

HAVE TROUBLE? BE PATIENT!

When trouble comes calling, what personal standard operating procedure (SOP) do you initiate? Most of us devise a mental action plan utilizing our intellect and other resources. Then we go into action. We battle the trial while coping with stressfulness. If we are successful, we pat ourselves on the back. If we fail, we call on the Lord to clean up our mess. Either result could be problematic for us.

God has a plan for each of us. When we problem-solve without Him, we have no way of knowing if we veered from His plan. This is especially true when we think we are successful without the Lord's guidance. Hmm ...

Each of us needs to change our SOP for problem solving. The first step in our newly revised SOP should be to pray to the Lord, asking Him to guide us through our trial. We should look to the Lord and wait for Him. He is listening, and He will hear our prayer. (See Micah 7:7 below.) Yes! As promised, He will hear us and guide us.

God's directions to you could be any specific action, including waiting on Him. Obedience to His guidance comforts you and gives you joy. I see your quizzical expression. The apostle James said that we should consider it joy while experiencing problems, trials, and such. We will be blessed with patience when we do. (See James 1:2–3 below.)

While wading through problems God's way, we have joy and develop patience, which makes us perfect and complete. This is all we need. (See James 1:4 below.) Wow! Your troubles can create joyfulness and patience, making you perfect and complete.

A problem will strike. You can go alone while being stress laden and offending God, or you can pray for God to lead through the situation and follow His lead. Two choices: Disobedience induces stress and sadness. Obedience brings joyfulness and patience. Which will you choose?

Action: At the first hint of trouble, pray for God to lead you through the problem. Then revel in your confidence, be patient, and pray to the Lord often. (See Romans 12:12 below.) Praise the Lord for your joy and patience.

Scripture Meditation: Micah 7:7: "Therefore I will look to the Lord; I will wait for the God of my salvation; my God will hear me." James 1:2–4: "My brethren, count it all joy when you fall into various trials, knowing that the testing of your faith produces patience. But let patience have its perfect work, that you may be perfect and complete, lacking nothing." Romans 12:12: "Rejoice in our confident hope. Be patient in trouble, and keep on praying."

TRADE DESPAIR FOR SINGING

Many, if not all, of us have wallowed in the mire of despair. It may have been self-pity that was born out of worrying over troubles. Maybe some lost heart by continually facing one trial after another. Others may have felt all alone as they felt there wasn't anyone to whom they could turn. An unlimited number of situational thoughts can cause despair. The cure is more important than the cause though.

Do you take action when you are despondent? Do you seek help from family or friends? Or do you battle despair alone? Regardless of your course of action, have you found misery is too difficult to completely overcome by your methods? I'm guessing your answer to each question is yes. There is a surefire method to totally overcome despair, even while the trouble still exists. Let God handle it.

King David explained that he cried out to the Lord for help when he was despondent, and God lifted Him out of the muddy pit of despair. (See Psalm 40:1–2 [NLT] below.) Be like David. Cry out to God. Ask Him to make you despair-free. The benefits are great.

God goes beyond lifting you out of the despair pit. God will steady and place you on solid ground. He will even give you a new praise song to sing. Your experience will be a witness to many, and some will come to know the Lord. (See Psalm 40:2–3 [NLT] below.) Wow! His blessings will be flowing.

Think about this. Trouble arrives. Misery sets in. You cry out to God for help. He takes you out of the despair and steadies you. Your misery turns to singing. Your happiness amazes many people. God is glorified as the amazed ones become believers. And all this is possible because some trouble came your way.

Action: When you are slipping into despair, pray for the Lord to transform it into happiness. Rejoice in the results as your light shines brighter upon nonbelievers. Praise God for the transformation of your trials into witnesses for Him.

Scripture Meditation: Psalm 40:1–3 (NLT): "I waited patiently for the Lord to help me, and he turned to me and heard my cry. He lifted me out of the pit of despair, out of the mud and the mire. He set my feet on solid ground and steadied me as I walked along. He has given me a new song to sing, a hymn of praise to our God. Many will see what he has done and be amazed. They will put their trust in the Lord."

HAVE YOU PRAISED GOD LATELY?

We all probably know that many Bible verses instruct us to praise God. And I believe most of us do praise Him. I do wonder, though, whether our praises have become perfunctory so that we can check off a spiritual activity box. We all should evaluate how we go about praising the Lord, including the regularity of our praises.

How often do you praise God? Is it rarely? Occasionally? Weekly? Daily? Continually? The psalmist said that we should praise God from sunrise to sunset. (See Psalm 113:3 below.) Think about yesterday. Remember that beautiful sunset you enjoyed? Your child brought home a report card with all A's. You acquired three new clients. You probably thanked Him for these things. Did you praise Him, though, for allowing them?

God is sovereign. He showers us with unearned blessings as He sustains us. He deserves our ongoing praises from morning to night. If we do not regularly praise the Lord, we are keeping some of His deserved glory for ourselves. Praising Him gives Him glory.

Think about this. What if God only blessed us after we sincerely praised Him after receiving a blessing from Him? It is likely that we would quickly miss His love and grace and resulting blessings. Also, God might question the sincerity of our few praises of Him.

The way we praise God reveals our sincerity. Another psalmist said that we should praise Him for His greatness, sovereignty, and awesome acts. Also, praise Him with the sound of all kinds of musical instruments, dancing, and any other kind of joyful way. (See Psalm 150:2–5 below.) Sincere praise has an obvious jubilated and excited tone, while mundane-sounding praise usually seems to be forced and insincere.

Ask yourself if you are praising the Lord regularly and with faithful sincerity. Answer honestly. Praising God the way the psalmists described will bring you closer to Him.

Action: Be intentional in praising the Lord. Set a goal to offer joyful praise to Him for His mighty acts, no matter how small. Never take some of God's glory by failing to praise Him. Revel in the now being closer to Him.

Scripture Meditation: Psalm 113:3: "From the rising of the sun to its going down the Lord's name is to be praised." Psalm 150:2–5 "Praise Him for His mighty acts; praise Him according to His excellent greatness! Praise Him with the sound of the trumpet; praise Him with the lute and harp! Praise Him with the timbrel and dance; praise Him with stringed instruments and flutes! Praise Him with loud cymbals; praise Him with clashing cymbals!"

BEING REMEMBERED

Most people want to be known and remembered. It makes us feel good and needed. The remembrance part may be short-lived though. For many, the remembering of others fades away over time. However, this is not true with our God.

The prophet Isaiah said that God has written our names in the palm of His hand. (See Isaiah 49:16 below.) Our Lord remembers you. By inscribing you in His hands, God has set His heart to always be conscious of you and your interests. He will not forget you. Count on it.

Some people think that God does not know them well enough to remember them. They are wrong. He knows you better than you know yourself. Do you know the number of hairs on your head? God does. (See Matthew 10:30 below.) He knows if you are strong or weak, happy or sad, comforted or anxious, healthy or sick, and all else about you. God even knows your thoughts. His knowledge of you is much greater than you know yourself.

Not only does God know you extensively, He values you. Jesus said that you are worth much more than many sparrows, yet God remembers and protects the sparrows. So, He will definitely remember and protect you. (See Matthew 10:29, 31 below.) The Lord places a high value on you. You are one of His children—a created treasure.

As the psalmist said, God made sure that we are treasures—His treasures. (See Psalm 139:14 below.) Wow! You and I are wonderfully created treasures. What a blessing.

Think about it. God went out of His way to create you as a treasure. He knows you better than you do. Your name is listed in His palms. The Lord always remembers you. His remembrance is everlasting. The world's remembrance is temporary at best.

Action: Praise God for remembering you. Pray for guidance in humbling yourself before Him in seeking His will for you, presenting your petitions to Him, and persevering in overcoming any self-centeredness. Take comfort in being God's wonderfully made child.

Scripture Meditation: Isaiah 49:16: "See, I have inscribed you on the palms of My hands; your walls are continually before Me." Matthew 10:29–31: "Are not two sparrows sold for a copper coin? And not one of them falls to the ground apart from your Father's will. But the very hairs of your head are all numbered. Do not fear therefore; you are of more value than many sparrows." Psalm 139:14: "I will praise You, for I am fearfully and wonderfully made; Marvelous are Your works, And that my soul knows very well."

SWIMMING IN THE SEA OF CARNAL LIFE ...

Do you feel as though you are surrounded by sin because carnal activity seems to be escalating rapidly in your community? The increase of sin creates more and more temptations. Satan appears to have a lot of reasons to be happy.

Sin has also grown by leaps and bounds nationally, creating two differing results among fellow Christians. Some say, "The same old temptations are more tempting than ever, causing me to fail more." Others say, "I have to work harder and harder to maintain my resolve to ward off temptations."

Neither result is good. Both can be resolved, though, with the same solution. We should stay focused on Heaven, where Lord Jesus is at the right hand of God. (See Colossians 3:1 below.) Setting and keeping our focus on Christ Jesus reminds us that He is ready and able to protect and sustain us. Also, we will easily remember to call upon Him for assistance.

Maintaining our sights on Jesus and other heavenly things will keep our minds on the scriptures and away from worldly things. (See Colossians 3:2 below.) Understanding God's Word allows applying the Lord's truths and obeying His commands. Thinking of earthly things only escalates temptations.

We also need to remember that our real life is spiritual in Christ. (See Colossians 3:3 below.) Never forget that we, like Jesus, have a secure spiritual life with God now and throughout eternity. This is why we accepted Christ as our Lord and Savior.

The constant sinning around us and accompanying temptations are disappointing to all Christians. Some are more disappointed than others. We can take comfort, though, in knowing that the state of our world is temporary and will end. Our Lord is coming again to gather His children. Then we will share in the glory of Christ and God throughout all of eternity.

We all have a choice. Trust the Lord and focus on Him and heavenly things, or trust the world and succumb to the temptations of the carnal things. Which will you choose?

Action: Pray for the wisdom and strength to keep your thoughts on Jesus and heavenly things. Take comfort in knowing you share a spiritual life with God. Enjoy peace while waiting for Jesus to come again to rescue all Christians.

Scripture Meditation: Colossians 3:1–3: "Since you have been raised to new life with Christ, set your sights on the realities of heaven, where Christ sits in the place of honor at God's right hand. Think about the things of heaven, not the things of earth. For you died to this life, and your real life is hidden with Christ in God."

DO YOU EVER DOUBT YOUR SALVATION?

What is your answer to today's topic? I'm guessing your answer would be yes. It seems to be common for many individual Christians to sometime doubt their salvation. We shouldn't. Yet we do. But why?

Maybe your current situation is difficult because of some problems that have come along. Satan is bending your ear, saying, "You have these difficulties because God has abandoned you." Doubt of your salvation has entered into your mind.

May I remind you that trials happen because you and I are living in a fallen world? Do not listen to Satan. His goal is to take you away from the Lord. Instead, listen to Christ Jesus. He said that anyone who listens to Him and believes in Him will have eternal life. There are no other requirements. (See John 5:24 below.) Jesus promised you will not be judged for your sins, nor will you experience the second death. Listen to Jesus rather than the evil one, Satan. Your salvation is secure. Believe it. Accept it. Don't doubt it.

Jesus emphasized the security of the salvation of all believers when he said that they belong to Him. He also said that no physical or spiritual being is able to take any of His followers away from Him or God the Father. (See John 10:28–29 below.) Your salvation cannot be taken away. Jesus promised and confirmed it. This should provide a lot of comfort for us.

Did I hear you correctly? You said, "I can't help it. Doubt arises in me at times." Read John 5:24 and John 10:28–29 again. Your salvation cannot be snatched away from Jesus or His Father. If you still have doubt, Satan has tricked you into doubting the Lord's Word by telling you your salvation may be taken from you.

Do not listen to Satan. Send him packing. *Listen to Jesus.* Do not doubt Him.

Action: Memorize John 5:24 and 10:28–29. Recite the verses at the hint of any doubt of your salvation. Rejoice in the comfort of knowing with certainty that your salvation will not be revoked, and you are heaven bound. Praise God for the surety of your salvation.

Scripture Meditation: John 5:24: "'Most assuredly, I say to you, he who hears My word and believes in Him who sent Me has everlasting life, and shall not come into judgment, but has passed from death into life.'" John 10:28–29: "And I give them eternal life, and they shall never perish; neither shall anyone snatch them out of My hand. My Father, who has given them to Me, is greater than all; and no one is able to snatch them out of My Father's hand."

REVEALING GOD'S GRACE AND GLORY

You may be thinking, *I am only one person. What can I do to reveal the grace and glory of God? I know evangelism is important, and I try to share the good news of Jesus with others. I also help others in any way that I am able. I do not have that many opportunities though.*

Consider this. Remember that unshaven, raggedy-clothed, and dirty-looking man you passed on the sidewalk yesterday? Did you share the Gospel with him? Did you put your arm around him and tell him you loved him and would like to help him?

You say, "No, I did not stop him. I feared him, and I have little money." Jesus was so fearful of the cross He sweated blood. Yet He allowed the nails to be driven through His hands and feet. Jesus and His disciples had very little money, but He found ways to meet the needs of many. Jesus revealed God's grace and glory with fear and very little money.

We can reveal the Lord's glory and grace by humbly serving others as Jesus did. This is how we worship and serve the Lord. Jesus said that every time we serve and help the needy, we are serving Him. The needy could be young or old, but they have some type of need. (See Matthew 25:40 below.) Jesus called the needy the "least of these." We need to be about serving others.

Jesus even gave us examples of serving others. He said that we should feed the hungry; give water to the thirsty; visit the sick, shut-ins, and prisoners; and provide shelter and clothing to the needy. (See Matthew 25:35–36 below.) The needy are everywhere. Let the Holy Spirit guide you to them. Then serve them.

Are you willing to unveil God's grace and glory to others? You can. Humble yourself. Assist, love, serve, and share the Gospel with others.

Action: Serve and worship the Lord by humbly helping those who need assistance of some kind, including hearing the Gospel. Pray for the Holy Spirit to lead you to service opportunities and to guide you in serving them.

Scripture Meditation: Matthew 25:35–36, 40: "'For I [Jesus] was hungry and you gave Me food; I was thirsty and you gave Me drink; I was a stranger and you took Me in; I was naked and you clothed Me; I was sick and you visited Me; I was in prison and you came to Me.' And the King will answer and say to them, 'Assuredly, I say to you, inasmuch as you did it to one of the least of these My brethren, you did it to Me.'"

IF GOD CALLS, HOW WILL YOU ANSWER?

Think about this possibility. God has called your church to plant a new church on the other side of town. Your pastor has called for congregational members to help in the effort. God, through the Holy Spirit, is tugging at your heart to take part. What will you do?

You might be thinking, *I need more information before deciding whether to participate.* What type of information do you need? *I need to know what I will be doing in the planting effort. There are certain things I physically cannot do and some other things for which I am not qualified.* God knows all of your limitations. He still called you though.

We all need to be like Isaiah and Abram (Abraham). God wanted a prophet during the days of Isaiah. So the Lord asked Isaiah, who would go and who could He send? Isaiah told God that he would go. (See Isaiah 6:8 below.)

God wanted to build a nation. He picked Abram to be the father of the nation. The nation-building project began by God telling Abram that He wanted Him to take his family and go to a country, which he would be shown later. (See Genesis 12:1 below.) So Abram obeyed the Lord without even knowing where he was going. (See Genesis 12:4 below.)

Isaiah and Abraham were given far greater assignments than you and I will probably ever receive from the Lord. Yet their responses were yes. Not maybe, depends, lack of personal qualifications, or a conditional yes. Just yes.

We have an advantage over Isaiah and Abraham. We have the Holy Spirit to lean on. So when God calls, why do we have so much trouble saying yes without any qualifications or conditions? Maybe, just maybe, our faith is not strong enough to trust God with our yes.

Is your faith strong enough?

Action: Strengthen your faith in the Lord by reading, obeying, and living His Word. Pray for the Holy Spirit to guide you in building your faith. Always use your faith to trust and obey God. Praise Him for the honor of assisting in extending His kingdom.

Scripture Meditation: Isaiah 6:8: "Also I heard the voice of the Lord, saying: 'Whom shall I send, and who will go for Us?' Then I said, 'Here am I! Send me.'" Genesis 12:1, 4: "Now the Lord had said to Abram: 'Get out of your country, from your family and from your father's house, to a land that I will show you.' So Abram departed as the Lord had spoken to him, and Lot went with him. And Abram was seventy-five years old when he departed from Haran."

DO YOU FEAR PERSECUTION?

Do you realize our society is an enemy of God and His people? It is. The world has standards that oppose the Lord's standards. The world endorses and enables a lot of sin. God hates sin. The world promotes pride. God despises pride. The result is the world having a warlike attitude toward God that spawns persecution of His followers.

Persecution of Christians comes in many forms. It could be verbal abuse, lying about us, or physical harm—including being slain. Persecution of some kind will occur against all of us. Believe it. Do not fear it though.

God knows when we are persecuted. Jesus said that we will receive blessings from God when we are persecuted by one or more evil things just because we follow Him. (See Matthew 5:11 [NLT] below.) How about that? Not only is God aware of our being persecuted, He blesses us for it. He appreciates our faithfulness. Knowing we will be blessed should inspire us.

Jesus went even further. He issued a command that we should be happy about being persecuted. (See Matthew 5:12 [NLT] below.) Be obedient. Replace fear with happiness, because rewards will be given to us in Heaven.

Pause and think about it. Every believer will be persecuted in some way. Some more than others. Some might even pay the ultimate price—their life. However, all believers share a common reason for being persecuted—being followers of our Lord, Christ Jesus. God will not abandon us though. He will bless us now and reward us later in Heaven.

We should be comforted by God's promise to bless and reward us. Know that our obedience to Jesus in being happy of our persecution will bring His peace to us. So, there is no reason to fear persecution. Fear will not prevent it. God's comfort and peace will significantly build our faith, desire, and ability to persevere in overcoming the persecution.

Now, do you fear persecution? If you do, are you willing to replace it with a comforting peace and joy inspired by God?

Action: When persecution strikes, do not fear. Instead, pray for the Holy Spirit to guide you in persevering. Be strong. Stand fast. Praise God for allowing you to be His follower.

Scripture Meditation: Matthew 5:11–12 (NLT): "'God blesses you when people mock you and persecute you and lie about you and say all sorts of evil things against you because you are my followers. Be happy about it! Be very glad! For a great reward awaits you in heaven. And remember, the ancient prophets were persecuted in the same way.'"

IS YOUR SPIRITUAL LIFE WITHERING AWAY?

Think about the title of today's topic. How would you answer the title's question? Sadly, many Christians could admit that the correct response would be yes. Most of them, though, would attempt to excuse their unwanted spiritual status.

Many believers would say something like, "I try to glorify God, be like Jesus, and work hard at doing good things for other people. Most of my efforts seem to fail though. I even try to seek God's will, but His will has not been revealed to me. I am left with questions of how to serve God according to His will."

We all have had questions in our walk with the Lord. What is the will of God for me? Should I accept that job promotion offer? In which church ministry should I be involved? How can I determine who is the right person for me to marry? Where should I live? These are but a few examples and can be answered by consulting with God through His Word. Never forget that His major way of communicating with us is through the scriptures.

Paul said that God's Word equips us to do His work while serving Him. The Bible gives us proper doctrine, righteous instruction, and corrective guidance so that we will be completely equipped to serve the Lord. (See 2 Timothy 3: 16–17 below.) There is nothing for which God's word cannot equip us.

God's Word is vital to you. Consider its importance this way. You are like an oak tree that provides shade and oxygen to our environment. To fulfill its purposes, the oak tree must be fed with water. Remove its water source, and the oak begins to wither. Its shade and oxygen production diminish. Like the oak tree, you need the Word of God to feed you so you will be thoroughly prepared to serve our Lord. When you are not absorbing God's spiritual food, your spiritual walk with the Lord begins to wither.

Now, is your spiritual life diminishing or growing?

Action: Commit to reading and absorbing the scriptures daily. Pray for the Holy Spirit to convict you when you falter in your commitment. Know that if you obey the scriptures, you will have wisdom, and your walk with Him will be stronger. (See Matthew 7:24 [NLT] below.)

Scripture Meditation: Second Timothy 3 16–17: "All Scripture is given by inspiration of God, and is profitable for doctrine, for reproof, for correction, for instruction in righteousness, that the man of God may be complete, thoroughly equipped for every good work." Matthew 7:24 (NLT): "'Anyone who listens to my teaching and follows it is wise, like a person who builds a house on solid rock.'"

ONE GOD, TWO GODS, THREE GODS ...

How many gods do you have? This is not a trick question. Examine your heart. Think about how you spend your time. Can you find one activity that always has priority over all other activities? If you cannot, you may have multiple gods. If you can, it means you have one god. Is your one god the Lord though?

You say, "Wait a minute. I have only one god, the Lord." A friend thought the same thing. Then he remembered he skipped the corporate worship of God in church one Sunday so he could play golf with three buddies. Have you similarly placed the Lord in second place?

Maybe money has top billing for keeping your attention. Then again, you may be chasing several joys of the secular world. Or sports may be occupying the uppermost part of your mind. These are but a few of many, many examples of things that are sometimes held to be the dearest. These activities have become false gods. They push God downward to second place or lower, causing a damaged relationship with Him.

Christians should heed Joshua's advice and decide whom or what we will serve. (See Joshua 24:15 below.) Everyone, through worship, will serve someone or something. It is part of our nature, whether we realize it or not. We have a choice, and it is decision time.

Our choice should be a no-brainer. We can choose a false god that cannot do a single thing for us beyond temporary happiness. Or we can choose the Lord, who is the living God of all Heaven and earth. Choosing a false god is not acceptable to God. Opting for the Lord perpetuates a holy relationship with God now and throughout eternity.

Joshua set the example for a wise choice. He said that he and his family were going to serve the Lord. (Again, see Joshua 24:15 below.) Will your decision be based on worldly desires? Or will you choose the Lord?

Only you can make your selection. Choose wisely.

Action: Be intentional. Make the Lord the object of your worship. Pray for the Holy Spirit to convict you when you may be allowing a false god to creep in. Enjoy the peace and comfort of being a child of God.

Scripture Meditation: Joshua 24:15: "And if it seems evil to you to serve the Lord, choose for yourselves this day whom you will serve, whether the gods which your fathers served that were on the other side of the River, or the gods of the Amorites, in whose land you dwell. But as for me and my house, we will serve the Lord."

SENDING PEOPLE TO HELL

There is a question that has been asked of many Christians. "Why does a loving God send people to hell?" It is a question usually raised by non-Christians. Some ask sincerely. Others use the question as an implication that the Lord is not a loving God. Consider how you would answer the question.

The apostle Paul said that everyone is a sinner because all have sinned. (See Romans 3:23 below.) We are born sinners ever, since Adam and Eve sinned first. It is part of our DNA. We came out of the womb as natural sinners and headed to hell.

Remember Adam and Eve? Blaming them for our destiny will not change it. Neither are we able to change it ourselves. Our Lord can change our destiny though.

Jesus explained that God loves us so much that He sacrificed His Son, Jesus, so we could live in Heaven forever. (See John 3:16 below.) God intervened through love by giving to us two options. We can accept Jesus by believing in Him, which will change our destiny to eternal life in Heaven with God. Or we can reject Jesus and perish in hell forevermore, separated from God and living in agony. We are free to choose our eternal path. Continue marching to hell, or walk with Jesus to Heaven. The choice should be a no-brainer.

God loves us, but He will not force us to choose Jesus. He is, however, encouraging us to believe in Jesus and eternal life. Jesus confirmed this by saying that God did not send Him to earth to condemn the world. God sent Jesus into the world to save the people. (See John 3:17 below.) God yearns for us to be with Him throughout all eternity.

Have you grasped what God has done? He demonstrated His love by providing a way for everyone to overcome sin and live with Him forever. So, the answer to the opening question is "God does not send anyone to hell. Nonbelievers send themselves to hell by rejecting Jesus."

Action: Accept Jesus as your Lord and Savior, if you have not done so already. When asked, "Why does a loving God send people to hell?" use the question as an opportunity to explain the good news of Jesus. Praise God for His love and saving grace.

Scripture Meditation: Romans 3:23: "For all have sinned and fall short of the glory of God." John 3:16–17: "For God so loved the world that He gave His only begotten Son, that whoever believes in Him should not perish but have everlasting life. For God did not send His Son into the world to condemn the world, but that the world through Him might be saved."

I WAS SAD, BUT THEN . . .

We were probably never happier than at the moment when we sincerely repented of our sins. "But," you say, "I've had several joyful experiences with the Lord since that time." It is wonderful that your walk with the Lord brings you happiness. Surely, though, your joy at the time of your repentance was even greater.

The apostle Paul said God's extraordinary kindness, tolerance, and patience toward us is fueled by His love and is intended to spur us to repent of our sins. (See Romans 12:4 [NLT] below.) It was this great love of God that created your burning desire to turn from the sorrow of your sinful ways and turn to the ways of the Lord. Your feeling and understanding of the fullness of His love created an extraordinary happiness.

"Why can't I maintain that extraordinary happiness?" you ask. You, like me, probably have heard Satan reminding you of just how bad and plentiful your sins are, though you repented long ago. The devil is determined and relentless. He keeps hammering those thoughts into you. You begin to feel haunted by your past. Sorrow then sets in.

We can overcome the sadness. The psalmist said that we are to always remember the wonderful things God did for us, including the forgiveness of our sins. (See Psalm 103:2–3 [NLT] below.) The goodness of God is so great that we cannot remember what He did without feeling very joyful.

Remembering God's forgiveness is especially jubilant. When He forgives, He forgets the offense. Satan then causes us to remember our sins that God has forgotten.

Do you see what happens? Repentance creates extreme happiness. Satan constantly reminds us of the nature of our sins. Our glee turns to sorrow. However, our joy can be reestablished by remembering all the great things God has done for us. This entire cycle occurs only because we are reminded of our sins that God has forgotten. Ignore Satan and think of the great things God has done for you.

Action: Be ever mindful of the good things the Lord has done for you. Start by praising Him in prayer. Then pray for assistance in recalling God's love, mercy, and grace. Rejoice in your walk with Him.

Scripture Meditation: Romans 12:4 (NLT): "Don't you see how wonderfully kind, tolerant, and patient God is with you? Does this mean nothing to you? Can't you see that his kindness is intended to turn you from your sin?" Psalm 103:2–3 (NLT): "Let all that I am praise the Lord; may I never forget the good things he does for me. He forgives all my sins and heals all my diseases."

BE HAPPY! SMILE!

Do your troubles have you down in the dumps, causing you to wonder if the ever-present trials will end? A friend said to you, "Smile." You responded by asking, "Why? I have no reason to smile." You seem to think, *If I had more money, I could pay my bills. I need a miracle to rid me of health problems. All I see are bad issues. I cannot find joy amidst the troubles.* Do you hear yourself? Your concentration seems only to be on your trials.

Maybe—just maybe—you need to look beyond your problems. You can start by kicking your self-pity in the rear to get rid of it. As you turn from the self-indulging sorrow, look to the one who is the creator of joy.

Regardless of no fruit being on the trees and vines, while there are no flocks or cattle and the fields are not producing, we can and should rejoice in the Lord. (See Habakkuk 3:17–18 [NLT] below.) No matter how dire your situation is, rejoice in the Lord. His joy will enter your heart until the self-induced pity is forced out. Then smile your way through your trials.

I can almost hear you saying, "I am not strong enough to rejoice while I am suffering." Yes you are. God's Word says so. God, in all of His strength and sovereignty, is your strength. He will make you as stable as any deer so that you can easily tread in the low, high, muddy, and rocky places. (See Habakkuk 3:19 [NLT] below.)

Have faith in God's strength. He will not leave you stumbling along your path. He will make you surefooted and steady so you can rejoice in Him.

Are you content in wallowing in self-pity? Don't be. Let your faith guide you through your troubles with gladness in your heart and a smile on your face.

Action: Overcome the pity. Rejoice in the Lord. Pray for strength to continually rejoice in God during all the turbulent times as well as the good days. Let your joy shine before others, and praise Him for your happiness and your witness.

Scripture Meditation: Habakkuk 3:17–19 (NLT): "Even though the fig trees have no blossoms, and there are no grapes on the vines; even though the olive crop fails, and the fields lie empty and barren; even though the flocks die in the fields, and the cattle barns are empty, yet I will rejoice in the Lord! I will be joyful in the God of my salvation! The Sovereign Lord is my strength! He makes me as surefooted as a deer, able to tread upon the heights."

GOD THE COMFORTER

We spend a large amount of time, energy, and resources to make ourselves contented. For our efforts, we usually end up with a temporary happiness and its consequences.

Remember all the money you spent on entertainment this year. The joy from being entertained has now waned, and you are worrying over the dent in your personal budget. You put in a lot of extra time at work. Yet you are stressed, worrying if your best is good enough. Maybe you are frustrated because your son seems to not understand the value of an education. The point is that contentment is elusive because you are struggling with a lot of mental stress and medical issues.

Frustration, anxiety, stress, worry, and medical problems are hard on anyone. There is good news though. (See Proverbs 21:21 below.) You can have a lasting contentment, including a peaceful life, personal honor, and righteousness, by seeking mercy and righteousness. Then you can put stress, worry, and such in your rearview mirror.

Some Christians wonder just how they can seek righteousness and mercy. It seems so hard. Do not fret. Jesus told us how. (See Matthew 6:33 below.) Seek God's righteousness and His kingdom by accepting His free gift of salvation. God is a comforter. He will trade life, righteousness, and honor for your worries, stress, anxieties, and frustrations. Wow, what a deal! You would be trading your problems for a true, everlasting contentment.

God's great deal is available to you. You may even receive more than you seek. Jesus also said that blessings come to those who seek God's righteousness rather than being self-righteous. Also, blessings flow to those who are merciful. (See Matthew 5:6–7 below.) Wow! The blessings resulting from the above trade just keep on flowing to you.

Are you ready to have a continuous contentment that exceeds the world's understanding? God wants you to have it, and you can have it. Go for it.

Action: Seek God and His righteousness. Turn your problems over to Him. In prayer, praise and thank the Lord for the contentment you will receive. Ask for the Holy Spirit to guide you in seeking God. Enjoy the peace and comfort from being truly contented. Remain mindful of your new witness to others.

Scripture Meditation: Proverbs 21:21: "He who follows righteousness and mercy finds life, righteousness, and honor." Matthew 6:33: "But seek first the kingdom of God and His righteousness, and all these things shall be added to you." Matthew 5:6–7: "Blessed are those who hunger and thirst for righteousness, for they shall be filled. Blessed are the merciful, for they shall obtain mercy."

THERE ARE NO SHORTCUTS

Most of us look for shortcuts to our goals. Shortcuts usually save time. Sometimes, though, the lessening of time creates a lessening of quality. Consider whether the loss of quality is worth the time saved. The importance of this question is revealed in our walk with the Lord. As Christians, we are disciples of Jesus. Our common goal is to become Christlike. The goal is consistent with the will of God. So, the quicker we act to get there, the greater our walk with Jesus. Right? Wrong.

Some believers hasten their quest to be Christlike by being in church every time the doors open and participating in most ministries inside the church. They do little, though, outside the walls of the church. They are following their own path rather than God's path and become easy targets of Satan. They blame God for not blocking the devil from doing his damage. Their shortcut to become like Jesus does not allow God to mold them to be like Christ. Their shortcut actually slows or prevents progress in becoming more Christlike.

There is no shortcut to become Christlike. God uses our trials to mold us into a stronger and more established believer. (See 1 Peter 5:10 below.) All Christians need to understand that our trials are tools for God to use in shaping us into a Christlike state. He uses our pain in the present time to perfect and strengthen us for the future.

We will have problems and trials. Do not respond by being angry with God, but rejoice in Him, show patience while suffering, and be faithful in prayer. (See Romans 12:12 below.) We should be happy that God is molding us to be like Jesus, and be patient while He works. Our submission to God's work in us glorifies Him. (See 1 Peter 5:11 below.) Give glory to God continually for all the work He is doing in you.

Are you attempting to develop a Christlike nature through some shortcut(s), or are you being patient while allowing God to shape you?

Action: Avoid shortcuts in your walk with Jesus. Be patient and rejoice in your tribulations as God transforms you into a better disciple of Christ. In prayer, praise God for taking your pain and using it for His purposes.

Scripture Meditation: First Peter 5:10–11: "But may the God of all grace, who called us to His eternal glory by Christ Jesus, after you have suffered a while, perfect, establish, strengthen, and settle you. To Him be the glory and the dominion forever and ever. Amen." Romans 12:12: "Rejoicing in hope, patient in tribulation, continuing steadfastly in prayer."

TONGUE OR SWORD?

Sadly, the most accurate spelling of tongue is s-w-o-r-d, tongue. The statement may seem at first to be overly harsh. At least the secular world might think so. The Word of God, though, does not think that the statement is overstated.

Solomon, a very wise king, said that our tongue could cause death or save a life, and all who love to talk will live with the tongue's effect. (See Proverbs 18:21 [NLT] below.) He described the tongue as a powerful tool. Wow! The tongue is a tool that can create very strong and opposing results, and we must live with the results, whatever they may be.

The apostle James's statements were just as strong. He said that the tongue is a deadly poison and cannot be tamed by humans. (See James 3:8–9 below.) The tongue is a powerful tool indeed that can cause death or life, praise or curse people, and actually bless God. Whether the tongue is used for good or bad depends on its owner's intent and self-control.

The tongue is a sword, a two-edged sword. One edge honors, edifies, encourages, or elates. The other edge tears down, saddens, hurts feelings, or does other damage. Which edge do you use when speaking to or about others?

You said, "I would never use my tongue's bad edge to hurt anyone." That is a good and worthy goal. However, how does your neighbor's short and skinny kid feel after hearing your oft-stated reminders of his stature and overly lean physique? Were those coworkers hurt when you angrily ranted at them with highly inappropriate language? When that church member hurt your feelings, did you retaliate verbally?

Think about the different atmosphere that would exist if we all tried to use only the good and helpful edge of our tongue/sword. Neighborhoods would be friendlier and more joyful. So would our workplaces. Worshipping God would be more intense. Relationships would be considerably more loving.

Taming the tongue is difficult. Are you willing to try though?

Action: Remember that your tongue can damage and destroy. Pray for guidance and wisdom in your efforts to be an edifier and encourager. Seek forgiveness from God and the offended person(s) when you fail to keep your tongue under control.

Scripture Meditation: Proverbs 18:21 (NLT): "The tongue can bring death or life; those who love to talk will reap the consequences." James 3:8–9: "But no man can tame the tongue. It is an unruly evil, full of deadly poison. With it we bless our God and Father, and with it we curse men, who have been made in the similitude of God."

DO YOU TEMPT YOURSELF?

We know that we tempt ourselves sometimes. That is, if we admit it. The self-tempting by some people is rare. For some others, it is often. Many times, we tempt ourselves without realizing it. And there are times when we know we are self-tempting, but we convince ourselves that we are strong enough to resist the temptation.

Ponder this. We Christians have recited the Lord's Prayer so many times that we cannot count the number. One clause in the prayer asks God not to cause us to be tempted. (See Luke 11:4 below.) So, we pray, asking God to not tempt us. Yet we tempt ourselves. Isn't our self-tempting foolish?

Foolishness? Yes. Still, we continue to lead ourselves into temptation. The temptations can come in many different forms and circumstances. One may be hanging out with the ungodly while they are sinning. You knew what they were going to do. Yet you hung with them. Another could be laughing at dirty jokes. You may think they are funny, but God doesn't.

"I would never tempt myself because I have enough temptations coming at me without my adding to them," a man said. Did he forget about the time he flirted with a coworker? He said, "She flirted first. It felt good knowing someone else was attracted to me." That might be fine in the secular world but not in God's world. The Lord knows you both tempted yourself and each other.

We should be heeding the advice Jesus gave to His disciples when He told them that they should be aware of their mind-set and pray to avoid temptations. (See Mark 11:38 below.) We need to be alert to our own thoughts before they turn into temptations. The Lord will help us. The apostle Peter said that the Lord is able to take us out of temptations. (See 2 Peter 2:9 below.) God stands ready to assist us.

Do you tempt yourself? I'm guessing you do. You can stop though, if you are willing.

Action: Always be alert to any potential self-temptation. Ask the Lord in prayer to lead you away from self-temptations. Praise God for His assistance and seek His forgiveness when you fall to your temptations.

Scripture Meditation: Luke 11:4: "And forgive us our sins, for we also forgive everyone who is indebted to us. And do not lead us into temptation, but deliver us from the evil one." Mark 14:38: "Watch and pray, lest you enter into temptation. The spirit indeed is willing, but the flesh is weak." Second Peter 2:9: "Then the Lord knows how to deliver the godly out of temptations and to reserve the unjust under punishment for the day of judgment."

A RACE YOU CAN WIN

You probably have seen world-class sprinters competing against one another on television. Some are men. Some are women. All are fast. Between races, they train to become even faster. They all have the same goal—to be the fastest in the world. They have a coach or coaches to prepare them for races.

We have a race to run. We do not compete against one another. We are running to achieve full sanctification—perfected Christlikeness. We each have the same coach, Jesus, and assistant coach, the Holy Spirit, to train us.

We should think like Paul, who knew he could not achieve perfection in this world but strived for perfection anyway. (See Philippians 3:12 [NLT] below.) Perfect Christlikeness will not be achieved until we enter Heaven. We know this. Yet the more we strive for it, the more we will be like Jesus prior to arriving in Heaven. We need to press on each and every day.

As we run our race, stumbling blocks will appear along our racecourse. Satan's trickery and our sin are just a couple of hazards. Our coaches will assist us in using God's Word to overcome the pitfalls. We can then put the past behind us and concentrate on our goal. (See Philippians 3:13 [NLT] below.) Forget the past. Running toward the final goal sanctifies us more and more, so we sin less and less. Once in Heaven, we will sin no more.

Think about living in eternity and being completely sanctified without sin. This is perfection, which is why we all should work hard until we finish the race and receive our trophy—full sanctification and eternal life with God. (See Philippians 3:14 [NLT] below.)

Are you pressing on in your race? Are you utilizing Jesus and His assistant to train you to run harder? Is your eye on the final prize?

Action: Strive to be more like Christ each day by serving and worshipping God the way Jesus did while He walked the land as fully man. Pray for Jesus and the Holy Spirit to guide you in your race and for wisdom in following their guidance.

Scripture Meditation: Philippians 3:12–14 (NLT): "I don't mean to say that I have already achieved these things or that I have already reached perfection. But I press on to possess that perfection for which Christ Jesus first possessed me. No, dear brothers and sisters, I have not achieved it, but I focus on this one thing: Forgetting the past and looking forward to what lies ahead, I press on to reach the end of the race and receive the heavenly prize for which God, through Christ Jesus, is calling us."

IT IS FINISHED! NOW WE LIVE!

Much has been written about the words Jesus uttered while dying on the cross. Each statement He made is important. None, though, is as important as Jesus's three words right before He died. He uttered that it is finished. (See John 19:30 below.)

What was finished? God's redemption plan, which He devised before time began, was completed by Jesus's death on the cross. His spilled blood is a sacrifice that takes away our sin. Earlier, John the Baptist said that Jesus is the Lamb of God who saves us from our sin. (See John 1:29 below.)

Prior to Jesus's death on the cross, all sacrifices of blood for sin were accomplished with animal blood, and it only covered sin. It could not remove sin. Jesus's sacrificed blood covers and takes away our sin. So, God's redemption plan is finished.

Jesus's "It is finished" statement was an announcement to God the Father and the world that His assignment was complete. The redemption plan was now installed. Jesus paid in full the penalty for our sin. He is our Redeemer. We can be freed from the bondage of our sin and have eternal life with Him and God the Father.

There is another benefit from Jesus's sacrifice. We now have direct access to Him. Jesus is our Priest. As He died, His spirit left Him. Immediately, the temple veil was torn from the top downward to the bottom. (See Matthew 27:51 below). Previously, only certain priests could enter the temple's holy of holies—God's residence. The veil kept people out. The priests represented the people before God. The tearing of the veil from top to bottom was God's way of removing the need of designated priests as agents. Each Christian now has direct access to the Lord, our High Priest.

You may claim your receipt for the payment of your sin. You register your claim by believing in Jesus and accepting Him as your Lord and Savior. Do you believe in Him?

Action: Be confident in believing in Jesus. Accept Him as your Savior and Lord. Praise God for sending His Son, Jesus, as a sacrifice to set us free from sin.

Scripture Meditation: John 19:30: "So when Jesus had received the sour wine, He said, 'It is finished!' And bowing His head, He gave up His spirit." John 1:29: "The next day John [the Baptist] saw Jesus coming toward him and said, 'Look! The Lamb of God who takes away the sin of the world!'" Matthew 27:51: "Then, behold, the veil of the temple was torn in two from top to bottom; and the earth quaked, and the rocks were split."

DO YOU UNDERSTAND GOD'S LOVE?

The Gospel is the greatest love story of all time. Hollywood has churned out hundreds of love story movies. Some were dubbed to be "the greatest love story ever." None measure up to the Gospel though.

Jesus summarized the Gospel when He taught that God, because He loved mankind so much, sacrificed His only Son so all who believe in His Son will have eternal life in Heaven. (See John 3:16 below.) This verse has been written, copied, and quoted so much that we may have unconsciously trivialized its meaning. The greatness of God's love is not fully realized in modern times. We need to reestablish our amazement of God's love by revisiting how He proved His love for us.

We were headed to hell because everyone was born as a sinner. (See Romans 3:23 below). God created us to be with Him, but we could not unless the penalty for our sin was paid. So God had a plan. He manifested Himself as Jesus, a child born of a virgin womb. He grew into a man and served mankind. Jesus paid the penalty for all our sins by allowing Himself to be crucified—the most painful death known to man. Why? Because of God's love for us. He sacrificed and resurrected Jesus so that we could be free of sin and have eternal life with Him.

Answer this question, "Do I understand God's love?" To develop an accurate answer, test yourself. What was your reaction the last time you committed a sin?

We generally react in one of three ways: 1) being shameless for having sinned; 2) having minor shame and thinking, *Whoops, I sinned. I need to ask God for forgiveness the next time I pray to Him*; or 3) hanging our head in shame until we ask for forgiveness from God and from the person sinned against (when appropriate).

The amount of shame we feel from sinning indicates how much of an understanding of God's love we have. The greater we see God's love to be, the more shameful sin is to us. How much shame do you have after sinning? Is it a little bit, a lot, or none at all?

Action: Develop and retain a deep knowledge of the greatness of God's love and how He used His love sacrificially so that we could have eternal life with Him.

Scripture Meditation: John 3:16: "For God so loved the world that He gave His only begotten Son, that whoever believes in Him should not perish but have everlasting life." Romans 3:23: "For all have sinned and fall short of the glory of God."

WILL YOU STAND FAST FOR JESUS?

Suppose your pastor asked, "Who do you say Jesus is?" Would you say "He is the Son of God" or "Jesus is my Lord and Savior"? Both answers are certainly correct. Yet consider this. Do these answers indicate that you will actually stand fast for Jesus? Think about some different scenarios before you form an answer.

Many people, including some Christians, now have different beliefs about who Jesus was and is. The beliefs include prophet, great teacher, great man, and radical. The truth is Jesus is God. The apostle John explained that the Word and God existed in the beginning; the Word was God; and God created everything through the Word. (See John 1:1–3 [NLT] below.) The Word (Jesus) crafted the world and its contents, including mankind.

You ask, "Is the Word really Jesus?" Yes, the Word is Jesus. John said that the Word became human and lived on earth. (See John 1:14 [NLT] below.) The Word became human by being born of a virgin. He was named Jesus pursuant to God's instruction.

Jesus was not created as mankind was. He, the Word, already existed. He is Jesus the Christ, the Son of God, the Messiah, and other worthy names. He is every believer's Lord and Savior. Never, ever forget that *Jesus is nothing less than Lord and Savior.*

Unfortunately, many nonbelievers promote the idea that Jesus was something much less than the truth. They now claim that they are offended by hearing Jesus's name. And they have had some success in preventing public prayer to be prayed in Jesus's name.

You may be asked sometime to pray or worship in public without any use of Jesus's name, so no one will be offended. If you comply, nonbelievers will not be offended. God will be though. You must choose whom you will offend. What would you do?

Will you stand fast for Jesus? Or will you offend Him?

Action: Pray for the strength and courage to stand for Jesus. Never think He is anything less than Lord, the Son of God. Assist in extending God's kingdom by explaining the Gospel to those who claim to be offended by Jesus's name.

Scripture Meditation: John 1:1–3, 14 (NLT): "In the beginning the Word already existed. The Word was with God, and the Word was God. He existed in the beginning with God. God created everything through him, and nothing was created except through him. So the Word became human and made his home among us. He was full of unfailing love and faithfulness. And we have seen his glory, the glory of the Father's one and only Son."

LIVE IN PERFECT HARMONY

Do you believe we all can live in perfect harmony? "I believe we can live mostly in harmony. But perfect harmony, no," you say. Why doubt perfect harmony? "No one is perfect. I sometimes unintentionally offend people. Then there are some who offend me in some way," you answer. You and I need to try the Lord's way to live in perfect harmony.

The Lord's way begins by being mindful that everyone has faults and then forgiving all who offend us. After all, the Lord forgave us, so we must forgive our offenders. (See Colossians 3:13 [NLT] below.) Overlook the faults of others and forgive those who are offensive to you or hurt you.

I know what you are thinking. *Some individuals make it very difficult to forgive them.* I agree. They disagree with most of what the church does. Even when they agree, they speak negatively. We should still forgive them. "Some, though, accept forgiveness as a license to keep being offensive. What should we do?" you ask. Keep on forgiving them. The reward is too great to miss out on it.

We are able to forgive properly and regularly if we exercise love, which can bring us together in perfect harmony. (See Colossians 3:14 [NLT] below.) Can you see it? God's way comes together through love when we exercise love the way He does. Love is the glue that binds us together spiritually with an ideal unity. This is living in perfect harmony.

King David said that perfect harmony is as refreshing as the water flowing into God's kingdom, where he pronounced eternal life and other blessings. (See Psalm 133:1, 3 [NLT] below.) Picture David's description. Can you imagine the joy that could emanate from the brothers and sisters in Christ living in perfect harmony? Also, think of the testimony for Christ this would create. We can live in perfect harmony, if we develop a Godlike love toward all others.

Action: Through love, forgive all who offend you. Pray for the wisdom to be ever vigilant in forgiving others, and praise God for leading you to live in perfect harmony.

Scripture Meditation: Colossians 3:13–14 (NLT): "Make allowance for each other's faults, and forgive anyone who offends you. Remember, the Lord forgave you, so you must forgive others. Above all, clothe yourselves with love, which binds us all together in perfect harmony." Psalm 133:1, 3 (NLT): "How wonderful and pleasant it is when brothers live together in harmony! Harmony is as refreshing as the dew from Mount Hermon that falls on the mountains of Zion. And there the Lord has pronounced his blessing, even life everlasting."

THE ROARING LION

When you hear a reference to a roaring lion, do you think of a large, wild, and very dangerous animal, the devil, or something else? If you are a Christian, I hope your answer is the devil or one of his other names—Satan, Lucifer, the evil one, and such.

The apostle Peter likened the devil to a roaring lion that wants to devour us. So, we should always be alert to the devil's presence. (See 1 Peter 5:8 below.) Peter had firsthand experience. A stalwart among the apostles, he failed to be alert at all times. He let his guard down, and Satan, like a roaring lion, jumped through the opening.

The devil induced anger in Peter, causing him to cut off a soldier's ear. Just hours later, Satan placed fear in Peter, resulting in the apostle denying Jesus three times. Then Peter learned to be vigilant against the devil's ways. We also are able to develop an ongoing alert system to prevent the creation of openings for the evil one. Satan hurts us without our opening doors for him.

Peter also said that we should fight the devil by remaining faithful to God. We can be comforted in knowing that Satan causes many other believers to suffer. (See 1 Peter 5:9 below.) We are able to resist, if we remember as Peter finally did. We are well equipped. We have the armor of God for defense. Put it on. And we have offensive weapons—the Word of God and prayer. Use them. Also seek encouragement from others who have like trials.

Above all, be patient while suffering. God will use your suffering to calm you and make you a stronger believer in Him. (See 1 Peter 5:10 below.) God will transform the devil's damaging work into a tool to mold you into a better disciple.

Never discuss anything with Satan. Eve and Adam did, and the result transformed a perfect world into a fallen world, causing everyone to be inherent sinners. Yet you can send the roaring lion packing, if you are willing to do so.

Action: Put on the armor of God. Study His Word. Pray for the strength to be alert and vigilant against the devil and for patience so God can mold you in your trials.

Scripture Meditation: First Peter 5:8–10: "Be sober, be vigilant; because your adversary the devil walks about like a roaring lion, seeking whom he may devour. Resist him, steadfast in the faith, knowing that the same sufferings are experienced by your brotherhood in the world. But may the God of all grace, who called us to His eternal glory by Christ Jesus, after you have suffered a while, perfect, establish, strengthen, and settle you."

TODAY, NEXT YEAR, OR NEXT GENERATION

The day of the Lord is coming. Most Christians would like to know when. None of us know though. Oh, some think they know, but they don't. Peter said that the Lord will come at an unexpected time. (See 2 Peter 3:10 [NLT] below.) God's Word clearly says that we will not know in advance when the day of the Lord will occur. Believe His Word.

Even though we do not know when the Lord will arrive, we do know what will occur according to Peter. The whole universe and earth will be consumed by fire that creates extremely loud noises. This is really bad stuff. Heaven and earth will be destroyed. We don't want to witness such a devastating event.

Christians, though, will not suffer through the destruction. Jesus will appear in the sky and gather His disciples (the rapture) just before the ruination begins. So we should not fear the day of the Lord, as many Christians do. Rather, we should be eagerly waiting for the Lord's Day. The destruction will be replaced with a new glorious Heaven and earth. (See 2 Peter 3:13 [NLT] below.)

I know you are wondering, "What are we Christians to do in the meantime?" First put aside any fear of the day of the Lord (end-times). Do not just mark time until the end-times arrive. Continue to grow in and serve Christ Jesus. Be stronger in your faith in Him. (See 2 Peter 3:18 [NLT] below.) God issued a command through Peter, not an option.

To grow in Christ, study the Word of God. Converse daily with Him in prayer. Obey the Lord's commands. Spread the good news of Jesus. Help the needy. Take care of widows and children. Try to be more like Jesus.

Will you continually work to make your personal relationship with Jesus more mature? Or will you in effect just wait on the day of the Lord and fear that day?

Action: Be intentional in learning about, growing in, and serving your Lord and Savior Jesus Christ. Pray for daily guidance in improving your closeness to the Lord. Expect His next coming.

Scripture Meditation: Second Peter 3:10, 13, 18 (NLT): "But the day of the Lord will come as unexpectedly as a thief. Then the heavens will pass away with a terrible noise, and the very elements themselves will disappear in fire, and the earth and everything on it will be found to deserve judgment. But we are looking forward to the new heavens and new earth he has promised, a world filled with God's righteousness. Rather, you must grow in the grace and knowledge of our Lord and Savior Jesus Christ."

PATIENCE AND THE CROSS

Think of Christ Jesus dying on the cross. What comes to mind? I suspect you would center on Jesus's death being a sacrifice for the sins of the world. You would be correct. Christ's sacrificial death for us is a foundational truth of Christianity. This truth cannot be overstated. Yet Jesus's death created an additional truth for Christians.

From the time of Jesus's arrest in the Garden of Gethsemane until His death on the cross, His conduct is a paragon of patience. The sacrifice called for His blood to be spilled. And it was spilled but in different and horrific ways. While Jesus was on the cross, He died in such great physical pain that it transcends our understanding.

Jesus's reaction to His spilt blood and horrific pain was truly remarkable. His handling of His suffering with complete patience is an example for us to use when we are persecuted. Jesus did not say any deceitful thing. He did not retaliate. He did not threaten anyone. But He did display a humble and faithful spirit. (See 1 Peter 2:21–23 below.) What a reaction it was. Jesus's reply to all the terrible things done to Him was silent patience.

Jesus stayed patient. How could He do that in the midst of such horrors? Jesus was committed to fulfilling the will of God the Father. Jesus knew the end of the story. He would be resurrected from the grave and return to Heaven. He had complete faith in God. May our strength be so strong.

It is the desire of God for all other believers to follow the example Jesus set for us when we are persecuted in some way. God knows why we would be under persecution. He also knows that it is very difficult to be patient when under such physical or mental stress. We can overcome the suffering with patience and glorify Him if we remain steadfast in our faith in the Lord.

Will you be patient when you are persecuted and suffering?

Action: Pray for wisdom, strength, and perseverance to be patient and to commit yourself to God when you are persecuted for following Jesus. Ask also for the light of Jesus to be reflected from your patience to both believers and unbelievers.

Scripture Meditation: First Peter 2:21–23: "For to this you were called, because Christ also suffered for us, leaving us an example, that you should follow His steps: 'Who committed no sin, nor was deceit found in His mouth'; who, when He was reviled, did not revile in return; when He suffered, He did not threaten, but committed Himself to Him who judges righteously."

IS YOUR LIFE GODLY?

Does your life seem as if it has had little change by accepting Jesus as your Lord and Savior? You were told that your life would become godly by knowing Jesus Christ and accepting Him. Yet you feel that little has changed.

You say, "I do not understand. I have the Lord's power because I accepted Jesus. I am a child of God. Why do I not have the comfort and peace like so many other Christians have as they go through each day?" Maybe you need to strengthen your faith in the Lord.

God did not create you to honor Him by being His puppet. You are to honor God by serving Him, which takes effort. The apostle Peter even reminded us of this. (See 2 Peter 1:5 [NLT] below.) You cannot spend your life just relaxing in knowing Jesus is your Lord. You must act using God's promised power and promised grace. This enables you to share His divine nature and to run from the corruption of the world.

Peter was specific in telling us that we are able to use God's grace to supplement our faith with perseverance, the ability to love everyone, a good knowledge of Him, sinless living, and obedience. (See Psalm 1:5–7 [NLT] below.) This is not easy, yet we can be like God wants us to be.

Yes, you can have a godly life, but it does not occur through happenstance. You should continually make every effort to react to the promises of God. He gave you the tools to add to and strengthen your faith. The tools are contained in His Word—the scriptures. The more you learn from His Word, the stronger your faith will be. The stronger your faith is, the more fruitful you will be. The more fruitful you are, the more godlike your life will be.

Living a godly life provides you with Christ's peace and comfort and glorifies God, but to have a godly life requires effort. Are you willing to put His promises to work for a godly life?

Action: Pray for the Holy Spirit to convict you of any straying from godliness. Be ever aware that your life is an ongoing witness for the Lord. Be intentional in developing godliness with assistance from the Holy Spirit.

Scripture Meditation: Second Peter 1:5–7 (NLT): "In view of all this, make every effort to respond to God's promises. Supplement your faith with a generous provision of moral excellence, and moral excellence with knowledge, and knowledge with self-control, and self-control with patient endurance, and patient endurance with godliness, and godliness with brotherly affection, and brotherly affection with love for everyone."

FOCUS, FOCUS, FOCUS

Yesterday is gone. No one can change it. We can learn from it though. Yesterday's thoughts and acts help determine the way we think and act today. We can look to yesterday to determine the object(s) of our focus during our nonsleeping hours. Reflect on your yesterday and where your focus was.

As you awoke, did you begin to mentally picture your day's scheduled activities? Maybe you then zeroed in on a planned afternoon meeting with a couple of attorneys to resolve a company legal question. Did you view the upcoming meeting as a stumbling block or as a way to prevent legal problems? Maybe your mind went directly to consideration of possible methods to improve your personal sales. Are lagging real estate sales fueling your desire to improve? Or could it be simply an inner greed that cannot be satisfied?

Note that situations or circumstances may be viewed differently. How we look at something can make a big difference. The things our thoughts are focused on influence our decisions. We are wired this way. So we have a responsibility to keep our thoughts focused on the right things.

Paul explained where we as believers should place our focus. (See Philippians 4:8 below.) Peter's writing is God inspired and tells us to stay focused on things that are God ordained, right, morally good, gracious, kind and courteous, virtuous, and praiseworthy. This is the will of God. But the hard part is knowing how to apply Peter's advice to our daily lives while confronting what the world throws at us.

Think about what God has done. He has characterized the type of things you should meditate on. Obeying God will result in better decisions and greater responsibility. The legal meeting would have been viewed as a right and good prevention measure. Sales methods would only change when an analysis showed a need for change. And you will be comforted by God's presence. (See Philippians 4:9 below.) So, are you focused on the right things?

Action: Be intentional in focusing on everything you learned from God's Word through meditation. Pray for guidance in maintaining your focus on the God-ordained things. Enjoy the comfort of knowing that God is with you.

Scripture Meditation: Philippians 4:8–9: "Finally, brethren, whatever things are true, whatever things are noble, whatever things are just, whatever things are pure, whatever things are lovely, whatever things are of good report, if there is any virtue and if there is anything praiseworthy—meditate on these things. The things which you learned and received and heard and saw in me, these do, and the God of peace will be with you."

BEING A LIVING SACRIFICE TO THE LORD

How much of your time do you spend serving God as a living sacrifice? Is it all the time, most of the time, half of the time, or little of the time? Pause and reflect on these questions. Your answer will reveal how much you serve the Lord.

The apostle Paul explained that our bodies should be used as a living and acceptable sacrifice to God. (See Romans 12:1 below.) "How is my body able to be a living sacrifice to the Lord?" you ask. You, like all Christians, should use your body and its members to worship, witness for, and glorify God. Your body is a temple because the Holy Spirit lives within you. "Ah, I do those things," you say. Are you sure?

Suppose you were drinking alcohol before going to theater rehearsal. You drank so much that you could not remember all your lines. Was that being a living witness for the Lord? Remember removing your Bible from your desk just before you were to meet with an important client who is a nonbeliever? Was that obeying God? Or maybe you have so many worldly responsibilities that the Lord had been lowered to second or third priority. How did this bring glory to God?

Our body is a temple, and we should use it to serve the Lord in a reasonable way. Through His grace, God has given to us the ability to be fruitful. So our service should be of the highest standard—everyday service to the Lord. Using our bodies as tools of righteousness is to be a full-time, not part-time, servant for God.

Every believer is able to use his or her body as a full-time, living sacrifice to the Lord. We can do this by working against being conformed to the world. Instead, we should achieve and maintain transformation to God's will by renewing our minds spiritually. (See Romans 12:2 below.) It is imperative that we conform to God's will, not the will of the world.

Are you willing to be a full-time living sacrifice?

Action: Be constantly aware that your body is a temple for God. Renew your mind spiritually. Pray for guidance in using your body as a full-time living sacrifice that God will accept. Avoid conforming to the world.

Scripture Meditation: Romans 12:1–2: "I beseech you therefore, brethren, by the mercies of God, that you present your bodies a living sacrifice, holy, acceptable to God, which is your reasonable service. And do not be conformed to this world, but be transformed by the renewing of your mind, that you may prove what is that good and acceptable and perfect will of God."

ONLY HE IS THE ONE TRUE GOD

The need to sometimes refer to the Lord as the True God is necessitated by the existence of false gods or idols. False gods are everywhere and come in many different forms. Some are things made by humans for the purpose of worship. Some are necessary things like money, cars, careers, and such that are placed above God. Some false gods are internal traits such as desires and pride that individuals place above the Lord.

The false gods that are the most difficult to overcome are internal traits. If one has an internal false god, he or she is the false god. Everyone has internal traits that define who he or she is. Have you become a false god?

You may be thinking that you are not a false god. Look within yourself to be sure. Maybe your desire to have a larger house has become so strong your entire being has become dedicated to satisfying the desire. You work so many hours you no longer have time for God. If this is true, your focus is on the dream house rather than on the Lord. Your desire has become a false god.

Has your pride gotten out of hand? Again, look within yourself. Be honest. Is your participation in church ministries dependent upon your receiving personal glory for your action? Maybe you have forgotten that the Lord deserves the glory from the ministries, not the participants. The desire to receive glory from the ministries is a false god.

There is good news though. False gods or idols can be removed by putting to death the sinful earthly things: envy, wrongful cravings, adultery, and such. These things are idols and false gods. (See Colossians 3:5 below.)

The solution is a necessity, not an option. The Lord God Himself said that He is the only real God. (See Isaiah 45:18 below.) All other gods are false. Are you willing to put God back in His place as the one and only true God?

Action: Through self-evaluation, identify and remove any of your characteristics that have risen above God. Pray for strength, sincerity, and wisdom while evaluating and acting on the self-analysis. Ask also for God's forgiveness for having false gods.

Scripture Meditation: Colossians 3:5: "Therefore put to death your members which are on the earth: fornication, uncleanness, passion, evil desire, and covetousness, which is idolatry." Isaiah 45:18: "For thus says the Lord, who created the heavens, who is God, who formed the earth and made it, who has established it, who did not create it in vain, who formed it to be inhabited: 'I am the Lord, and there is no other.'"

SATAN VERSUS THE LORD

We are living in the midst of a war. It is a spiritual war—Satan versus the Lord. All Christians should know this. Most do. This war is of vital importance. Yet a vast number of believers seem to have buried this knowledge so deep within their minds that they rarely, if ever, think about the war. We should be ever mindful that this war is all around us and involves us.

Satan leads the evil of the world. The Lord leads the goodness of the world. We were born into Satan's camp. We switched to the Lord's side when we accepted Jesus as our Lord and Savior. We know God will win in the end. So everything is good. Right? Wrong.

Satan will not give up. His evil workers continually tempt believers. A number of his followers seem to have prospered immensely when looked at from a worldview. Some believers become envious and give in to the temptations. Most Christians call this backsliding. We need to call it what it really is—changing sides in the middle of a war, albeit temporarily. How foolish is that?

One of the psalmists said that we should not crave the things or people of iniquity, for such will be destroyed. (See Psalm 37:1–2 below.) When a believer switches sides, they have chosen worldly benefits that are doomed to end in destruction. God will win the war at the perfect time for His purposes.

Most believers finally realize their mistake, repent, and turn back to the Lord. His benefits are true and real and lead to a better life and eternal rewards. The psalmist also said that we should trust in God, be faithful to Him, and believe in His faithfulness to His Word. If we do this, He will save us from Satan and his followers. (See Psalm 37:3, 40 below).

We must choose between God and Satan. There are no other options. Will you choose God?

Action: Trust the Lord's faithfulness. Through prayer, ask for the Holy Spirit to 1) lead you in being ever mindful of the spiritual warfare being waged all around you; and 2) warn you if you are about to fall to temptations from Satan's evil forces.

Scripture Meditation: Psalm 37:1–3, 40: "Do not fret because of evildoers, nor be envious of the workers of iniquity. For they shall soon be cut down like the grass, and wither as the green herb. Trust in the Lord, and do good; dwell in the land, and feed on His faithfulness. And the Lord shall help them and deliver them; He shall deliver them from the wicked, and save them, because they trust in Him."

REJOICE! I SAY REJOICE!

It is baffling. Many Christians hear the name of Jesus the Christ without rejoicing. Have we spoken and heard the name of Jesus so much that we take Him for granted? No one, not a single soul, has had a greater impact on our lives than Jesus. How can we be nonchalant about Him?

When you accepted Jesus as your Lord and Savior, you loved Jesus and trusted Him. Do you still love and trust Him? You say, "Yes, I do." Well, maybe your level of love and trust is just not as high as it was. You declare, "No, that is not true." Okay, but look at what the apostle Peter said.

We learned from the apostle Peter that even though we have not seen Jesus, we trust and love Him, and we rejoice with a great and mighty joy. (See 1 Peter 1:8 [NLT] below.) It should be easy for us to grasp. Loving and trusting Jesus inspires rejoicing with great joy. So again, why are we dispassionate at the sound of His name?

Jesus has taken our hand and led us through trials. He has protected us. He gave us a Helper to live within us to assist us continually. Jesus is our Redeemer and High Priest. He has set us on the correct path of life. And most of all, Jesus's reward for believing in Him will be our salvation, which is so great that even the prophets longed to know more about it. (See 1 Peter 1:9–10 [NLT] below.) Jesus gives us a perfect and eternal life with Him. A greater reward is not possible. So, why do we fail to rejoice when hearing His name?

Maybe Satan is the problem. He may be constantly asking us, "What has Jesus done for you lately?" Jesus continues to do plenty for us each day. He is our mentor, provider, and protector. He gave to us the power to overcome Satan's trickery while living with an inner peace and comfort that is unexplainable.

You have a lot of reasons to rejoice over Jesus's name. Rejoice in Him!

Action: Be intentional in keeping Jesus uppermost in your mind each and every day. Pray for perseverance in recognizing and remembering all that Jesus does in your life. Praise and thank Him for all that He does for you. Rejoice *every* time you hear His name.

Scripture Meditation: First Peter 1:8–10 (NLT): "You love him [Jesus] even though you have never seen him. Though you do not see him now, you trust him; and you rejoice with a glorious, inexpressible joy. The reward for trusting him will be the salvation of your souls. This salvation was something even the prophets wanted to know more about when they prophesied about this gracious salvation prepared for you."

THE VALUE OF KNOWING JESUS IS ...

Could you answer this question, "What is the value of knowing Christ Jesus?" You probably cannot measure the value in worldly standards. One possible answer that might be the most correct is infinite value that has no end. This answer is vague because the value of knowing Jesus is so great that it is not measurable. Yet each of us would be a better disciple of Christ if we were mindful that the value of knowing Him is infinite.

Even the apostle Paul could not measure the value of knowing Jesus. Though he did know the value was so great that everything else he had was trash. Paul also suffered greatly because he knew Christ. Yet he knew his suffering was worth knowing the Lord. (See Philippians 3:8 below.) Not being able to measure the value of knowing Christ did not hinder Paul's burning desire to know more and more of Jesus and His resurrection power. (See Philippians 3:10 below.) Paul wanted to know Jesus completely and to conform his life to be like Him.

Paul's knowledge of Christ went far beyond knowing who Jesus was. Paul had a personal relationship with Him. Paul rated his relationship with Christ to be higher than anyone else or anything. Paul also knew that to maintain a top value on knowing Jesus, he must learn from Christ's teachings and try to live like Jesus.

Think about this question: are you willing to think like Paul concerning the value of knowing Jesus? Before you answer, reflect on Paul's words. Then think about what the answer yes would mean.

For you to place top value on knowing Jesus, you must have a personal relationship with Him. You must try to live like Him. To live like Jesus, you should learn from His teachings, be obedient to His commands, and attempt to act like Him. You can do all of these things if you place focusing on Jesus your top priority each day. Are you willing?

Action: In prayer, ask for the Holy Spirit to guide you in developing the mind-set of giving Christ top priority each day over your life. Be intentional in following the precepts of the Lord. Praise Him for His faithfulness to you.

Scripture Meditation: Philippians 3:8, 10: "Yet indeed I also count all things loss for the excellence of the knowledge of Christ Jesus my Lord, for whom I have suffered the loss of all things, and count them as rubbish, that I may gain Christ that I may know Him [Jesus] and the power of His resurrection, and the fellowship of His sufferings, being conformed to His death."

I CHOSE THE PATHWAY OF ...

You probably have traveled on a small road and unexpectedly came to a fork in the road. You could not find signs to tell you which fork to take for your destination. So you had to guess while feeling stressed. You will also encounter a very important and possible life-changing fork in your path of life.

Everyone comes into this world by going directly from their mother's womb to the pathway of Satan—also known as the path to hell. "Oh? How can a sweet, innocent newborn baby be on the road to hell?" you ask. That beautiful baby is an inherent sinner. We all are. Everyone is headed to hell until we arrive at the most important pathway fork that we will ever encounter. The fork only has two prongs.

One prong is the same pathway we were born onto—the path to hell. The other prong is the pathway of God, known as the path to Heaven. Each of us must choose which road to take in completing our journey on earth. Two options face us. Will it be Satan's path, or will it be God's path? Hell or Heaven? We must choose. No one can decide for us.

It seems like a no-brainer. Heaven is the better choice. You must remember, though, that Satan will not accept defeat lying down. He wrote the book on deceit and trickery. Satan and his minions will work hard to trick you into staying on Satan's path. However, the psalmist David told us how we could stay on God's path.

David's enemies were after him, so he cried out to the Lord, asking to be led on the correct path. (See Psalm 27:11 [NLT] below.) Your enemies, Satan's forces, can be overcome. You can cry out to the Lord to lead you along His path by teaching you how to live.

Obedience to the Lord's teachings opens your heart to His righteousness. Another psalmist said that God's righteousness makes His footsteps to be our path. (See Psalm 85:13 below.) Obeying God transforms our footsteps onto His pathway. Have you chosen the pathway of God?

Action: Look within your heart. Have you chosen to follow God's path? If you haven't, pray for the Lord to lead you to His path to Heaven. Praise God for allowing you to choose Him, His ways, and His path to eternal life.

Scripture Meditation: Psalm 27:11 (NLT): "Teach me how to live, O Lord. Lead me along the right path, for my enemies are waiting for me." Psalm 85:13: "Righteousness will go before Him [God], and shall make His footsteps our pathway."

STANDING IN A CESSPOOL

Our nation that we have loved so much seems to have transformed into a country that Christians do not recognize. Many political leaders and judges have made decisions that pushed God aside. This coupled with our failure to properly spread the good news of Jesus has created havoc. Our nation has become repugnant to God.

Many are now looking at boarded-up churches that once proudly rang their steeple bells. Crime is taking a toll on citizens. The once-rare circumstance of a citizen carrying a gun is commonplace. More and more citizens are publicly reveling in their immorality. Many, many Christians feel as if they are standing in a cesspool.

The apostle Paul talked about similar situations. He said that ungodly people of his day were headed toward destruction because they did not think about an afterlife. (See Philippians 3:19 [NLT] below.) Today, the same types of sinners are also headed to hell unless they turn to Jesus. Believers, though, are bound for Heaven.

Paul said that believers' true citizenship is in Heaven, and we wait for Christ Jesus to come and take us there. (See Philippians 3:20 [NLT] below.) Earth is our temporary home. Our permanent home is in Heaven, where Jesus has prepared a place for us. We all should eagerly wait for Christ to come for us.

"How can we be eager about waiting for Jesus's return?" you ask. Trust in the Lord and obey His commands. Extend God's kingdom by spreading the Gospel to sinners and teaching them the commandments of Jesus. (See Matthew 28:20 below.) Sinners are easy to find.

You have two options: 1) You can be unhappy while standing in the mire; or 2) You can trust and obey Jesus while eagerly and happily spreading the good news of Jesus and making disciples. Are you willing to choose option two?

Action: Be a joyful beacon for Jesus each day. Pray for the Holy Spirit to guide you to opportunities to spread the Gospel. Be involved in discipling new and immature believers. Praise the Lord for the honor of serving Him.

Scripture Meditation: Philippians 3:19–20 (NLT): "They are headed for destruction. Their god is their appetite, they brag about shameful things, and they think only about this life here on earth. But we are citizens of heaven, where the Lord Jesus Christ lives. And we are eagerly waiting for him to return as our Savior." Matthew 28:20: "Teach these new disciples to obey all the commands I [Jesus] have given you. And be sure of this: I am with you always, even to the end of the age."

BUILDING UP OR TEARING DOWN?

One of the most-used words in our language is love. It is often a misunderstood word. Love is expressed positively and is steadfast. Love is both a thought and a word of action. A Godlike love is a reflection of the fruit of the Spirit.

You may think that your love is Godlike, but are you sure? Paul told us what love is and is not. Love is heartfelt, amiable, and long-suffering. Love is not proud, mean, or irritable. (See 1 Corinthians 13:4–5 [NLT] below.) Paul also told us what love does and does not do. Love forgives and rejoices over the truth. Love is always faithful. Love does not quit, is always upbeat, and perseveres. Love is not demanding and detests injustice. (See 1 Corinthians 13:5–7 [NLT] below.) How would you describe your love?

If your love is patient and kind, you are forgiving, rejoicing in truths, faithful, hopeful, and long-suffering. You build people up by edifying them. You spread the Gospel. This is what a Godlike love does. People enjoy your friendship. You reflect the light of Jesus.

If you tend to be jealous, proud, rude, or irritable, you tear down people. You appear to be loveless. Your thoughts and actions are mostly negative. Friendships are short-lived. Your most loyal friends remain but only because their love fuels their steadfastness.

Think about this. My wife and I know a teenage girl who did not respond to my wife's telling her about Jesus. Later, my wife learned that the girl had a change of heart and accepted Christ as her Lord and Savior.

The girl has a schoolmate who was routinely rude and irritable toward everyone. Then the classmate suddenly changed into a loving person who was helping others. The girl my spouse knows asked the schoolmate what changed her. The classmate said that she came to know Jesus and proceeded to the lead the girl we know to Christ. Hallelujah! Do you build up others through love like the transformed classmate?

Action: Pray for guidance in developing a Godlike love. Be intentional in putting your love into action. If you are not a Christian, ask Jesus to come into your heart and accept Him as your Lord and Savior.

Scripture Meditation: First Corinthians 13:4–7 (NLT): "Love is patient and kind. Love is not jealous or boastful or proud or rude. It does not demand its own way. It is not irritable, and it keeps no record of being wronged. It does not rejoice about injustice but rejoices whenever the truth wins out. Love never gives up, never loses faith, is always hopeful, and endures through every circumstance."

WATCHING AND PRAYING OR MARKING TIME?

A married couple accepted Christ Jesus as their Lord and Savior. Both were baptized a short time later. They knew each was headed to Heaven. Their joy was abundant. Then each took a different path to travel through their daily lives.

The husband decided there was no need for him to attend church every week. He felt secure in his salvation. He spent little time abiding in Jesus. He would do that full-time when he arrived in Heaven. He did little to please God. The man was just marking time while waiting on Jesus to come and gather His people.

The wife's path took her down the spiritual growth road. She matured. She knows that Jesus's return could be momentarily or a long time from now. In Sunday school, the wife learned that no one, including Jesus, knows when Jesus will return for His people. Only God the Father knows the return date for Jesus. So she obeys Jesus by watching for Him and praying for Him to direct her life while she watches. (See Mark 13:33 below.)

But how does the wife watch for Jesus? She watches by walking in the newness of life that she obtained when she accepted Christ as Lord and Savior. This is what Paul said all believers should do. (See Romans 6:4 below.) Because of her newness of life, the wife strives to obey Jesus's commands, including telling others about Him. This pleases and glorifies God.

The wife understands that she has been freed from her sins and that her heavenly life will be holy for all eternity. Unlike her husband, the wife knows that walking in the newness of life is being an active disciple of Jesus. So she strives for holiness while waiting for Jesus.

The wife is not alone in her quest for holiness. She allows the Holy Spirit to guide her as she watches and prays for Christ's return.

As Jesus's disciple, are you marking time or watching and praying?

Action: Do not mark time. Watch and pray. Pray for the Holy Spirit to guide you in abiding in Jesus each day of your newness of life. Pray for Jesus to come. Praise God for allowing you to have a little of Heaven while residing on earth.

Scripture Meditation: Mark 13:33: "Take heed, watch and pray; for you do not know when the time is." Romans 6:4: "Therefore we were buried with Him [Jesus] through baptism into death, that just as Christ was raised from the dead by the glory of the Father, even so we also should walk in newness of life."

ARE TROUBLES CLOUDING YOUR BLESSINGS?

Jesus said that we would go through trials and tribulations. Everyone is a living example of the truthfulness of Jesus's words. We have "been there, done that." Some have had more troubles than others. Also, the severity of the trials has been worse for some. There is probably a lot of variation in how we are each affected by our troubles.

Some have been affected to the point of being consumed by their trials. That is all they talk about. The trials' mental clouds have engulfed them and turned their concentration away from the Lord to their troubles. The more dreadful a trial is, the thicker the cloud. The thicker a cloud is, the more difficult it becomes to recognize God's blessings.

You can overcome the clouds of trouble. You ask, "How? While struggling with a trial, there seem to be multiple troubles waiting to take the trial's place. My joy seems lost." I know, but you still can overcome the clouds.

Refocus on the Lord. Your concentration on Him allows His light to shine through the clouds and reveal His blessings. You will again be joyful instead of joyless.

Praising the Lord will help you remember all of His blessings. (See Psalm 103:2 below.) The blessings have been flowing to you and continue to flow. The psalmist said that the Lord will continue to bless you in many ways. He will forgive your sins, restore your life after disasters, heal you, feed you, and sustain and protect you. (See Psalm 103:3–5 below.) God will take care of you. Do not let the clouds of trouble blind you to His blessings.

Understand this. Keeping your concentration on the Lord instead of your troubles will bring you His peace and comfort along with all the other blessings. God is faithful. He will continue to bless you in ways that renews your youth. (See Psalm 103:5 below.)

Will you focus on the hurt and fear of your trials? Or will you use the blessings of the Lord to guide you through the troubles?

Action: Intensify your concentration on the Lord at the onset of every trial or tribulation. Pray for the strength to persevere in maintaining your focus on God. Praise Him for the showering of blessings He sends to you. Relax in the peace and comfort of the Lord.

Scripture Meditation: Psalm 103:2–5: "Bless the Lord, O my soul, and forget not all His benefits: Who forgives all your iniquities, Who heals all your diseases, Who redeems your life from destruction, Who crowns you with lovingkindness and tender mercies, Who satisfies your mouth with good things, so that your youth is renewed like the eagle's."

ARE YOU WALKING IN THE SPIRIT?

How would you answer this question, "Are you walking in the Spirit?" Most Christians would say something like this: "Yes. I am, because I have had the Holy Spirit in me since I was saved." Having the Spirit within you is not the same as walking in the Spirit.

The Holy Spirit is the power given to us to use in serving God. We must use the power, though, to achieve the will of God. The Spirit leads and guides but does not dictate. Through each of us, the Holy Spirit wars against sinful temptations of all kinds. We activate the Spirit's power when we are walking in the Spirit. When we are not, we succumb to temptations. (See Galatians 5:16 below.) We simply cannot overcome our inborn sinful nature to sin without walking in the Spirit.

The blessings of walking in the Holy Spirit are enormous. He gives us His fruit, which reshapes our character. We become happier, more loving, and more patient. We have more self-control and kindness. (See Galatians 5:22–23 below.) These are great traits, but we are not able to develop them without the Spirit.

You cannot wake up one day and say, "I am going to have more love, and more faith, and more self-control." It will not happen without walking in the Spirit. Obedience to what the Spirit tells you is what develops the fruit of the Spirit.

The Holy Spirit is in you. Listen to Him. Godly traits will develop within you. Use the Spirit's guidance more and more. The fruit will multiply. Fruit have seeds that breed more fruit. Always remember that traits of fruit can be self-perpetuating.

All of the individual parts of the Spirit's fruit are both separate and intertwined. Note that the list of the Spirit's fruit begins with love and ends with self-control. These are the bookends. Once you have these two, you have them all. It is the entire shelf of fruit that will keep you on the path of pleasing God.

Is your walk in the Spirit rare, sometimes, a lot, or every day?

Action: In prayer, praise God for sending the Holy Spirit to you. Also pray for discernment in recognizing the guidance of the Holy Spirit. Listen to Him each day. Do what the Spirit urges. Have confidence in knowing you are pleasing the Lord.

Scripture Meditation: Galatians 5:16, 22–23: "I say then: Walk in the Spirit, and you shall not fulfill the lust of the flesh. But the fruit of the Spirit is love, joy, peace, longsuffering, kindness, goodness, faithfulness, gentleness, self-control. Against such there is no law."

HOW IS YOUR DAY GOING?

No doubt, there are many people having a problem-infested day. We all have bad days. It is the nature of a sinful world. Some troubles may be major, while others may be minor. Those days that we do not want will continue to occur.

When our days becomes trial laden, many people cannot seem to get past the worldly results of bad days. They become sad, afraid, anxious, and such. Worry consumes them. Simply put, they freak out. Their minds stay in turmoil. They just cannot find a way to manage the problems that ruined their day. Why though?

Have they forgotten about the Lord Jesus? He is just a prayer away and has an unlimited supply of assistance.

The apostle Paul taught that we should not worry about anything. Instead, we should give our problems to God through prayer with thanksgiving. (See Philippians 4:6 below.) Pray to the Lord and tell Him about your difficulties. He will intervene but only if He is asked. Just do it. He is ready to help you.

God will ensure that His peace enters your heart. (See Philippians 6:7 below.) You probably will not understand His peace, but it will give you comfort while you are surrounded by problems. This may sound somewhat oxymoronic. It is true though. Count on it. This is just the beginning. The Lord does not give you peace and walk away.

God, through Isaiah, gives you a calming assurance that there is no reason to fear trials. The Lord will take your right hand and lead you through the management of your problems. (See Isaiah 41:13 below.) Just ask Him.

Now, the best part is that the light of Jesus will shine through you. Nonbelievers will notice how you calmly and methodically solve your problems. Many of them will want to have the same inner peace that sustains you. Will your light shine during bad days?

Action: When trial-laden days appear, tell the Lord of the problems through prayer. Relax in the peace of God as you reach for the Lord's hand. Allow Him to guide you through the difficulties of all your bad days. Let Jesus's light shine through you.

Scripture Meditation: Philippians 4:6–7: "Be anxious for nothing, but in everything by prayer and supplication, with thanksgiving, let your requests be made known to God; and the peace of God, which surpasses all understanding, will guard your hearts and minds through Christ Jesus." Isaiah 41:13: "For I, the Lord your God, will hold your right hand, saying to you, 'Fear not, I will help you.'"

YES! THE ANCHOR HOLDS!

What a journey. There were times the journey seemed like a pilgrimage. Yet sometimes the journey felt more like running a gauntlet. Problems abounded from start to finish, but the Anchor held. To what journey am I referring? The journey of writing this book of devotionals.

Trials popped up throughout the journey. Most of the problems evaporated through the encouragement of knowing with certainty that Jesus is my soul's anchor. (See Hebrews 6:19 below.) Knowing that Jesus is my Anchor shouldered my faith and trust in Him.

My Anchor took my hand, strengthened me, upheld me, and led me through every trial, just as He said He would. (See Isaiah 41:10 below.) However, there were two trials that required a double dose of big-boy faith in the Lord.

A tragedy struck after my writing was off to a good start. A freak accident caused a deep third-degree burn on my ankle. Surgery was required and included a skin graft. The burn center said that considerable pain would occur throughout the multi-month recovery. Would I be able to write? "Yes," said my Anchor. He blocked the pain, so I did not have any. None. The would-be tragedy became a testimony of the Lord's faithfulness.

A year later, a horrific pinched-nerve pain struck me. I could not write, for the pain and meds took my concentration. My Anchor led me through six weeks of pain. I asked Him, "How can I ever finish the book?" The Holy Spirit began to teach me patience and reminded me that God would assist me in the task He assigned to me. (See Psalm 57:2 below.) My Anchor faithfully led me through the fulfillment of His task for me—this book.

My Anchor is also your Anchor. He is 100 percent reliable. He will lead you through your trials. He will assist you in fulfilling God's purpose for you.

Do you trust in Him to be your Anchor?

Action: Know that Jesus is your sure and steadfast Anchor. Pray for Him to lead you through your trials and tribulations. Praise Him for His faithfulness.

Scripture Meditation: Hebrews 6:19: "This hope perfect [Jesus] we have as an anchor of the soul, both sure and steadfast, and which enters the Presence behind the veil." Isaiah 41:10: "Fear not, for I am with you; be not dismayed, for I am your God. I will strengthen you, yes, I will help you, I will uphold you with My righteous right hand." Psalm 57:2 (NLT): "I cry out to God Most High, to God who will fulfill his purpose for me."

INDEX OF DEVOTIONAL CATEGORIES

ABOUT THE AUTHOR

Ron Crowe and his wife, Karen, are believers in Christ and have raised two sons who each, along with their wives, are raising two children. Ron is retired from a long career in governmental work and is known for his work in ethics oversight of state and local governmental officials and employees. One news outlet referred to him as "Mr. Ethics." This unofficial title stuck and followed him into his retirement life. Ron also is a veteran of the US Army and the National Guard.

Ron became a Christian more than sixty years ago. For a number of years, his maturing spiritually bounced between slow developing and stagnant. He even angrily ran from the Lord for two years, but God's love was far greater and stronger than Ron's anger. God brought him back into the fold. Ron learned that true joy comes from a deep faith in the Lord, and a deep faith results from regularly spending time with God and reading, meditating on, and applying His Word. This proved to Ron that the spiritual maturation of each Christian never ceases.

Ron then served the Lord through evangelism and missions and as a deacon, deacon chairman, a Sunday school teacher, and a member of numerous church committees. Later, God led Ron and Karen to their present church, where he serves the Lord as a deacon and in much the same ways as in his previous church.

Some medical issues began to limit Ron's physical activity, so at age seventy-two, he began to consider different ways he could still serve the Lord. God stepped in and in effect said, *No problem. I want you to write a devotional book for publication and give all the proceeds to assist in funding mission and evangelism projects.* The Lord also let Ron know that the financial part of the vision should be handled by a not-for-profit organization to be created.

Through Ron's obedience to the Lord, *The Anchor Holds* is the first project to bring funds into the newly created Our Anchor Ministries (OAM), which will distribute the proceeds pursuant to God's instructions. Other books and fund sources for OAM are already in the formulation stage.

Ron will readily tell anyone that *The Anchor Holds* is God's book because He inspired the creation of each devotional. Also, Ron says that the vision given to him demonstrates that believers do not retire from serving God and that serving Him becomes even more joyful as believers age.